THE
DELHI
MODEL

ADVANCE PRAISE FOR THE BOOK

'*The Delhi Model* is a very interesting and accessible account of how the Aam Aadmi Party (AAP) reformed the delivery of school education, healthcare, rations and other government services in Delhi. It offers an attractive template for those who want to put the human capital of our citizens at the centre of India's development agenda'—**Raghuram Rajan, eminent economist and former governor, Reserve Bank of India**

'The concepts and ideas are transformational. More importantly, many of them have actually been successfully implemented and have made a difference, particularly in matters of health and education. The Delhi Model has given meaning to these very important and basic fundamental rights'—**Justice Madan Lokur, former judge, Supreme Court of India**

'Education, health and service delivery are mainly the responsibility of state governments, and India needs stronger state-level leadership to improve human development, which is a critical foundation for broad-based prosperity and well-being. Having known Jasmine [Shah] for over a decade, I am delighted to see this documentation of a state-level model that combines attention to evidence and cost-effectiveness with a political commitment to better service delivery for all citizens. A highly recommended read for anyone interested in accelerating India's development'—**Karthik Muralidharan, author and Tata Chancellor's professor of economics, University of California San Diego**

'A thorough and well-researched account, *The Delhi Model* challenges India's obsession with trickle-down economics and advocates a bold new approach of investing in human capital first. Jasmine has an academic's eye and a literary auteur's flair when chronicling the unique development model shaped by the AAP in the last decade'—**Rajiv Bajaj, managing director, Bajaj Auto**

'The AAP has succeeded against brutal opposition from the established political establishment to show the feasibility of a fully democratic system of governance. Government is not just of the people (elected by them) and for the people (providing the neediest with affordable healthcare, education and essential services), but also by the people, with common people participating in the decisions that change their lives and winning their support in implementation. Governance systems are routinely corrupted by payments of money at many levels for obtaining favours illegally. However, they are fatally corrupt when the system's design is entrenched, providing political power to people with more resources to legally shape the rules of the game for their own interests. Successful movements of change that shift power to the people are always threats to an entrenched system of power. Jasmine Shah's insider account with facts of what the AAP government has accomplished in Delhi so far must be read by all who want India to achieve *poorna swaraj*—full political, social and economic freedom for all its citizens'—**Arun Maira, author and former member, Planning Commission of India**

THE
DELHI
MODEL

A BOLD NEW ROAD MAP
TO BUILDING A
DEVELOPED INDIA

Jasmine

JASMINE SHAH

**PENGUIN
BUSINESS**

An imprint of Penguin Random House

PENGUIN BUSINESS

Penguin Business is an imprint of the Penguin Random House group of companies
whose addresses can be found at global.penguinrandomhouse.com

Published by Penguin Random House India Pvt. Ltd
4th Floor, Capital Tower 1, MG Road,
Gurugram 122 002, Haryana, India

First published in Penguin Business by Penguin Random House India 2024

10 9 8 7 6 5 4 3 2

The views and opinions expressed in this book are the author's own and the
facts are as reported by him which have been verified to the extent possible,
and the publishers are not in any way liable for the same.

Please note that no part of this book may be used or reproduced in any manner
for the purpose of training artificial intelligence technologies or systems.

ISBN 9780143472131

Typeset in Sabon LT Std by MAP Systems, Bengaluru, India
Printed at Thomson Press India Ltd, New Delhi

www.penguin.co.in

Contents

Preface

Born out of a historic anti-corruption movement in 2012, the story of the unprecedented rise of the Aam Aadmi Party (AAP) in Indian politics is well known. What isn't clearly understood is what followed: the birth of a unique model of governance that has become the AAP's trump card in all its electoral battles henceforth—the Delhi Model.

The Delhi Model has, for the first time in independent India, brought the issue of transforming public education and healthcare from the margins to the centre of Indian politics. It prioritizes investments in building human capital while providing a social safety net for the most vulnerable. The Delhi Model lies at the heart of the AAP's political narrative of *'kaam ki rajneeti'* (politics of work) and its meteoric rise to become India's youngest-ever national party within a decade of its formation. A true understanding of AAP's success is, therefore, incomplete without understanding what really is the Delhi Model.

My association with the AAP government in Delhi began soon after they stormed to power in February 2015 with a historic mandate. Like many, I was intrigued by how AAP would go about delivering the transformative change they had promised. Back then, I was the South Asia policy head for one of the world's leading think tanks. I met Manish Sisodia, the then deputy chief minister and education minister of Delhi, and Atishi, his education adviser, for the first time in July 2015. That first meeting lasted three hours where we discussed what two decades of rigorous research on education innovations globally taught us, and how those lessons could be applied to Delhi's government schools. That one conversation was sufficient to convince me: this government genuinely wanted to walk the talk.

A year later, I joined Mr Sisodia's office full-time as a policy adviser. The journey thereafter has been nothing short of a dream. Growing up as a small-town boy in Silvassa in western India, I had aspirations similar to most middle-class Indians. After graduating from IIT Madras in 2004 and landing a plush corporate job, life was good. However, the disconnect between the two Indias I saw started gnawing at my conscience. In the post-liberalization era, Indian corporates were competing with the best globally, yet our governance resembled that of a third-world country. Living and working in Bengaluru, daily traffic jams lasting two to three hours en route to Electronic City, the epicentre of India's IT revolution, epitomized this mess. As an engineer, I knew the problem behind all such governance failures wasn't the lack of technical knowhow; it was a failure of policy imagination and political will within governments.

I quit my high-flying corporate job to join a non-government organization (NGO) working on urban governance. Over the next decade, as I worked on policy solutions to India's governance crisis finally landing up in the AAP government, my faith in the need for skilled, well-meaning people in public service and politics only strengthened. In 2018, I was appointed by the Delhi cabinet as the vice-chairperson of the Delhi government's policy think tank, the Dialogue and Development Commission of Delhi (DDC), a position I held till 2024. DDC was the brainchild of Chief Minister Arvind Kejriwal, who was also its chairperson.

Looking back at these eight years, serving the people of Delhi by working closely with all the ministers on deep policy reforms across almost every sector has been the greatest privilege of my life. I have witnessed the inner workings of a government led by a visionary chief minister who refused to believe that governments in India cannot deliver world-class outcomes in a short span of time; ministers who led from the front to deliver on this vision and a bureaucracy that was pushed to the hilt to implement it. I also saw first-hand how this progress was achieved despite constant attempts by the Bharatiya Janata Party (BJP)-ruled Centre to cripple the functioning of a democratically elected government. In spite of, and through all these tribulations, a unique model of governance was born, one that wasn't about fixing a specific set of issues but about fixing how governance itself worked in India.

I decided to write this book for two reasons.

First, though the Delhi Model occupies an exalted position in AAP's political narrative, it is often misunderstood or not understood at all. While parts of the Delhi Model, especially education, have been covered extensively by the national and international media, news cycles are transient and attention spans short. Having had the privilege of seeing the model unfold before my eyes, I took upon myself the responsibility to put together a true record of the genesis, successes and challenges of the Delhi Model.

The intention was to present a factual, policy-focused analysis of the Delhi Model substantiated through data. Every possible effort has been made to ensure the accuracy of data. Errors, if any, are unintentional and the author's alone.

It might feel overwhelming for some readers to believe that the scale of transformation across sectors presented in this book actually took place in a government in India, that too within a decade. I invite those readers, especially those of staunchly different political persuasions, to talk to the beneficiaries of the Delhi Model or to visit Delhi to see it in action—in the thousands of schools, clinics, hospitals and other facilities of the Delhi government.

It is not my intention to claim that everything has been fixed in Delhi, in all or even in a single sector. The attempt here is only to capture the true scale of change brought about by the AAP government over its two terms and how that has set new benchmarks in governance across multiple sectors even though much still remains to be done. I have also attempted to present a national road map for building a developed India, taking inspiration from the principles of the Delhi Model.

The second reason to write this book was to inspire hope among all those Indians, especially the youth, who have grown up believing that governments and politicians are no good. Their anger is justified, their cynicism or despair isn't. For it was a bunch of such angry, educated and middle-class Indians who decided to channel their frustration with status-quo politics into action in 2012, creating a political party and forming a government that transformed the lives of millions of the people living in the national capital—all within a decade. The story of the Delhi Model should be a constant reminder of the wondrous possibilities of what our governments can do, if they really want to, and what the voters ought to demand in return for their precious votes.

Introduction

What really is the 'Delhi Model', and how is it different from the way governance usually works in India? What challenges did Chief Minister Arvind Kejriwal and his cabinet of first-time ministers encounter while implementing the varied policies and programmes, and how were these obstacles overcome? What does the Delhi Model mean to the *aam aadmi* (common man)—across multiple sectors?

This book unpacks the Delhi Model, as it has come to be famously known, layer by layer. It tells the story of how it came into being, what were the ideas that powered it and the principles that underpin it.

AAP was born out of the historic India Against Corruption (IAC) movement, one of the largest citizen-led movements in independent India and the greatest in this generation. Driven by the anger and frustration over endemic corruption scandals in the Congress-led United Progressive Alliance (UPA) government, millions across India had rallied behind Anna Hazare—the octogenarian social reformer—and Arvind Kejriwal—one of India's leading anti-corruption activists and a key force behind the Right to Information (RTI) Act—seeking accountability. The movement demanded the legislation of a strong and effective Jan Lokpal Bill, which would ensure a truly independent federal anti-corruption watchdog with unfettered powers to take political corruption in India head-on, even at the Prime Minister's level. Despite widespread protests, street demonstrations and hunger strikes across the country between 2011 and 2012, the movement failed to accomplish its mission. Veteran politicians, unnerved by the audacity of the IAC movement, dared the activists to fight elections and form their own government if they wished to pass their bills.

This challenge was ripe for an undertaking. A section of IAC leaders led by Kejriwal decided to get into politics, form a government and clean up the system from within. The idea that a bunch of honest, patriotic and educated Indians with no political background could come together to form a viable political force seemed remote, perhaps even a pipe dream, to most Indians back then. Against all odds, the AAP was born on 26 November 2012 in New Delhi, which had emerged as the epicentre of the IAC movement.

Few political observers believed that the AAP would survive beyond the first few years. Yet, within a year of its formation, the party surprised everyone by securing twenty-eight out of seventy seats in the 2013 Delhi assembly elections. Arvind Kejriwal defeated Congress's three-time incumbent Chief Minister Sheila Dikshit by a record margin. With no other party mustering a full majority, the angry young man of Indian politics took oath as the Chief Minister of Delhi in December 2013, forming a minority government with the outside support of Congress.

Within days of assuming office, the first AAP government crystallized intentions to fight corruption through a slew of decisions: they launched a major anti-corruption campaign to catch corrupt government officials, announced a Comptroller and Auditor General of India (CAG) audit on Delhi's private electricity distribution companies and cracked down on private schools for exorbitant increase in school fees, among other steps.[1] The AAP government also announced major subsidies in water and electricity bills—the two issues it had campaigned aggressively on, alleging inflated bills were due to government officials colluding with stakeholders with vested interests. The word on the street was day-to-day corruption had visibly reduced.

The minority AAP government lasted only forty-nine days. The Chief Minister resigned in February 2014, after the

Delhi Jan Lokpal Bill failed to garner majority support in the Delhi assembly.

What happened next sent shock waves across Indian politics and captured global attention. AAP created history in the 2015 Delhi assembly elections by winning sixty-seven out of seventy seats—an unprecedented mandate of 96 per cent seats received by any party in the history of independent India. The Congress, which had ruled for three consecutive terms in Delhi from 1998 to 2013, was reduced to zero seats. The BJP, the group that won the maximum seats in the 2013 Delhi assembly elections and had obtained a huge mandate at the Centre less than a year ago under Prime Minister Narendra Modi, wound up with a tally of three seats. Shunned by Delhi voters in the 2014 Lok Sabha elections, AAP managed to achieve an electoral success beyond its or anyone else's wildest dreams.

A wide-eyed promise of change is perhaps what enamoured AAP to the people of Delhi. It wasn't just a commitment to rooting out corruption—a credential well established because of the legacy of the IAC movement and the performance of the forty-nine-day AAP government—but also a promise of *vyavastha parivartan,* a systemic change. In other words, AAP pledged a wholesale retooling of the government machinery in itself, and Kejriwal came to be the man people trusted to deliver on this bold promise. AAP had caught the pulse of Delhi's aam aadmi, who was frustrated with the establishment parties and their silence over issues that plagued people's daily lives—crumbling government schools, overcrowded and unreliable healthcare system, constantly rising water and electricity bills, long power cuts and rising pollution, among others.

Kejriwal and AAP had successfully convinced the Delhi voters that the problem lay in the DNA of all existing parties. It wasn't the case that the solutions to these challenges didn't exist; the truth was the existing parties had no intention to act on them. In many cases, politicians were in cahoots with vested interests, who profiteered by ensuring the system stayed unchanged. For example, most private schools are owned by politicians themselves, and it was in their self-interest to ensure a gradual deterioration of government schools such that even the poorest are compelled to send their children to private schools. Water supply lines in the national capital hadn't reached one-third of its population living in the outer areas; these regions were serviced by private water tankers, many owned by local politicians.

With AAP in power, the stage was now set for the unveiling of a brand-new model of governance, one that wasn't about fixing a specific issue but about fixing how governance itself worked in India. But how does a promise of systemic change of the government machinery translate to reality? Just like no template existed for the rise of AAP as a political force, no governance template existed thus far for what the AAP government set out to do.

When they assumed office on 14 February 2015, Chief Minister Kejriwal and his cabinet did not have any grand plan or a five-year blueprint to deliver the transformative change they had promised. Yet, they had every intention and commitment to do whatever it took to get the job done. Therein began the journey to create, day by day, brick by brick, a unique model of governance, which the AAP refers to as the 'Delhi Model'. Over the next five years, deep reforms were initiated in multiple sectors—particularly education, health, water, electricity, transport and air pollution—that had the most direct impact on the daily lives of the people.

As soon as Chief Minister Kejriwal took over the reins of the Delhi administration, a war on corruption was announced, and government budgets were redesigned from scratch to deliver the outcomes that none before had thought to be even possible.

Can government schools perform better than private schools? Is it even conceivable that students will drop out of private schools to stand in queue for admission to government schools? Can quality primary healthcare be available free of cost in every neighbourhood—for the rich and the poor? Can a public healthcare system provide free and quality healthcare to all citizens for any ailment, irrespective of its cost? Can free and 24 x 7 electricity be available to every household? Can our cities succeed in substantially reducing air pollution? Can we make rapid progress in transitioning to electric vehicles (EVs) and renewable energy? Can free public transport become a tool for empowering India's women, enabling them to better access education and job opportunities? Can India have inflation lower than developed nations?

The answer to any of these questions in 2015 would have invariably been: 'Not in India, not at least in our lifetime'. Yet, over the course of its two terms, the AAP government in Delhi managed to turn most of these dreams to reality. Such was his confidence in delivering upon his promises to the people that Kejriwal approached the 2020 Delhi assembly elections with a bold declaration to voters: 'Vote for me only if you think I have done work, do not vote for me if I have done no work.' Few incumbent Chief Ministers or even Prime Ministers may have made such a direct appeal to voters based on their work alone.

So how did the Delhi voters respond? They created history once again. AAP became the first incumbent party in independent India to be voted back to power with yet another historic mandate of sixty-two out of seventy seats—around 90 per cent seats. What was to be the biggest test of whether the Delhi Model impacted the lives of the people of Delhi turned into its greatest endorsement. Starting out as an avowedly anti-corruption party in 2015, the AAP asked for the people's vote in the 2020 Delhi assembly elections on a much broader platform of *kaam ki rajneeti* (politics of work), which has come to be identified as its political ideology ever since. Here was a party that shunned talk of grand ideologies and instead prided itself on having the capability to transform the daily lives of citizens in ways that no other party could.

The Delhi Model is often caricatured as an exercise in freebie politics by political opponents, yet nothing could be further from the truth. For sure, the Delhi Model has enabled the aam aadmi to access a range of welfare goods for free, allowing them to live a life of dignity, while the state government has been consistently delivering a revenue surplus state budget since 2015. It is also true that the Delhi Model has brought the issues of education and healthcare from the margins to the centre of Indian politics. Since Independence, experts and political parties have sermonized about prioritizing social sector spending, yet no party has showed a willingness to do so while in power. For the first time in Indian history, Delhi's AAP government allocated nearly 40 per cent of its annual budget to education and health—nearly 25 per cent to education and 15 per cent to health—as compared to an average of 18–20 per cent for all other Indian states. AAP is also the only political party that places education and healthcare as a central plank across its election manifestos. While some parties may have started copying the freebies that are one pillar of the Delhi Model, none have come close to replicating the scale and ambition of the entire Delhi Model.

The model also puts forth a profoundly new approach to governance. It rejected the fetish for gross domestic product (GDP) growth and glossy infrastructure projects—an article of faith for most Indian governments—as the primary marker of progress; it instead put a full stop to decades of neglect faced by the Indian people, especially the less privileged, from their governments. By pivoting the focus of the entire government on issues that directly impact the lives of the lower- and middle-classes and furthers their human potential, the Delhi Model stands in sharp contrast with existing governance templates, particularly the Gujarat Model.

After receiving a record mandate in the 2020 Delhi assembly elections, the Delhi Model of governance has been AAP's trump card in all its electoral battles henceforth. AAP famously fought the 2022 Punjab assembly elections on the platform of replicating the Delhi Model in Punjab, winning ninety-two out of 117 seats—the largest mandate for any political party in Punjab's history. It was the promise of implementing the Delhi Model during the 2022 Gujarat and Goa assembly elections that endeared AAP to their voters too.

Despite being a completely new entrant to a fiercely contested political space, the AAP secured a 13 per cent vote share in Gujarat, winning five MLA seats and a 7 per cent vote share in Goa, winning two MLA seats. With this, it achieved the distinction of becoming India's youngest-ever national party, as per the Election Commission of India (ECI).[2]

The book begins by defining the Delhi Model, decoding the key principles underpinning it and contrasting it with the dominant thinking of economic growth being pursued by the two established parties in India—the BJP and Congress—over the past three decades. The subsequent six chapters dive deep into six key sectors—education, health, air pollution, transport, electricity and water—to portray how the Delhi Model has delivered transformational results over the first nine years of the AAP government's rule i.e. until mid-2024. These sectors have been chosen, for they matter the most in the day-to-day life of any citizen and fall under the domain of the Delhi government. The issues of crime and women safety, among the most important issues in the national capital, have been left out since the Central government exercises jurisdiction over law and order in Delhi through the Delhi Police.

The first section under each sector gives an overview of the key reforms initiated by the AAP government over the past decade and how have they transformed the lives of the people of Delhi. The subsequent sections dive deeper into many of these key reforms, tracing their exciting journey from ideation to execution. The final section under each sector draws out the implications for scaling up the Delhi Model nationally. It attempts to critically analyse the policy failures of our successive governments at the Centre, especially the BJP-ruled government since 2014, and provides a road map for building a modern India by leveraging the principles of the Delhi Model. In doing so, I do not presume that Delhi has all the answers for a country as vast and diverse as India. The intention is only to draw out what lies at the heart of Delhi's transformation and how might those policy lessons scale up nationally.

The eighth and the final chapter gives a round-up of the confrontation between the AAP government in Delhi and the BJP government at the Centre, acting through the Lieutenant Governor (L-G) of Delhi, which has shadowed the entire term of the AAP government's rule. The confrontation has been precipitated by the Centre in two major ways. First, through the fight to wrest control over Delhi's bureaucracy away from Delhi's elected government, despite a unanimous verdict of a five-judge constitutional bench of the Supreme Court in 2023 favouring the Delhi government. Second, by unleashing the full wrath of the Centre's investigative agencies upon the AAP government and its leaders. An understanding of the impediments faced in the implementation of the Delhi Model due to constant interference by the Centre is critical to truly appreciate the constraints under which the AAP government had to deliver, and why some of the progress still remains pending.

Chapter 1

What Really Is the Delhi Model?

The Birth of the Delhi Model

As the sun dawned on Delhi on 14 February 2015, the air was suffused with hope and optimism. To the people of Delhi, the day felt different from any other in recent memory. An overwhelming number of them—across divides of class, caste and religion—had rejected the two grand old parties that dominated the capital's politics for decades, the Congress and BJP, and instead voted to power a new party born barely two years ago. The AAP won 96 per cent seats in the Delhi assembly—charting a verdict that shocked all veteran political observers and made global headlines.

AAP's sudden rise, 'next to BJP's and Congress's obliteration, marked a clean break from Delhi's 'politics-as-usual' electoral climate. People's anger and frustration wasn't just with corruption endemic to Indian politics but extended to the neglect and alienation embedded in the way elected governments functioned. Even after seven decades of independence, all prior governments in the national capital appeared either unable or unwilling to fix issues that animated the household conversations of an average aam-aadmi. Government schools were crumbling; healthcare systems were overcrowded and unreliable; water supply was deficient and sewage systems hardly serviced Delhi's outer areas; power cuts were long and rampant. Pollution rose, so did inflation, and crimes against women made daily headlines.

Arvind Kejriwal had successfully convinced Delhi voters that the AAP had answers to all these problems. People's frustration with establishment parties had found an outlet in a rookie party formed by a group of zealous, honest and educated Indians with little money—truly the aam aadmi— who campaigned extensively on the promise of eliminating corruption and a wholesale retooling of the government itself. A *vyavastha parivartan*, as they called it. Mr Kejriwal and the AAP caught the pulse of Delhi voters that nobody else could.

That morning, as Arvind Kejriwal took oath as the Chief Minister, tens of thousands of people across Delhi and India thronged the precincts of the Ramlila Maidan to watch the historic event unfold before their eyes.

Doubt subsisted in this atmosphere: how exactly would the next five years unfold remained a matter of conjecture. Naysayers were aplenty. Delhi's political elite held the AAP and Arvind Kejriwal too anarchist and inexperienced in the ways of running a government to achieve anything substantial. In AAP's political promise of honesty and aam aadmi-oriented governance, which made it extremely popular among average Delhi voters, critics saw naïve idealism. Many mocked the newly elected CM, saying he had promised something that could never be delivered. Take electricity costs: the outgoing Congress Chief Minister Sheila Dikshit had once infamously told the people of Delhi to use less power if they couldn't afford hiked charges, holding the inflated electricity bills as a fact of life.[1]

AAP offered the first peek into its proposed scale of transformation in its manifesto for the 2015 Delhi assembly elections. Prepared after months of consultations with subject matter experts and hundreds of meetings with citizens from all sections of Delhi's population—an exercise called Delhi Dialogue—the AAP came up with seventy action points that aimed to make Delhi a better place to live for every Delhiite.[2] The consultative process adopted while formulating its first manifesto would later become an inherent feature of AAP's governance model through its newly established government think-tank, the DDC.

The 2015 manifesto included some of AAP's most popular promises while campaigning, including legislating the Delhi Jan Lokpal Bill, ensuring free water upto 20,000 liters per month to every household, cutting electricity bills by half, among others. Health and education sectors found cursory mention as the party promised to increase their respective budgets. However, the document offered sparse details about the nature or magnitude of the reform agenda as part of AAP government's *vyavastha parivartan*.

The first definitive signal that the new AAP government meant business came on 24 June 2015, during the maiden budget speech of Delhi's new deputy chief minister and finance minister Manish Sisodia. The new government, announcing its decision to double the spending on education and increase the spending on health by 45 per cent over the previous year, took many within and outside the government by surprise.[3] It became clear in the subsequent years that this decision was not a flash-in-the-pan moment: the AAP government continued to prioritize spending on education and health above all others. In its first nine years in power, the party has consistently increased the allocation to education; as of 2024, education spending accounts for 25 per cent of the total budget. Explaining why, Arvind Kejriwal said on more occasions than one, 'If good education is provided to every child in the country, they can eradicate poverty in their families within one generation.'[4] The belief ran deep within the party's leadership —world-class education for all children was perceived as the foundation to build a modern India and to rid the country of poverty.

The Delhi Model of governance was yet to take shape. The first glimpse came from the unlikeliest of places—a Twitter reaction between CM Arvind Kejriwal and PM Narendra Modi, during the latter's launch of the Make in India campaign in September 2015. Countering the PM's call to global investors to set up manufacturing units in India and avail generous incentives, the Delhi CM shot back on

Twitter: the goal cannot be achieved without 'Making India' first by investing in education, health, water, safety, justice and infrastructure for all citizens, he said. 'People are our best asset. Invest in them and the world will follow us.'[5]

This honest, even if spur of-the-moment, response from Mr Kejriwal highlighted the drastically different visions of two of contemporary India's tallest political leaders. Mr Modi with his Gujarat Model held an image for attracting big investments and building shining new infrastructure. Mr Kejriwal, on the other hand, barely seven months into his term as Delhi's Chief Minister, expounded a profoundly different vision of investing in *people* first to build a modern India. From here began the monumental task of shaping the Delhi Model of governance.

So what really is the Delhi Model?

At its core, the model rests on three principles. First and foremost, prioritize investments in building human capabilities and improving the quality of life of the aam aadmi—the lower and middle classes. The nation prospers only if all its people prosper. In other words, make India, first. Second, declare a war on corruption, for corruption eats into the government's limited budgets and directly compromises the delivery of government schemes and programmes meant to transform the lives of the aam aadmi. Third, make a firm commitment to fiscal prudence. The aforementioned gains can be sustained *only* if government budgets continue to grow on the back of a healthy state economy without pushing the state into a debt trap.

Let's look at these three principles in greater detail and how have they been applied by the AAP government in Delhi.

Make India, First

It's hardly a secret that even after seventy-eight years of independence, India ranks pathetically low in global human development indices. India's rank in the United Nation's Human Development Index (HDI) dropped in the last 10 years—from 130 in 2014 to 134 in 2023–24.[6] On the 2023 Global Hunger Index, India ranks 111 out of 125 countries. The 2024 Global Gender Gap Index of the World Economic Forum places India at 129 out of 146 countries.[7] Sure, there have been overall gains in health, education and other parameters nationally, but other countries seem to be making faster progress in far lesser time than India. For example, Bangladesh has historically trailed India in HDI rankings; yet, in 2023–24, Bangladesh was ranked at 129, five spots above India. China (75), Sri Lanka (78), Bhutan (125) and Iraq (128) all rank above India.[8]

These rankings mirror a truth known only too well among development experts and politicians alike. No nation of unhealthy and poorly educated people can ever become a great and powerful nation; no amount of foreign direct investment (FDI) or rhetoric around GDP growth is going to fix these issues automatically, only elected governments can do so through wilful and thoughtful interventions. Countless government committees and policies since independence, including the National Education Policy 2020, have recommended prioritizing education and health above all else. Leaders in the current and past generations have sung paeans over it, yet no political party has made these issues their singular focus while in power. Neither BJP nor Congress—who ruled at the Centre and in several states for decades since Independence—can claim to have transformed the public education and healthcare systems in a single state. While world-class education and healthcare are foundational to develop a nation's human capabilities, it is also unthinkable that societies can flourish without access to cheap and 24 x 7 electricity, clean and affordable drinking water, clean air, public safety for women and public transport systems accessible to all.

As Chief Minister, Arvind Kejriwal made these issues his government's mission when setting about the promise of transforming Delhi—not for global investors or tourists, but for the people living in Delhi. Deep reforms were initiated in all areas that affected Delhi's aam aadmi the most, such as education, healthcare, water and sanitation, electricity, public transport, air pollution, social welfare and inflation. The results speak for themselves.

Throughout its two terms, the AAP government in Delhi was the only one nationally to consistently spend over half of its budget on social sectors—with education and health receiving the largest push.[9] Expenditure on social welfare quickly became an article of faith for the government. Former Education Minister and Deputy Chief Minister Manish Sisodia, in a *Hindustan Times* interview in 2016, challenged the traditional definition of infrastructure as one limited to constructing flyovers and roads, and said the 'understanding of economy and development' should also include building modern government schools or laying water pipelines to unserved areas.[10] Mr Sisodia said to this author once that he was willing to build one road or flyover less if it allowed him to build a world-class government school first.

Driven by this radical vision, the AAP government built over 22,700 new classrooms in Delhi government schools in its first nine years, compared to 24,100 classrooms built in the preceding seven decades. The school infrastructure in all existing schools was fundamentally transformed and upgraded to world-class standards with many schools sporting AC auditoriums, modern libraries, swimming pools and some even housed hockey turf grounds. An all-out focus on pedagogy and teaching quality saw government schools consistently trump private schools in Class 12 CBSE results from 2016 onwards. Bucking the national trend of reducing enrolment in government schools, over 2,00,000 students have left Delhi's private schools to join government schools. An increasing number of government school students clear JEE and NEET examinations every year—their numbers touching a record high of 730 and 1,414 respectively in 2024.[11] Government schools have also become laboratories of curriculum innovations, developing frameworks such as the Happiness Curriculum and Entrepreneurship Mindset Curriculum, which attract global attention. The transformation caught the attention of the former US First Lady Melania Trump who chose to visit a 'happiness class' in Delhi in 2020 during President Donald Trump's official visit to India. In a rare international recognition, the *New York Times* in 2022 carried a front-page feature on how AAP's education model transformed the lives of millions of poor families in Delhi.[12]

The AAP government made parallel strides in healthcare. It created India's first health guarantee model through a three-tier system comprising *mohalla* (neighbourhood) clinics, polyclinics and tertiary care hospitals that provide free-of-cost care to every citizen, rich or poor, for any kind of ailment. The novel concept of mohalla clinics, introduced for the first time in India, received much global acclaim for its ability to make affordable and quality primary healthcare available at the doorstep of every citizen. Over nine years, Delhi's 540 mohalla clinics have registered over seven crore outpatient visits, serving over 60,000 patients every day through free consultations, tests and medicines. Government hospitals underwent a makeover too to cater to increased demand. The preceding governments over seven decades had created a capacity of 9,523 beds in Delhi's government hospitals by 2015; the AAP government added 4,185 beds or nearly 44 per cent capacity in the next nine years, with construction projects expected to add another 16,000 beds by 2026 at an advanced stage.

The government also made substantial headway in water, sanitation and hygiene facilities. Free lifeline water was provided to every household of Delhi for upto 20,000 litre per month to secure a basic human right. The government made unprecedented investments in expanding the reach of the water supply network and sewage network to unserved areas, especially unauthorised colonies that house a third of Delhi's population. Over 5,200 km of water pipelines were laid, increasing the share of unauthorised colonies having access to piped water supply from 54 per cent in 2015 to 99.6 per cent in 2024.[13] Another 2,100 km of water pipelines were laid to service rural areas and resettlement colonies, while 3,500 km of old pipelines were replaced. Put together, the AAP government installed over 1,000 km of water pipelines every year in the national capital. Additionally, over 4,400 km of sewer lines were laid in unauthorised colonies during this period, increasing the share of colonies connected to the sewage network from just 13 per cent in 2015 to 57 per cent in 2024.

In the power sector, the electricity distribution network was upgraded and made reliable—Delhi transitioned in five years from a region witnessing long power cuts every summer to the first Indian state with 24 x 7 power supply.[14] To make electricity affordable for all, the AAP government kept the electricity tariffs in check over both its terms, even as the tariffs continued to rise year on year in most Indian states over the last decade. In 2015, the AAP government decided to provide 50 per cent subsidy on domestic electricity bills up to 400 units. Expanding the subsidy, from 2019 onwards, it started providing free lifeline electricity up to 200 units to every household and 50 per cent subsidy on bills between 200 and 400 units. A massive expansion in solar and renewable energy was initiated with the result that its share in Delhi's installed capacity increased from virtually nil in 2015 to one-third by mid-2024. Plans are underway to switch to 50 per cent renewable power by 2027.

Air pollution was perhaps the toughest challenge for the AAP government—not due to a lack of will or knowledge, but because the problem is truly regional in nature and requires coordinated actions from all the state governments in the National Capital Region. Yet, the AAP government took a series of unrivalled bold actions. First, it shut down all thermal power plants within Delhi's boundaries. Second, it ensured all 1,627 industrial units in Delhi transitioned from polluting fuels such as coal, diesel, etc. to clean Piped Natural Gas (PNG). Third, it initiated a massive greening drive planting nearly three crore trees and increasing Delhi's green cover to a record 23 per cent in 2021. Fourth, it implemented an ambitious electric vehicle policy, which allowed Delhi to emerge as the EV capital of India with a 12 per cent registration rate among new vehicles, the highest in India so far. Fifth, it modernized and increased the fleet of Delhi's public bus system to a record 7,700 vehicles, including nearly 2,000 electric buses. The collective net result is an unprecedented decline by 45 per cent in pollution levels over the last decade—contrary to the gloomy picture usually painted about Delhi's air pollution.[15]

Public transport is usually the lifeline of any city and the backbone of its economy. It became AAP government's mission to create a public transport system that is convenient, accessible and affordable for every Delhi resident, rich or poor. During AAP's tenure, Delhi has emerged as the city with the largest fleet of public buses as well as electric buses across India: the capacity of the public bus fleet was expanded from 6,100 buses in 2015 to 7,700 buses by mid-2024—25 per cent of these were zero emissions electric buses. There is a plan underway to increase the fleet size to 10,480 buses by the end of 2025, with electric buses accounting for nearly 80 per cent of them. Similarly, the government doubled the Delhi metro network with an addition of 200 km network length between 2015 and early 2024, as compared to 193 km network developed over the previous 17 years. In a move that promised to encourage women's mobility and improve their access to education and work, the AAP government in 2019 became the first globally to make bus rides free for all women—a policy decision at first derided by political parties, but later adopted by several Indian states. As of early 2024, Delhi's women had availed almost 170 crore free bus rides.

Apart from sectoral reforms, the AAP government also undertook steps to create a strong social safety net for marginalised populations in the city. In March 2017, the Delhi cabinet approved a hike of 36 per cent in Delhi's minimum wages, making it the highest in India.[16] The step reportedly benefited more than 50 lakh workers in Delhi. With annual hikes to reflect inflation, an unskilled worker in Delhi in mid-2024 was legally entitled to a minimum wage of ₹17,494 per month—compared to the national minimum wage of ₹5,340 per month, and ₹10,250 per month in the neighbouring Uttar Pradesh. The government also expanded the coverage of seventeen social welfare schemes, designed for construction workers, from a mere 39,000 in 2015 to over 12 lakh people in 2022; the AAP government's financial assistance to construction workers hit by Covid-19 lockdown reached ₹280 crores. For over 9,00,000 senior citizens, women in distress and disabled individuals covered under the government's social security pension schemes, the AAP government hiked the pension amount from ₹1,500 to ₹2,500 per month—the highest in India.

The AAP government's roster of reforms was not only recalibrating the rhythm of life in Delhi, but also provided to its people a resilient shield from retail inflation. Delhi has reported the lowest retail inflation figures pan India for years now: as of April 2024, its year-on-year inflation stood at 2.18 per cent, which was less than half of the national average of 4.83 per cent and two-thirds lower than the neighbouring BJP-ruled states of Haryana and Uttar Pradesh (Figure 1).[17] Interestingly, Delhi's inflation in April 2024 was lower than many industrialised economies, including the US (3.5 per cent), the UK (3.2 per cent), Japan (2.7 per cent), France (2.4 per cent) and Germany (2.3 per cent).[18] The AAP government has thus laid a template to fight soaring inflation that has persistently dogged the Indian economy, and managed to register advances far ahead of other Indian states as well as advanced economics globally.

Figure 1: Retail inflation (year-on-year, in %) for Indian states in April 2024

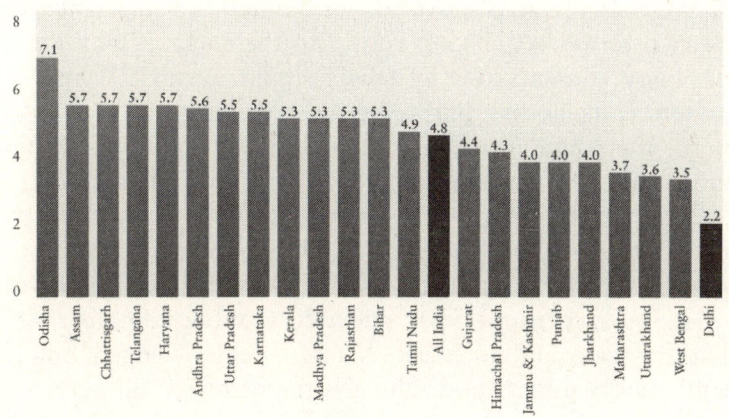

Source: Ministry of statistics and programme implementation[19]

The Delhi Model of governance, with a commitment to building human capital and promoting social welfare pledged into its core, rejects the fetish for GDP numbers and glossy infrastructure projects as the primary marker of progress. The subsequent chapters will elaborate on the untold story of transformation and reform in key sectors in greater detail. If the model's first principle was a humane plea to improve the way of life for the aam aadmi, the second proposition was more hawkish in nature: to declare a war on corruption.

War on Corruption

Looking at the AAP government's outcomes in Delhi over the two terms, a question rushes to the surface: why aren't more governments able to deliver similar results? Why have governments across party lines since independence failed to fix the foundational issues of health, education, water, and power, which determine the quality of life for voters? The answer lies in plain sight: corruption, charged by the nexus between vested interests in every industry and political power, which has managed to corrode intent and initiative.

In India, corruption is so endemic to public administration that its scale and intensity is often acknowledged but its depth rarely understood. There is the ordinary, all-pervasive kind of retail corruption that plagues almost everything the government touches. Like a chameleon, this corruption changes colours and faces: an average middle-class citizen may pay off an official to expedite work, the poor could use a bribe to get their fair share of government entitlements such as MGNREGA wages or old-age pension or a street hawker might be compelled to bribe cops every week to protect their cart from seizure. Then there are the headline-grabbing, big-ticket corruption scandals in massive public projects that define and diminish government regimes—including the Bofors Scam, Coal Scam and Commonwealth Games Scam. Here, a well-defined 'cut' typically goes to all key officials in the food chain, leading its way back to the political bosses.

The bitter truth, though, is that corruption is even more pervasive than this: like a moth, it chews every fibre woven into the fabric of governance in India. Much of the decay is hidden from public view, but graft silently compromises the delivery of every single government programme or scheme meant to transform the lives of the aamaadmi. Additionally, it eats into the limited budgets of governments in a large, populous country like India. Name a sector and you will find well-entrenched vested interests—operating as brazenly as mafias—who call most of the shots. These external forces ensure government schools don't improve; water pipelines don't reach the last mile, pushing people to purchase water at exorbitant rates; public infrastructure projects overshoot budgeted costs and electricity tariffs keep rising year on year. Corruption is not a passive enemy—it is a culture of perversion obstructing every project the government undertakes where nothing gets done without bribes or kickbacks.

Therefore, the platitude of 'zero tolerance on corruption' that all political parties these days serve in their election manifestos, rings hollow. For a government that intends to transform the lives of its people, the only credible response is to declare a war on corruption.

That is exactly what the AAP, with its well-established identity of an anti-corruption crusader, set out to do when it assumed office in February 2015. The Anti-Corruption Branch (ACB) and the soon to be enacted Delhi Jan Lokpal Bill were going to be its two primary weapons. Within a year though, the BJP-ruled Centre would snatch both these tools from the AAP government's arsenal.

AAP's vision for the ACB was blunted in less than 70 days. The sequence of events was such: Mr Kejriwal upon taking office in 2015 set about reviving the defunct ACB and tasking it with stamping out corruption from every government department in Delhi. As per the constitutional scheme of governance, the Delhi Police reports to the Central government without any involvement of the elected Chief Minister; however, ever since Delhi achieved partial statehood in 1993, the ACB reported directly to the Delhi Chief Minister, upholding its mandate of checking corruption among government officials. With this express knowledge, Mr Kejriwal vowed to weave into the ACB a fresh purpose and resilience. Budgets and strength of inspectors were doubled with immediate effect; global best practices of anti-corruption units studied and implemented and staff were trained to handle the deluge of corruption complaints the AAP expected.[20]

Mr Kejriwal, while launching the dedicated anti-corruption helpline in April 2015, encouraged citizens to participate in this noble war. Take sting videos or audio recordings of any government official demanding bribe, and the ACB would respond within 48 hours, he promised. The helpline was soon flooded with over 3,000 calls every day—although few missives provided actionable evidence. The ACB within two months arrested 35 and suspended 152 officers, sending shock waves across government departments. Mr Kejriwal had earlier promised that 'Delhi will be ranked among the five least corrupt cities in the world in the next five years.'[21] The message rung loud and clear among officials and the public alike.

But these activities came to an abrupt halt on 8 June 2015, when the BJP-ruled Centre sent paramilitary forces to ACB's office to snatch its authority away from the Delhi Chief Minister for the first time in 22 years.[22] The ACB was put under the control of the Centre. Commentators ascribed the purported motive to stymie the threat ACB presented to Central government ministers and officials, but if that were the case, the Centre could have put guardrails around ACB's scope of operation. The more plausible cause, one gleaned, was of political anxieties: the BJP-ruled Centre feared the soaring popularity of Mr Kejriwal and his anti-corruption drive and used its disproportionate powers to clip his wings. 'Centre took away my most potent weapon against graft by taking control of ACB,' Mr Kejriwal rued, a year later.[23]

Did the ACB lose its might? In the two months the ACB functioned under the AAP government, the body arrested 35 people, an average of 17 per month. Under the Centre's command, between 2015 and 2023, the ACB has managed to arrest only 104 government officials—approximately two per month—of which, conviction was secured in only 30 per cent of the cases.[24]

A similar trajectory was awaiting the Delhi Jan Lokpal Bill, the other centrepiece of Mr Kejriwal's war against corruption and among his most prominent election promises.

The legislation aimed to establish an effective, expeditious and independent anti-corruption authority—a public ombudsperson—chaired by a retired Supreme Court or High Court judge empowered to inspect corruption at every tier of the government. Mr Kejriwal, during his 49-day coalition government in early 2014 had failed to pass the Bill, but this time around, the Bill was passed easily and with much fanfare in the Delhi assembly on 4 December 2015.

The Centre intervened at once. Since Delhi is not a full-fledged state, the Constitution requires all bills approved by the Delhi assembly to be further approved by the Centre before they get notified as laws. The Centre used its veto to block the Delhi Jan Lokpal Bill 2015; just like it stonewalled the approval of 19 bills passed by the Delhi assembly in its first term.[25] The AAP government's marquee legislation to fight corruption never saw the light of day. Unsurprisingly, the BJP-ruled Centre also dragged its feet in implementing the consequential Lokpal and Lokayuktas Act, 2013, passed by the UPA government at the culmination of the historic India Against Corruption movement. The Centre took six long years before appointing the first Lokpal under the Act, and resorted to dilatory tactics ensuring the body remained toothless and irrelevant.[26] The public faith in the institution declined drastically: the body received 1,427 complaints in 2019–20, 110 complaints the next year, and by July 2021, registered no more than 30 grievances.[27]

With both its key moves stalled, the AAP government found itself in a bind and was impelled to change course. It shifted focus towards administrative corruption, which compromises the delivery of nearly every government initiative. Challenging this rot also happened to fall under the government's complete jurisdiction. To do so, the AAP government relied heavily upon technology and process innovations.

From compromised government tenders to shoddily built roads and bridges to non-delivery of essential services such as water supply and electricity, administrative corruption takes many forms. Such actions are led by vested interests—better known as mafias—in every sector and is entrenched into the system with the sanction of officials at ministerial levels. Within days of a new government assuming office, the compromised chain of officials are either assured about the safety of the status quo or get a signal if some adjustments have to be made. Administrative corruption, in other words, is sustained on the back of political corruption.

Any serious attempt to eliminate administrative rot must, therefore, start by rooting out political corruption—a settled question in the AAP government under Mr Kejriwal. The aggressive anti-corruption campaign made AAP's message clear, and the six Ministers that comprised the Delhi cabinet, apart from the Chief Minister, further reinforced this unyielding commitment to stamp out corruption in their daily dealings with department officials. Faltering from this ethos was not an option, even more so for members of the AAP administration. And in the one occasion that a Minister was found to falter from this ethos, the step taken by CM Arvind Kejriwal surprised everyone.

In October 2015, an audio clip emerged of Asim Ahmad Khan, the food and civil supplies minister, of allegedly accepting a bribe of ₹6 lakh. Mr Kejriwal immediately assessed the evidence and found it to be prima facie genuine. The misdemeanour, committed and caught within AAP's first year in office, could have been potentially very damaging to AAP's credibility. Mr Kejriwal's response, however, created a storm; without waiting for a media leak or an investigative agency raid, he held a press conference sacking the Minister then and there and referred the matter to the Central Bureau of Investigation (CBI).[28] The significance of his actions wasn't lost on Mr Kejriwal. It was possibly the first time a sitting Chief Minister had *suo-moto* sacked his own cabinet minister for he failed to live up to the standards of honesty the party had set for itself. 'Voters may overlook anything but not corruption. If our officer, minister, MLA or even my son or Manish is found involved in corruption, we will not spare anyone. This is the message we want to give to the entire administration,' he said, using the occasion to reaffirm AAP's commitment to running a clean administration.[29]

The stage was set for the AAP government to undertake the promised overhaul of administrative corruption. Eliminating this nexus of fraud requires a careful re-engineering of governance delivery itself to ensure vested interests have little control over outcomes—akin to design thinking. An illustration of a few striking case studies will show how the AAP government, with young, educated leaders at the helm, generously leveraged technology and innovation to achieve its desired goal.

Eliminating Touts Through Doorstep Delivery of Public Services

The AAP government's flagship initiative to tackle administrative corruption was a radical solution conceived to address the problem of touts that dot every government office in India. Much of the retail corruption that exists in government offices has nothing to do with the nature of the service but the opacity of the process that creates space for rent-seeking. From applying to documents such as income and caste certificates to availing benefits under a government scheme, the aam aadmi remains at the mercy of the local government official to get their work done. This direct contact created a flourishing industry for lakhs of middlemen, or touts—individuals seen hanging outside every government office to get the same job done *smoothly* albeit for a fee. AAP proposed eliminating touts through the doorstep delivery of public services, a simple yet radical solution. Instead of the citizen approaching the government office for a service, the government would send a mobile *sahayak*—a well-trained outsourced employee—with a mobile or a tablet to the citizen's home for a small fee of ₹50. Citizens could call the new toll-free helpline 1076 to enquire about services, documents required and schedule pick up appointments as per the citizen's convenience—just like what Amazon or Flipkart offer.

Resistance hit from every sphere. The bureaucracy was sceptical of the feasibility of such a complex effort; the L-G of Delhi found the solution an unnecessary waste of resources and refused to give his assent and lakhs of touts outside government offices stood furious. A mobile sahayak model, inspired by a shift towards doorstep delivery of private services such as e-commerce and food delivery, was indeed a complex idea to execute; it required bringing to a common IT platform diverse processes scattered across 35 government departments. AAP stood its ground, with Chief Minister Kejriwal firmly backing the massive reform. The initiative was launched in September 2018 starting with 30 services across 14 departments, and gradually expanded to 100 of the most in-demand services within a year.

The mobile sahayak model was an instant hit—the call centre received 11,000 calls the first day. Within one year, over 2.16 lakh requests for documents were serviced through the helpline with a 99.5 per cent success rate, as compared to a 57 per cent success rate for documents requested after a visit to a government office.[30] As if offering further validation of the initiative's success, a body representing touts filed an official complaint with the Delhi government for being rendered jobless and sought rehabilitation![31] By early 2024, the initiative had serviced over 6,00,000 requests for documents and was in the process of adding another 58 services to its list. The initiative has since received global recognition; the *Berkeley Public Policy Journal* called it 'a notable example of smart design thinking . . . a transformation from bureaucracy to technocracy'.[32]

Shutting Down RTOs and Automating Driving Tests to Curtail Transport Mafia

In Delhi, nearly three million service requests are received annually by the Regional Transport Offices (RTOs) for issues ranging from vehicle registration and issuing driving licenses to road transport permits. The need for physical verification of applicants in many service requests meant the doorstep delivery model couldn't completely eliminate the need for a physical visit; as a result, the proliferation of touts continued.

The AAP government dealt a decisive blow to the nexus at RTOs in August 2021. It became the first government to transition from in-person visits to faceless delivery of services using AI-based technology. To move the citizen to a completely self-reliant mode, the AAP government equipped the online process with e-sign and biometrics-based authentication, apart from instituting an e-learners license test through AI-based facial recognition, to help citizens adopt self-reliance. Those struggling with the technology could place a call to the 1076 helpline to connect with mobile sahayaks for assistance. Within a year, over 2.2 million service requests were received with pendency staying below 2 per cent at all times.[33] While launching the faceless services initiative in August 2021, Mr Kejriwal locked up Delhi's RTO offices, symbolizing the end of an era.

Driving tests, for which a physical visit proves unavoidable, presented an obstacle. It is common for RTOs pan India to issue driving licenses to an applicant if they approach through touts—a practice bound to have ramifications on road safety. The AAP government used technology to address this loophole. In 2018, it became the first government to transition away from conducting manual driving assessments to fully automated driving test tracks (ADTTs). ADTTs assess driving skills over 24 driving tests through sensors and CCTV cameras using video analytics technology and with zero human intervention—all within ten minutes. As of April 2023, for the first time in any Indian state, all Delhi's driving test tracks have been automated. Official records show the number of people clearing the test since automation has gone down—the average pass percentage at ADTTs is 50 per cent against the manual pass percentage of 70–80 per cent.[34]

Shutting Down Ration Mafia—an Unsuccessful Attempt

In Delhi, nearly 72 lakh families avail subsidised food grains through ration shops under the Food Security Act, 2013. However, ration distribution is plagued with challenges prevalent across India: shops receive poor quality of food grains, which are often stored in inferior conditions, and many ration shop owners engage in malpractices such as overcharging and black-marketing. Mr Kejriwal had closely witnessed the workings of the ration mafia when he was an activist working in Delhi's slums for a decade, and was determined to find a permanent solution to this perennial problem.

In line with the doorstep delivery template, the AAP government in 2018 conceived the ambitious Mukhya Mantri Ghar Ghar Ration Yojna, a scheme that delivered monthly pre-packaged ration packets directly to Delhi's citizens. The new model would scrap the role of ration shop owners, and beneficiaries were no longer required to wait for the ration shops to open or stand in long queues to access their entitlements. The plan was executed in two steps. The government sourced grains from the Food Corporation of India (FCI) godowns and sent it to the mills for processing and packaging. As an added convenience, packaged atta was provided instead of wheat. Food packages then reached the delivery agencies that planned distribution schedules and doorstep deliveries after successful biometric authentication. Existing beneficiaries were asked to choose between receiving ration through shops or through the doorstep delivery model. An overwhelming majority opted for the latter. 'People are asking if pizza, burger, smartphone and clothes can be home delivered, then why can't the poor citizens of Delhi get their share of ration home delivered?' said Mr Kejriwal, summarizing the initiative's appeal.

In addition to implementation challenges, the scheme was promptly challenged in the court by the ration shop mafia who had the most to lose. However, the AAP government won all cases and received a nod from the Delhi High Court to implement the scheme in September 2021. Tenders were successfully floated, milling units and delivery agencies onboarded and history was about to be made that would take India one step forward towards achieving food security. Political stars, however, were on a collision course. Since the rations were being distributed under a Central act, the L-G of Delhi refused to approve the ambitious rollout without the clearance of the BJP-ruled Centre—which never came. The AAP government reasoned that ration distribution was under state government jurisdiction, and the Centre's approval was unneeded, but the Delhi L-G did not relent. Petty politics won, and a pro-poor initiative that could have eradicated the ration mafia syndicate lost. In early 2024, the AAP government in Punjab, under Chief Minister Bhagwant Mann, launched the same initiative—finally creating history.

A Half-Won Battle

These examples highlight the effort and innovation it takes to defeat vested interests that have infiltrated every sphere of governance. More case studies in subsequent chapters will exemplify AAP government's long and continuous battle to eliminate administrative corruption—a fight which demands unyielding political will and a capacity to innovate. It is ironical that between 2022 and 2024, key members of the Delhi cabinet including Mr Kejriwal, who spearheaded these progressive changes, were arrested on trumped-up corruption charges by the Centre's investigative agencies and kept in jail without a trial for periods lasting up to two years. We will discuss this in detail in the concluding chapter of this book.

While there is little comparative data to measure the levels of corruption across states, a survey by Transparency International India and LocalCircles in 2019 revealed Delhi to be among the top five states where citizens reported low instances of corruption.[35] Incidentally, two of the top three departments that citizens reported paying a bribe to get work done in Delhi, per the survey, included the Delhi police (33 per cent) and the municipal corporation (21 per cent)—both administered by BJP-ruled governments. Globally, India's rank in the Transparency International's Corruption Perceptions Index has declined over the past decade, from 85 to 93 out of 180 countries.[36]

Delhi is undoubtedly far from finding its place in a list of the least five corrupt cities in the world, but AAP's government's doggedness to fight daily corruption—despite the Centre's continued hurdles—has contributed to a perceptible improvement in the level of transparency. For now, it can be said half the battle is won.

Commitment to Fiscal Prudence

The third principle underpinning the Delhi Model, fiscal prudence, acknowledges the need for sustained public investment in building human capital over decades to be able to envision and deliver transformational change. This commitment is not just desirable but essential—it allows governments to introduce new subsidies for vulnerable groups besides ensuring all citizens have universal access to basic services.

When the AAP government assumed power in early 2015, a common refrain amongst the naysayers was that the party promised too much. Where was the money to deliver on these promises? Unperturbed by the criticism, Chief Minister Kejriwal got down to business. Electricity and water subsidies were rolled out within days. In its first budget, presented in June 2015, the allocation for education was doubled and health's share was increased by 45 per cent. The message was clear: this government was going to walk the talk on social welfare. Simultaneously, the government initiated sustainable measures to meet these commitments, by expanding the budget pie and shoring up higher revenues through tax reforms. Delhi's economy is driven by the services sector; as a result, the Value Added Tax (VAT), precursor to the present Goods and Services Tax (GST), contributed 70 per cent of the government's total revenue collections. It was, therefore, the first target of fiscal reform.

Corruption is commonly understood to take place at the stage of programme or project implementation. However, venality enters the system even before the taxpayers' money hits government's coffers—at the stage of tax collection itself. Across India, a culture of 'raid raj' is pervasive in tax departments that sanctions incessant raids on businesses with the purported motive of catching tax evaders and shoring up government revenues. In reality, however, much of the hunt is a front, allowing tax inspectors to collect bribes for themselves and their superiors. The chain leads up to the political bosses, and the state exchequer gets shortchanged in the process.

Mr Kejriwal, having worked as an IRS officer in the income tax department, was familiar with the administration's intricate workings and its fault lines. He was convinced that for the state revenues to rise substantially, the current antagonistic culture between the VAT department and the business community will have to be replaced by a culture of trust and mutual respect. Individuals and businesses would willingly give their due share of taxes if they are treated not as thieves but with respect, and if they are assured that the taxpayers money will be put to honest use by the government. Meetings with market and trade associations in the run-up to the 2015 elections further reinforced this belief, with stakeholders unequivocally clamouring for an end to the fear-infested culture of raid raj.

This demand eventually found its way to the AAP manifesto, and Mr Kejriwal followed through when AAP's time came. The plug was immediately pulled off: tax inspectors no longer had the liberty to arbitrarily storm a business premise, requiring departments to gather sufficient evidence and get approval from the senior officials. Raids by Delhi's VAT department fell drastically from approximately 150 raids a month earlier to almost none.[37] Simultaneously, deputy chief minister and finance minister Manish Sisodia met with all prominent market and trade associations to get assurance that they will voluntarily comply with their tax obligations and rein in tax evaders. Tax collection goals were collectively set for each market area and honest officers were posted in the most sensitive areas. The transparent, efficient and effective tax administration system yielded results: VAT revenues rose by 17 per cent in the first year (compared to a mere 2.6 per cent in 2014–15)[38] and grew further by 19 per cent in 2016–17. The bold move had in turn forged a new partnership between the traders and their government.

This process of dialogue also further streamlined Delhi's tax administration. VAT rates were slashed across a range of products based on feedback from traders. Officials in the VAT department resisted initially, but the government persisted.

The revenues for wood and timber, whose tax rates were brought down from 12 per cent to 5 per cent, increased by 1 per cent the following year. Emboldened by the positive trend, Mr Sisodia and his team reviewed other tax slabs, mined the available data, carried out multi-level consultations and eventually decided to slash VAT rates from 12.5 per cent to 5 per cent across 44 products in 2016–17. No previous government had carried out such a tax reform in one sweeping stroke. A government under pressure to increase revenue collections chose to forgo the beaten path of increasing tax rates, and instead adopted an unorthodox decision to encourage tax compliance.

The government further tweaked the compliance mechanism to make it business-friendly and less expensive based on feedback from associations.[39] Ambiguities in filling out VAT returns were resolved; unique rewards schemes introduced; a cash reward of ₹5 lakh each announced for the top ten performing market associations, to be utilized for the overall benefit and maintenance of public conveniences.[40] A similar transparent and efficient mechanism was set up in all other major revenue streams to shore up collections. Within the first year, state excise revenues increased by 31 per cent as compared to 8.6 per cent growth in the previous year, and stamps registration fees increased by 21 per cent as compared to a negative 4.3 per cent growth in the previous year.[41]

It's the nature of corruption that it rears its head every once a while. Eternal vigilance is, therefore, not just the price of liberty but also a corruption-free state. AAP's feedback loop with city traders had in some ways bolstered the government's ability to stay vigilant. In October 2018, Mr Sisodia disbanded an entire 25-member team of tax inspectors (including commissioners and GST officers) based on a tip from trade associations. During Diwali that year, some tax inspectors sensing an opportunity to make a quick buck, resorted to the old ways of raid raj, with the cover that 'the (Lok Sabha) elections were round the corner and those running government needed money'.[42] This time-tested scheme had but one fatal flaw: the inspectors did not realize that most of the trade associations were directly connected to Mr Sisodia over WhatsApp.

Mr Sisodia verified the tip, swung into action, disbanded the team and sought new officers. He convinced representatives of various trade associations of strict action, and urged them to continue sharing WhatsApp photos of the officers who ask for money in the name of raids. 'I will not let him go scot-free,' Ms Sisodia's assured them.[43] This one incident shows how reforming a tax department needed a strong political will, devoted attention, trust and direct communication with citizen groups.

What did the AAP government's efforts in trust building amount to—did they create the necessary fiscal space required for the ambitious Delhi Model? The numbers bespeak a tale of triumph. In absolute terms, the Delhi government's budget under AAP has increased by two-and-a-half times within nine years (see Figure 2), an unmatched achievement in Delhi's history. The budget swelled by nearly ₹5,000 crore every year, from ₹30,940 crore in 2014–15 to ₹74,900 crore in 2023–24, as compared to the ₹1,200 crore yearly budget increase between 2009–10 and 2014–15. In annualized terms, the budget multiplied at a Compounded Annual Growth Rate (CAGR) of 10.3 per cent during AAP's tenure, almost two times faster than the 4.4 per cent during the five years before the AAP government came to power. To AAP and its supporters, this extraordinary growth in the state budget felt nothing short of a miracle and a testament to its promise of running an honest, transparent, and corruption-free administration.

Figure 2: Delhi government budget over the years
(in ₹ thousand crores)

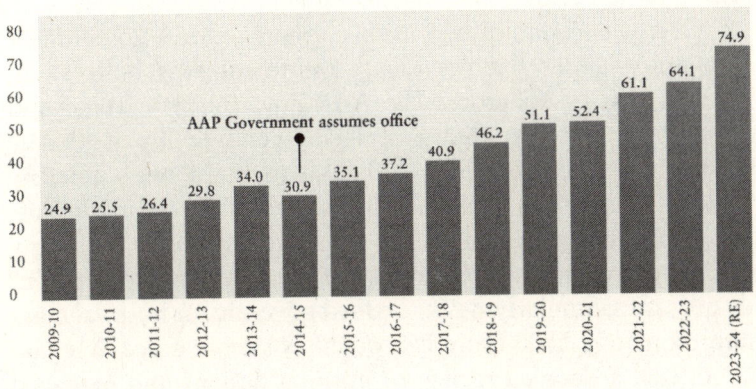

Source: Finance department, Government of NCT of Delhi

With tax reforms and revenue collection on track, the AAP government turned to optimising fiscal expenditure. Inefficiencies in spending are commonplace in government projects, some by design to generate kickbacks and some by sheer incompetence, and the next piece of AAP's puzzle was to minimise waste and stretch each penny of the taxpayer's money. History is crammed with examples of public projects that ended up costing many times over their original estimates. As many as 448 major infrastructure projects nationally were plagued with cost overruns of more than ₹5.55 lakh crore—almost 65 per cent of the sanctioned cost—during the quarter ending December 2023.[44]

Cutting costs without compromising on quality is not unattainable. It is possible by carefully scrutinizing projects at the design stage, axing elements that add little value to the people and meticulously monitoring implementation to rein in escalations—a guiding principle the AAP government put to action. The large infrastructure projects under the former public works department (PWD) minister Satyendar Jain are a case in point. Detailed design reviews at the Minister's level coupled with close monitoring during implementation ensured that the AAP government constructed 30 flyovers over nine years with a combined total savings of ₹557 crore—a rare feat.[45]

Cost was economised in other spheres too. A government dispensary under the previous government was built at an average cost of ₹5 crore. The AAP government's frugal and innovative mohalla clinics slashed spending by a drastic 96 per cent—it takes only ₹20 lakh to build one clinic. By building over 540 mohalla clinics over nine years in just ₹11 crore, the government has saved the spending of nearly ₹2,700 crore that would have gone into building government dispensaries. Similarly, a 500-bedded government hospital costs approximately ₹500 crore i.e. roughly ₹1 crore a bed. Mr Jain conducted a detailed review of hospital designs and managed to bring the construction cost down to approximately ₹30 lakh a bed.

When asked in an interview about his mantra for saving taxpayers' money, Mr Jain, an architect by profession, said:

'There's no rocket science to it. The biggest reason for cost overrun in any public infrastructure project is delays. Let's take the case of a ₹500 crore flyover project. Most public tenders have an in-built escalation clause for delays due to government inaction. This suits the contractors. Within two to three years, the same project will cost ₹1,000 crores. We put an immediate stop to this by ensuring there are no delays and if there are any, make the contractor accountable for it and pay a penalty to the government. Second, there is a practice in governments that if a project gets completed under the sanctioned cost, the contractors are encouraged to submit bills for the entire project cost since no questions will be asked anyways. We don't allow this in the AAP government.'[46]

For a government spending around ₹75,000 crore annually, systemically optimizing cost and monitoring projects required planning and precision. Mr Sisodia and his team came up with outcome budgeting, a unique and innovative idea to usher in transparency and accountability in public spending. The idea was fairly simple: to shift attention to results and outcomes that matter most to citizens. Annual planning and monitoring of programmes in Indian governments typically revolves around budget allocation, and periodically checking if the money is being spent and activities completed. 'Did they do it?' is the operative question to judge performance— did they build enough toilets, did they open schools and clinics? This approach, as pervasive as it is in public administration, misses the difference between doing the job, and doing it well. An outcomes-based approach shifts the perspective to the short and long-term outcomes of governance. The AAP government turned the operative question to instead ask 'So what?': so what if toilets were built, are they clean and functional and did open defecation reduce? So what if clinics were built, how many patients are served every day and are they satisfied with healthcare delivery?[47]

An outcome budget enshrines the 'so what' approach within governance by linking budgetary outlays to specific outputs (tangible services or infrastructure provided) and outcomes (short or long-term benefits to the people). It arms citizens with data to hold governments accountable, and in turn, empowers the elected leadership to identify inefficient spending and better orient the bureaucracy towards results. To borrow a corporate analogy, it is the equivalent of defining key performance indicators (KPIs) across government departments and tracing the value delivered for every rupee of taxpayer's money spent. [48]

Delhi's first comprehensive outcome budget report for 2017–18 reflected a herculean task lasting several months and involving hundreds of officials. Under Mr Sisodia's guidance, a team of officers from the planning department linked approximately 80 per cent of the budget across 34 departments to 1,900 unique performance indicators. The report also contextualised each indicator by including a baseline performance from the preceding year, and the envisioned targets for the next cycle. For a government in India, this was a bold act of *suo moto* disclosure.

It is now an annual ritual for the AAP government to publish and put in the public domain an outcome budget report every budget session, while also taking stock of the previous year's achievements. As if a rite of passage, city newspapers have a field day covering performance across departments and ranking the best to worst performing departments based on outcome budget indicators.

To date, Delhi's AAP government is the only state or union territory that carries out such a rigorous exercise of performance monitoring and disclosure, another testament to its commitment to fiscal prudence. The initiative has placed Delhi in the league of global cities that rigorously measure their governments' performances and make the data available in the public domain. A notable example of civic openness is New York City's budgeting exercise: the government has since 1977 released a half-yearly mayor's management report tracking the city's 44 agencies against 1,649 performance indicators.

This third principle of the Delhi Model also counters a common and lazy criticism of the AAP government's welfare governance—that subsidising water, electricity and transport will push the state into debt and eventual economic collapse. Look closely, and such critics will find the sum total of Delhi's subsides adds up to a mere 7 per cent of its annual budget; the remaining is reserved for the national capital's holistic development.

The 2021 CAG report on state finances further validated AAP's approach to fiscal prudence, noting that the Delhi government was the only one across India to run a revenue surplus budget every year for the period 2015–20, an achievement sustained till date.[49] Mr Sisodia remarked in the Delhi assembly: 'When every state government is facing a huge revenue deficit, it's only and only the Arvind Kejriwal government that is running revenue surplus since 2015. Honest politics brings prosperity.'[50]

Indians are used to hearing about piling government debts, but here was AAP, running a revenue surplus while making unprecedented investments into its people. A debt-free approach towards growth has been a distinctive feature of the AAP's fiscal model. Even as Indian states and the Centre continue to accumulate enormous debt to fund an ever-increasing gap between revenues and expenditure, Delhi is the least indebted state. The AAP government has managed to substantially reduce its debt to GSDP ratio (the preferred indicator to compare debts across governments), from 6.6 per cent to 3.9 per cent over the period 2015–23.[51] In contrast, the Central government's total debt has ballooned over the past decade, charting a 300 per cent rise from ₹53 lakh crore in 2014 to ₹169 lakh crore in 2024. In 2024–25, the Centre's budget will be financed by loans worth ₹14 lakh crores, constituting around 30 per cent of its annual budget. As of March 2023, the average debt to GSDP ratio for Indian states stood at 27.5 percent (see Figure 3).

Figure 3: Total Debt to GSDP ratio of Indian states/ UTs as of March 2023

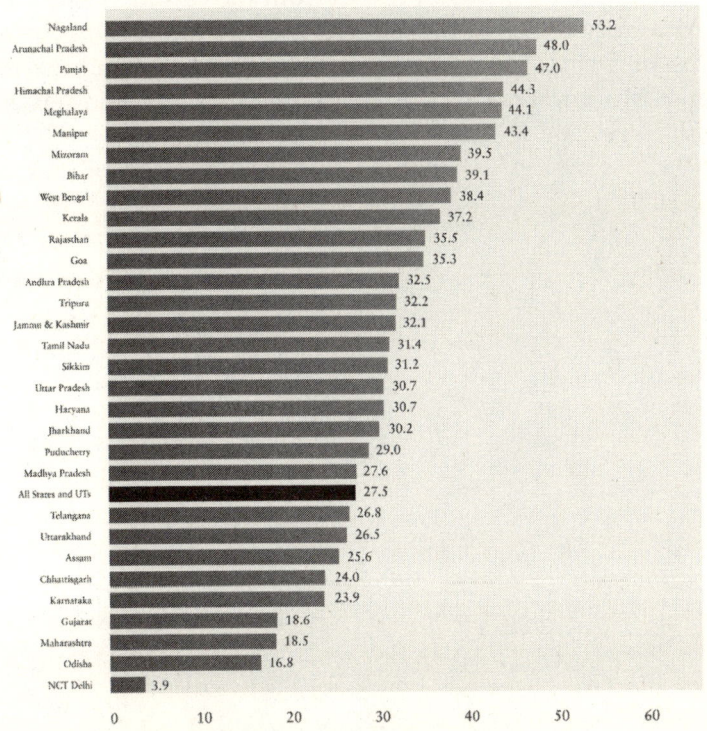

Source: State Finances: A Study of Budgets, RBI[52]

An interesting facet of the Delhi Model is its synchrony. Its three governing principles—investing in people, declaring a war on corruption and committing to fiscal prudence—work only in tandem. Remove any pillar from this model, and the model collapses. It is impossible to transform people's lives by reforming key sectors such as healthcare or education without declaring a war on corruption that directly compromises the delivery of almost every government scheme or without a robust financial plan to back the sustained investments it takes to see meaningful change over years. Take out fiscal prudence, and you are left only with idealism and empty promises. The Delhi Model succeeded only because the AAP government under Mr Kejriwal's leadership showed the political will and persistence to deliver on all three fronts, year after year, for nearly a decade.

A legitimate question comes from those well-versed with AAP's story in Delhi: the model may have improved people's lives in Delhi, but what is the long-term economic vision here? More importantly, is it scalable to states and nations with large economies?

Trickle-Down vs Trickle-Up Economics

Ahead of the final leg of the 2024 Lok Sabha elections, Prime Minister Narendra Modi in an interview was asked about India's growing inequality. The Prime Minister shot back: 'Do you want everybody to be poor? If everyone is poor, then there will be no difference.' He proceeded to explain his theory of economic growth: first a few will become rich, then their prosperity will reach the next layer, and so on until everyone reaps the benefits. The economic tide will shift gradually, not overnight, he said.[53]

This isn't a novel proposition: the 'rising tide lifts all boats' idea has been around for at least half a century and is what the economists call 'trickle down economics'. The hypothesis holds wealth creation at the top as the only way for an economy to grow; one cannot redistribute wealth or help the poor if there is no growth, the proponents of this theory argue. A government should thus focus through its taxation policies and economic reforms to support the rich—large corporates, businesses and entrepreneurs—for these resources should eventually 'trickle down' to the rest, benefitting everyone.

It is a tempting theory except for a small problem—it doesn't work.

Take the US, the poster child of the failure of trickle-down economics. For nearly four decades, from the start of the Reagan era, through Obama's presidency and till today, the US has drastically cut taxes on the rich, decreased social spending and deregulated the economy to boost economic growth. The result? The Nobel Prize-winning economist from Columbia University, Joseph Stiglitz, in his book wrote the trickle-down economic model has only increased income inequality and benefitted the richest 1 percent in the US.[54] Their share in the national income has more than doubled—from 10 per cent in 1980 to 21 per cent in 2015—while the median income of an average US citizen, adjusted for inflation, has stagnated. For those at the bottom of the pyramid, the outcomes were even worse: an inertia has beset the minimum wage, which has remained unchanged for 45 years. Any economic system,

Mr Stiglitz argues, that doesn't increase the standards of living of the majority of its people for a quarter of a century and makes those at the bottom worse off than they were almost half a century ago, is a failed economic model.[55]

Another seminal study analysed 50 years of tax cuts for the wealthy across 18 developed countries—from Australia to the UK and the US—in the hope that such measures will boost jobs and incomes for everyone else.[56] The researchers at the London School of Economics (LSE) and King's College found that the per capita gross domestic product and unemployment rates were nearly identical after five years in countries that slashed taxes on the rich and in those that didn't. The only change: the income of the rich grew at a faster rate in countries with lowered tax rates. Instead of trickling down to the middle class, tax cuts had largely helped the rich keep more of their riches while exacerbating income inequality.

Others like Robert Reich, a former US secretary of labour and a professor of public policy at the University of California, Berkeley, have lambasted trickle-down economics as a gonzo economic theory that continues to live on, notwithstanding its repeated failures.[57] He explains the fatal attraction of this repeatedly failed economic theory lies in its ability to satisfy politically powerful, moneyed entities who want to rake in even more wealth. These forces also ensure that a portion of their gains are invested in an intellectual infrastructure of economists and pundits who continue to promote a failed doctrine, thus confusing the public.

India too has held a long fascination with this failed economic theory. Ever since economic liberalisation in the 1990s, both Congress and BJP-led governments at the Centre have skimped on social sector spending and instead gave massive tax breaks, subsidies and interest-free loans to big corporate groups and foreign investors, in the hope their investments will raise overall economic growth. The Congress-led UPA regime arguably did invest into social sector schemes such as the Mahatma Gandhi National Rural Employment Guarantee Act (MGNREGA), 2005, and the Food Security Act, 2013, but its economic policies bore a distinct imprint of the trickle-down approach. The government promoted Special Economic Zones (SEZs) with massive tax breaks and awarded indiscriminate loans to large corporate houses that created the original bad loan crisis in India's public sector banks. While India recorded a sustained GDP growth at around 6.8 per cent during this period, inequality widened, and human development indicators remained dismal.

After 2014, the BJP-ruled Centre under Mr Modi has gone further than any other government in independent India to staunchly promote trickle-down policies. In 2019, the Centre unprecedently reduced the corporate tax rate from 30 per cent to 22 per cent for existing domestic companies, and to 15 per cent for new manufacturing companies. The decision wiped off ₹1 lakh crore from the Centre's annual revenues, shrinking the allocation to two dozen social sector schemes, including the midday meal scheme that caters to 12 crore school children, and the Pradhan Mantri Awas Yojna that has crores of poor families in the waiting list for free housing. The Centre has also pursued industrial policies that offered huge subsidies to investors, such as its flagship Production Linked Incentives (PLI) scheme that gives big corporates an incentive package of ₹2 lakh crores—more than the combined annual spending on education and health.[58]

India is also far from tiding over the bad loan crisis. Over the last decade, banks have written off nearly ₹15 lakh crore of bad loans of rich corporates from their books, with seemingly little consequences for over 12,000 wilful defaulters responsible for it.[59] Over two-thirds of these write-offs were done by public sector banks, which operate under the government's close supervision.[60] The Centre has reiterated that write-offs do not mean loan waivers and the recovery process with the borrower would continue; however, only 14 per cent of this amount was recovered until 2023. The remaining 86 per cent of bad loans, now written off, function as an equivalent of a freebie to the big corporates.[61] As the large corporate sector basked in this generous debt relief, India's public debt exploded from ₹53 lakh crore in 2014 to ₹169 lakh crore in 2023—an increase by 300 per cent.

Did India's idealised experiment with trickle-down on boosters yield results?

The largest study on India's income inequality in India holds some answers. Conducted by the World Inequality Lab and led by famed economist Thomas Piketty, the analysis reviewed trends over the past 100 years (1922–2023) to find that for the first time since independence, India is more unequal than it was under British rule. That's not all, the share of India's richest 1 per cent in its national income in 2022 exceeded all the G20 nations, surpassing even the US for the first time (Figure 4). Between 2002 and 2022, this group's share in the national income rose from 15 per cent to 23 per cent. In contrast, the share of the bottom 50 per cent population in the national income declined from 20 per cent to 15 per cent during this period. Even the share of the middle 40 per cent population dropped from 38 per cent in 2002 to 27 per cent in 2022. The study further found that during 2014–2022 under the BJP-led Central government, only the richest 10 per cent benefitted while the shares in the national income of the bottom 50 per cent or the middle 40 per cent population either stayed stagnant or declined (Figure 5).

Figure 4: Share of India's top 1 per cent in national income is highest among G20 nations

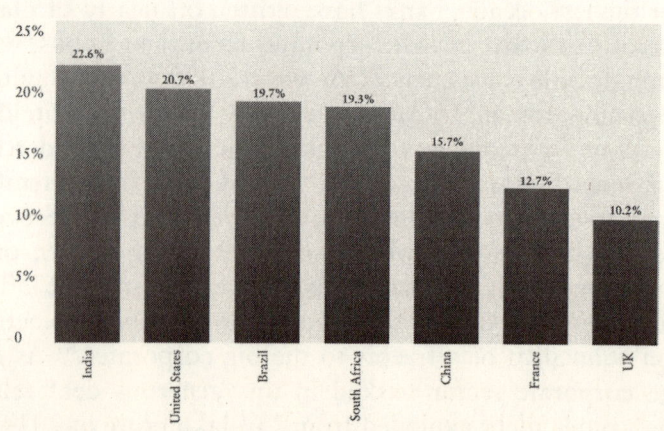

Source: Analysis by World Inequality Lab, 2024[62]

Figure 5: Trends in India's income inequality
from 1952 to 2022

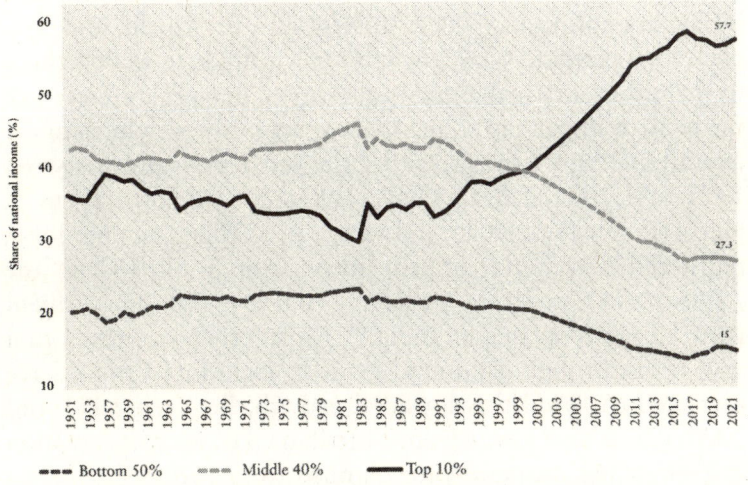

Source: Analysis by World Inequality Lab, 2024[63]

The fact that the economic conditions of India's middle classes and the poorest have stagnated over the past decade, even while the overall economy grew, was made out in the India Employment Report 2024 released by the International Labour Organisation (ILO) and the Institute for Human Development (IHD). The study uses official government data to reveal that over the decade 2012–22, the real wages (inflation adjusted) of regular salaried workers declined by 1 per cent each year, with the wages in urban areas dwindling at a faster pace than in rural areas.[64]

To make things worse, the Indian economy has over the last decade failed to create enough jobs, registering the highest unemployment rate of 6.1 per cent in 45 years in 2017–18. News stories abound with stories of young people, their numbers estimated in lakhs, competing for a handful of government job vacancies. Out of the 20 million jobs Mr Modi promised every year back in 2014, the Centre admitted in 2023 that it was able to generate only 1.5 million jobs every year during its tenure.[65] It's amply clear that India's GDP figures belie an unprecedented wage, jobs and consumption crisis.

Yet, the BJP-ruled Centre has sung hollow praises of the Indian economy, now the fifth largest in the world, and its 6 per cent aggregate GDP growth rate. It made little difference to them that, as far the prosperity of the masses is concerned, the growth in per capita income carries more weight than the overall GDP growth (driven by the top 1 per cent). Between 1991 and 2021, India's GDP rank ascended from 17 to 5. However, on the metric of average per capita income, India registered a minimal improvement from rank 161 in the 1990s to 159 in 2021—reflecting that it is only the affluent who have prospered in India.[66] Most other countries that saw breakthrough economic growth, including China, have managed to avoid this lopsided growth. Between 1991 and 2021, China's rank rose from 11 to 2 in GDP, while its position in average per capita income climbed from 158 to 75.[67]

One wonders if there is a way to remedy the present crisis borne out of two decades of failed trickle-down policies. What alternate economic model can deliver prosperity for all Indians, not just the richest 1 per cent or 10 per cent?

Many economists, including Mr Stiglitz, advocate for replacing trickle-down economics and its embedded fetish for aggregate GDP growth with 'trickle-up economics'. Give more money to those at the bottom and the middle, and everyone will benefit. The model is straightforward: economic and social policies need to be directly aimed at those in the middle and lower classes to increase their wages and earning capacity. For it is the demand for goods that powers the economy, and when there is demand for goods, the rich will automatically have an incentive to satisfy the demand without waiting for government dole outs. If there is no demand for goods, even the best of entrepreneurs will not make investments.[68] Conversely, therefore, if the bottom 90 per cent have higher spending power, the top 10 per cent will automatically do well.

To achieve this, Mr Stiglitz recommends a sustained public investment in education as key to addressing inequality and growing the economy. Since the quality of education is the strongest determinant of an individual's income, and public investment can provide equal opportunity to every child, it follows that any individual, rich or poor, can develop their abilities and claim an equal stake in the economy. On the contrary, if only the rich have access to the best education, one generation's inequality will pass on to the next.[69] He also recommends increasing minimum wages, widening social protection and providing for the essential needs of the citizens.

A similar proposition comes from the 2019 Nobel prize-winning MIT economists Abhijit Banerjee and Esther Duflo in their book, *Good Economics for Hard Times*. The duo advocate for treating GDP as a *means* to creating jobs and raising wages, not an *end*. The ultimate goal for any government, they say, should be one of raising the quality of life of the average person and especially the poorest person, which includes addressing their concerns about the health of their families and education of their children. A clear focus on the well-being of the poorest offers the possibility of transforming millions of lives much more profoundly than from the recipe of increasing GDP by a few decimal points. [70]

As scholarly gaze urgently shifts towards trickle-up economics, it bears noting that the AAP government in Delhi has been an early proponent of the model. From its first year in office, the party held an uncanny clarity of its principles of development, but it was Mr Sisodia who put a definition to AAP's economic model. In his 2018 budget speech, he termed the AAP government's approach in Delhi as a 'unique and important experiment' in trickle-up economics. In his 2018 budget speech, Mr Sisodia further implored the Delhi assembly:[71]

'What use is it to be among the fastest growing economies globally if our government expenditure on education and health as per cent of GDP is the least among all BRICS countries and even some SAARC countries?

'What use are the countless MoUs signed with corporates in mega-investor summits, when over a third of our children under five years of age are malnourished and three-fourths of our children studying in Grades 6, 7 and 8 cannot even read their textbooks?

'What use is to be attracting billions of dollars of FDI if only 7 per cent of our engineering graduates are employable and we have a huge shortfall in skilled manpower in almost every sector?'

Mr Sisodia summarized the trickle-up model as one where government policies directly benefit the poor and middle class citizens leading to better education, health and income growth. Governments should have faith that the prosperity of the poor and middle classes will find its way up to the overall economy, he said.[72]

The Delhi Model's trickle-up economic approach has unfolded through two major pathways. First, the government has made unprecedented investments in human capital, particularly education and health that account for nearly 40 per cent of Delhi's budget thereby laying the economic foundation for Delhi's economy for decades to come. Second, several of the AAP government's decisions, such as raising minimum wages to the highest in India, have directly improved the spending power of Delhi's poorest citizens. Targeted subsidies like free public transport, water and electricity also serve to boost people's spending power and productivity, besides allowing them to live a life of dignity.

A household sample survey among 70 per cent of Delhi's households receiving full electricity subsidy revealed that families saved an average of ₹2,464 per month due to the combined policies of the AAP government.[73] Almost 76 per cent of the families benefitted from zero water bill, 65 per cent from free treatment in government hospitals,

58 per cent from free bus rides for women and 44 per cent from free public education. If one adds up these savings for the entire population of Delhi, this increase in disposable incomes translates to an additional buying power of over ₹10,000 crore per annum in 2020—a staggering value indeed.

A small incident from late 2019 provides a glimpse into how this additional buying power fuels the economy. Soon after implementing the free bus rides scheme, Mr Sisodia ran into a young woman and her family outside the Delhi Zoo and got talking. The woman and her little sister, mother and father had just finished visiting the zoo and were enjoying an ice-cream. She told Mr Sisodia that they lived their entire lives in Najafgarh in outer Delhi and had never visited the Delhi Zoo before because the family couldn't afford the long travel. But now, since three of her family members could travel for free, she decided to buy a bus ticket for her father and took the entire family to the zoo for the first time. For this woman, a free bus ride was an adequate nudge to plan a fun evening out with her family resulting in higher revenues for the zoo, the ice-cream vendor and, maybe, a few other local businesses. Imagine millions of such decisions by families every day and you get a picture of what it does to the economy.

Delhi's experiment with trickle-up economics offers evidence of the theory championed by global economists. Between 2014–15 to 2022–23, Delhi's economy (inflation adjusted GSDP) grew from ₹4.28 lakh crore to ₹6.26 lakh crore at an average growth rate of 4.9 per cent. In the same period, the Indian economy grew at 5.4 per cent. Delhi has also managed to almost halve its public debt to GSDP ratio, from 6.6 per cent to 3.9 per cent—the lowest in Delhi's history—whereas India's public debt as a share of its GDP skyrocketed to the highest it has ever been, at 82 per cent. The 2022–2023 data from the Centre's Periodic Labour Force Survey (PLFS) shows that Delhi reported an unemployment rate of 1.9 per cent against the national average of 3.2 per cent.[74] As of April 2024, Delhi registered the lowest year-on-year inflation across India. In summary, AAP's approach has managed to grow Delhi's economy almost at par with the rest of India while reducing its debt burden and trumping most states and the all-India average in inflation and unemployment rates. The Delhi Model's success offers the surest proof that trickle-up economics works—for the economy and for the people.

It is important to understand that AAP's economic approach isn't opposed to capitalism or private enterprise, but one that opposes giving excessive concessions and dole outs to a chosen few in the private sector at the cost of others. The emphasis rather is to create a hurdle-free and supportive environment for all private enterprises to prosper without worrying about the next tax raid or constantly running around government offices to obtain compliances to run a business. Experts have called this as the difference between being market-friendly and business-friendly. While market-friendly economies minimize interventions by the state, in business-friendly economies, politicians (and "their" bureaucracies) intervene in favour of the companies they seek to favour—their cronies. [75] By 2022, the AAP government had either eliminated or simplified over 460 compliances in Delhi to ensure ease of doing business. It doesn't take more than 31 days for any new establishment to get an electricity connection in Delhi, which is the lowest in Asia.[76] The results have started showing. Delhi, for the first time in 2022, dethroned Bengaluru as the startup capital of India, by adding 5,000 startups between 2019–22 as compared to Bengaluru's 4,515.[77]

The AAP government's approach has ensured Delhi's economy continues to generate jobs for lakhs of local youth and those migrating in large numbers to the national capital every year. The low unemployment rate attests to Delhi's flourishing private sector, especially small and medium enterprises, which have benefited from the government's unprecedented investments in social and physical infrastructure besides efforts to improve the ease of doing business. An initiative launched by the AAP government in July 2020 provides a window into the job generation potential of Delhi's private sector. To address the economic crisis arising out of Covid-19, the DDC—the policy think-tank of the Delhi government—conceptualized the Rozgar Bazaar portal that helped entry-level job seekers connect with employers at a time when lockdown left many people unemployed. The platform has successfully provided jobs to over 10 lakh people in its first two years.[78] By 2022, the government had created 1.8 lakh new government jobs too by filling up long-pending vacancies and creating new positions in government schools, universities and hospitals.[79] In 2022, Mr Sisodia laid out an ambitious plan called 'Rozgar Budget' with an aim to create 20 lakh new jobs in Delhi to revive Delhi's economy hit by the pandemic. Informed by the trickle-up approach and months of groundwork by the DDC, the plan sought to boost demand and consumption in Delhi's economy through a range of initiatives targeting sectors such as retail, food and beverages, real estate, travel and tourism.[80]

Delhi isn't alone in pursuing the less-trodden path of trickle-up policies. During Covid-19, US President Joe Biden in 2021 announced a $1.9 trillion American Rescue Plan Act and $2.2 trillion American Jobs Plan to pacify the Covid-19 ravaged economy. The two initiatives put dollars directly in the hands of consumers who are most likely to spend them, creating demand for products and services.[81] According to a White House statement in 2023, the policies moved '. . . beyond the failed trickle-down policies and fundamentally change the economic direction of our country . . . by growing the economy from middle out and bottom up'. The statement further said these policies created 13 million new jobs, reduced inflation while reducing deficit and improved real wages for all workers with the largest-wage gains among low-wage workers.[82]

In 2022, Mr Kejriwal, on the eve of AAP's first full term in office, defended his government's economic policy:

'In the past five years, I did not increase anyone's taxes, instead we reduced taxes on many goods from 12 per cent to 5 per cent. I have kept Delhi's budget in the surplus, never in the deficit. So if I have eliminated corruption in the government and saved some money which I am returning back to the people of Delhi by reducing their electricity bills, water bills and public transport fares, did I commit any crime? Instead, if I had eaten away this money, many would have said I am a good Chief Minister (because I did not give freebies) . . . the money that people are saving through the freebies is the money that the government has put into their pockets, which creates demand in the economy.

'Today, the biggest problem of our economy is paucity of demand, not production. Giving big concessions to a few top corporates isn't good economics, what we have done by putting money into the pockets of the masses to create demand in the economy is good economics.'[83]

It's becoming clear that the crisis of the Indian economy is due to a flawed economic model adopted more than a quarter of a century ago. India cannot muddle along this path any longer, ignoring the most fundamental issues of human development, while still hoping to become a modern, developed nation by 2047 or even 2147. The Delhi Model is a template of possibility and promise for all Indian states and the nation as a whole that an alternate approach exists and that it works.

Having discussed the Delhi Model threadbare, let's now look at how it fares next to the most popular state model of the past decade and the showpiece of the present BJP regime under Prime Minister Narendra Modi—the Gujarat Model.

Determining India's Future:
Delhi Model or Gujarat Model?

The Gujarat Model of development seized national imagination in the run-up to the 2014 Lok Sabha elections as Chief Minister Narendra Modi staked his claim to the prime minister's chair. So relentless and powerful was BJP's propaganda that many Indians, without understanding what the Gujarat Model actually was, came to perceive it as a catch-all for overall development and what the whole of India should aspire to. In the Lokniti-CSDS post-poll survey conducted in five states in 2014, Gujarat was ranked first when voters were asked *'In your opinion, which state in India is doing best on development indicators?'*[84]

Over the past fifteen years, there has been plenty of discussion and dissection of the Gujarat Model in academic circles but not much of this has filtered through to India's middle classes largely because the media has failed to scrutinize its claims. To begin with, let's define what the model is or isn't. The Gujarat Model is an example of trickle-down economics taken to the extreme. It reduces the primary role of the state to facilitating rapid economic growth by promoting big industry at all costs and at the exclusion of almost everything else, especially expenditure on human development. The result has been stark: Gujarat experienced a sharp jump in growth rate over the decade 2001–02 to 2011–12—the Modi years—but simultaneously saw itself underperforming when compared to most Indian states in social indicators. This has led many critics like the French political economist, Christopher Jaffrelot, to define the model as 'growth without development'.[85]

Let's discuss Gujarat's economic performance first. For several decades since its formation as a state in 1960, Gujarat was known to be a business-friendly state with big corporate houses having a huge influence on the governments.[86] In the decade preceding the Modi years, from 1990 to 1999, Gujarat's economy (GSDP) grew faster than all major Indian states at 8 per cent as against the all-India average of 5.9 per cent. In the subsequent decade 2000–2010 under Chief Minister Modi, Gujarat's economy grew at 9.8 per cent as compared to the all-India average of 7.7 per cent.[87] Gujarat's growth rate was 2.1 per cent above the national growth rate in both these periods indicating no further acceleration of growth in the 2000s relative to the 1990s. However, achieving a near 10 per cent growth rate for a decade starting 2000 was a rare feat by any Indian state.

This was achieved by an unprecedented rise in incentives to the corporate sector to attract investments—virtually free land, large loans at nearly-zero interest rates, generous tax breaks and no-fuss environmental clearances.[88] For example, to woo the Tata Nano project, Gujarat offered a soft loan of ₹9,570 crore at 0.1 percent interest rate and repayable in twenty years, for an investment of ₹2,900 crore—a third of the loan amount. Media reports called it a 'sop opera'. Most of these investments focused on capital intensive industries that didn't create enough jobs. The Nano plant never had more than 2,200 employees—in other words, a ratio of one direct job for over ₹1.3 crore of investment. Until the Centre banned it in 2007, 40 per cent of the revenue from sales tax in Gujarat was forgone in the form of corporate subsidies. The government complemented this big-business bonanza by establishing a single-window mechanism for clearing investment proposals and focusing on infrastructure development to attract corporates, primarily roads, power and airports.[89] Apart from a sharp rise in industrial and manufacturing output, Gujarat also saw its agriculture output double between 2001 and 2011.[90]

However, not everyone gained from this 'development on steroids' model, least of all labour. Only 6.8 per cent of the workers in Gujarat are in the formal sector with the rest in informal and traditional sectors with low incomes and poor social security.[91] Throughout the past two decades, Gujarat had among the lowest wages across India. The Centre's

Labour Bureau data shows that the average daily wage for non-agriculture rural labour in Gujarat was ₹273 in 2023 as compared to ₹697 in Kerala and the national average of ₹348.[92] Gujarat stood at nineteen out of twenty states in this list.

The fact that the average daily wages in rural Gujarat were substantially lower than the state-notified minimum wages of ₹462 per day in 2023 shows that the government did little to remedy this situation that favoured big businesses. As a result, Gujarat had a high multi-dimensional poverty rate (that measures deprivations in health, education and living standards, rather than income) of 11.7 per cent in 2021, as compared to other large states with similar per capita incomes such as Maharashtra (7.8 per cent), Telangana (5.9 per cent) and Tamil Nadu (2.2 per cent). West Bengal, which had only 40 per cent of the per capita income as Gujarat, had a similar share of its population below the poverty line.[93]

Besides furthering social inequalities, the prioritization of corporate sops meant that little was left to spend on education and health. Between 2006–2007 and 2022–2023, Gujarat spent an average of just 14.2 per cent of its budget on education, lower than the national average of 15 per cent, leading to steady deterioration of the government school system. As of February 2024, 1,606 government primary schools in Gujarat had only one teacher.[94] The government had failed to recruit full time teachers since 2009, resulting in 19,000 teacher vacancies. Remote districts were the worst hit. While 95 per cent of teacher posts were filled in fifteen developed districts, this figure dropped to 50 per cent in ten remote districts. 'Schools in tribal districts like Dahod and regions of central Gujarat, or far-out villages of Kutch are empty boxes, with one or no teacher,' said Digvijaysinh Jadeja, the president of the Gujarat State Primary Teachers Association.[95]

The condition of education infrastructure wasn't acceptable either. In 2014, after twelve years of the Modi government, over 12,000 of 34,000 government schools operated from a single room.[96] In 2021, the government disclosed that over 10,500 schools were in dilapidated conditions with tin-shade roofs.[97] Poorly-run government schools have led to a steady exit of students leading to government shutting down or merging schools, citing low student enrolment. Just between 2020 and 2022, the Gujarat government closed down around ninety government primary schools and merged nearly 500.[98] Gujarat continues to be at the bottom of the table on most education outcomes. As per the Economic Survey 2023–2024, Gujarat ranked twenty-second among twenty-eight Indian states with only 75 per cent children enrolled in secondary schools as compared to the national average of 80 per cent, and 100 per cent in Delhi. It ranked twenty-third with only 48 per cent enrolment in higher secondary schools as compared to 58 per cent national average and 95 per cent in Delhi—the highest nationally.[99] The Annual Status of Education Report 2023 revealed that only a third of the children in rural Gujarat in class five could read class two texts; lower than the national average.[100]

Gujarat's track record in public health is equally poor. From 2006–2007 and 2022–2023, Gujarat spent an average of just 4.8 per cent of its budget on health, just about making the national average. The spending from 2006–2007 and 2013–2014 under Mr Modi's tenure was even lower at 3.9 per cent.[101] For years, Gujarat has faced a severe shortage of doctors in rural primary health centres and hospitals with a 99 per cent vacancy of specialists.[102] When Covid-19 struck, only thirteen of the thirty-three district hospitals in Gujarat had CT scan machines and only one had an MRI machine. Chronic underfunding has had devastating consequences on Gujarat's health outcomes. In 2020, Gujarat had an infant mortality rate of twenty-three out of 1,000 live births placing it at sixteenth among twenty-eight states.[103] According to the National Family Health Survey 2019–2021 (NFHS 5), Gujarat ranked fourth in terms of stunted children at 39 per cent, and second in terms of underweight children at 40 per cent.

Overall, Gujarat stood at twenty-one out of thirty-six Indian states and union territories in the Human Development Index (HDI) in 2019–2020 despite having the highest per capita income (GSDP per capita) among larger states.[104] Such poor performance on human development indicators could have been defended by saying that, like all good things, the Gujarat Model cannot deliver overnight. But not in this case. The Gujarat Model had been the subject of BJP's relentless pursuit for three consecutive decades, ever since it stormed to power in 1995. What Joseph Stiglitz, the Nobel Prize winning economist, said of the United States between 1980 and 2015, holds true for the Gujarat Model under the BJP regime too: an economic system that doesn't increase the standard of living of the majority for a quarter of a century, even if it works miracles for the top 1 per cent or 10 per cent, is a failed economic system.

Delhi's trickle-up model stands in sharp contrast to the Gujarat Model's faith in trickle-down theory. A head-to-head comparison between the performance of the AAP government in Delhi and the BJP government in Gujarat since 2015 on select economic and social indicators shows us how (Table 1).

In terms of economic indicators, Delhi outperforms Gujarat hands down on two indicators that matter the most to the masses—inflation and minimum wages. Over the first eight years of AAP's rule in Delhi, minimum wages increased by a staggering 95 per cent as compared to an increase by 33 per cent in Gujarat in this period. On inflation, Delhi was at par with Gujarat in 2015, but by early 2024, Delhi reported inflation of less than half of Gujarat. On both these parameters, the Delhi Model leads the nation. Delhi and Gujarat both perform similarly on the unemployment rate, both doing better than the national average of 3.2 per cent in 2022–23.

Table 1: Performance of Delhi Model vs Gujarat Model

	Unit	Delhi		Gujarat	
		2014-15	2022-23	2014-15	2022-23
Economic Indicators					
Minimum wages	₹	8,632	16,792	6,968	9,238
Annual retail inflation (CPI)	%	4.9	2.3*	5.4	4.9*
Unemployment rate	%	3.3	1.9	0.9	1.7
Total government debt	₹ crore	32,498	40,018	2,02,511	4,21,018
GSDP growth rate over 2015 to 2023 (Real)	%	-	4.9	-	7.8
Social Indicators					
Enrolment rate in higher secondary schools	%	92	95	45	48
Pass % in Class 12 in government schools**	%	88	92	61	72
% of underweight children	%	27	22†	39	40†
Rank on multi-dimensional poverty index	Number	28	28†	15	15†
Rank on human development index	Number	-	1†	-	21†

*Reference period 2023-24 ; †Reference period 2019-21 ; **All Gujarat state board schools included

Source: Official records of Government of Gujarat, Government of NCT of Delhi; Periodic Labour Force Survey (PLFS); Ministry of statistics and programme implementation; Economic Survey of India; National Family Health Survey, NITI Aayog, RBI.

The only economic indicator where the Gujarat Model outperforms Delhi as well the national average is GSDP growth rate, also its stated obsession. However, there's ample evidence to suggest that this growth was cornered by big industry who were the prime beneficiaries of the state's largesse, while average workers saw little improvement in their wages or the quality of jobs due to rising informalization. For example, in the Nano plant in Gujarat, out of 2,200 employees in 2016, only 430 were 'permanent workers' earning ₹12,500 per month. The rest were informal workers earning about ₹3,300 a month.[105] This high economic growth on the back of decades of incentives to big industry has exacted a huge toll on the state's finances. Over the period 2015 to 2023, the Gujarat government's debt doubled, leading the Comptroller and Auditor General (CAG) to warn that the state may risk 'falling into a debt trap'.[106] Rising indebtedness has further reduced Gujarat's ability to invest in sectors that affect the productive capacity of its people, such as health or education, raising questions on the long-term sustainability of such an approach.

Delhi's economic growth reflects a more sustainable approach as it happened on the back of record investments in building Delhi's human capital, while outperforming most Indian states, including Gujarat, on economic indicators that impact the masses. An important factor to bear in mind when analysing Delhi's performance on growth rate is that it is the Centre and not the Delhi government that controls land, urban planning and law and order in the national capital—intrinsic to delivering standout economic growth.

It is the social indicators, however, where the Delhi Model stands heads and shoulders above the Gujarat Model. In each of the indicators barring poverty index (where it ranks fifteen), Gujarat figures in the bottom half of Indian states and in some cases, the bottom five. Sure, Delhi had a better start than Gujarat in 2015 when AAP came to power. But over the past decade, the Delhi Model has consistently pushed the boundaries of human development and significantly improved the quality of life of the majority of Delhi's residents. Delhi's performance in HDI, where it ranks first among thirty-six Indian states and union territories, places it ahead of countries like China and Mexico and equivalent to countries in Eastern Europe. Throughout this book, as we unpack the Delhi Model across multiple sectors, we will see numerous instances of how it has successfully delivered on a wide range of social indicators and created new benchmarks in governance.

On the other hand, even after three decades of implementation of the Gujarat Model, the state has little to show besides high economic growth and progress in provisioning basic infrastructure such as roads, electricity etc. In HDI, Gujarat ranked twenty-one among Indian states and union territories, below Arunachal Pradesh and Jammu & Kashmir. With this backdrop, it should be fair to conclude that BJP's success in winning seven consecutive assembly elections in Gujarat is primarily a triumph of its political strategy rather than its approach towards development. In a telling incident from October 2022, when Prime Minister Narendra Modi visited Gujarat to launch the 'Mission Schools of Excellence' initiative, he did so from a made-up classroom built in a studio environment for better photo-op rather than a real classroom of a Gujarat government school.[107]

The past three decades have demonstrated that the Gujarat Model is nothing but a poster child of the failure of trickle-down economics. Although several eminent economists, notably Amartya Sen and Jean Drèze, have been making this case since the early 2010s, few Indian states could stake a claim to offer an alternate development model that delivered resilient economic performance while substantially improving human development indicators and the quality of life of its people. The singular achievement of the Delhi Model could be that it has filled this national vacuum.

Let's now dive into the journey of the making of the Delhi Model, sector by sector.

Chapter 2

Education

Mission Impossible: Transforming Delhi's Government Schools

'Mehnat-mazdoori karne wale log pehele sapne dekha nahi karte the. Magar Dilli sarkar ne education ke liye toh unko sapne dekhne ka mauka de diya hai. Ab sab khoob bade bade sapne dekhte hai.'

Working-class people never dreamed earlier.
But the Delhi government has made it possible
for them to dream—especially for education.
Now we can dream big.

—Parent in a Delhi government
school, 2020[1]

Even the poorest in India understand that good education is a ticket out of deprivation and poverty. Even the poorest know that government schools are the unlikeliest places for turning such dreams to reality. Many of them dig deep into their pockets to send their children to private schools, while

53

those who can't, are forced to rely on government schools. While the Indian economy has grown commendably over the past three decades, much of this prosperity has failed to change the fate of our government schools. The number of successful political parties too has grown steadily in India since Independence, many winning elections at the state or centre on the promise of poverty eradication, yet none have made public education their calling.

Much before Arvind Kejriwal and Manish Sisodia rose to prominence in Indian politics, they were troubled by the questions concerning the state of education in India: why was education not at the centre of Indian politics? Why do governments allocate paltry budgets to education? How long would India remain a country with two education models: one for the classes and another for the masses?[2] With AAP's historic victory in the 2015 Delhi elections, the spotlight was turned upon them to answer these questions. Their ability to transform Delhi's government schools would test the faith of millions supporting clean and alternative politics. It would also test their own faith in being able to deliver upon a core tenet of the Delhi Model of governance—building human capital as the fundamental means to address inequality and grow the economy.

From the day he assumed office in 2015, Chief Minister Kejriwal put education at the top of his government's agenda. In Mr Sisodia, he was gifted with a perfect education minister. The son of a retired government schoolteacher who grew up studying in his village government school in Uttar Pradesh, Mr Sisodia was passionate about education and the role it can play in shaping society. Over a decade in journalism had brought him face-to-face with the true state of our public schooling system. Back then, he had submitted many RTIs to understand why the system failed the country's children. In an attempt to figure out the solutions, he also got in touch with some of the leading schools of thought in education.

Mr Sisodia became Delhi's education minister in the first forty-nine days of the AAP government in 2013–14. Even before he was sworn in as a minister, he asked the education director to present the state of Delhi's school system. In a meeting that ran over two hours, he recalls the bureaucracy presenting beautiful pictures of five to ten schools and claiming everything was fine. A day after he took oath, he went for a surprise inspection with the officials to one of the government schools in Patparganj—his assembly constituency—to show the true state of the remaining 1,000 Delhi government schools that don't make it to the department's presentations. The doors and windows were broken, fans did not work, electrical wires were dangling and ceilings were leaky.

In 2015, Mr Sisodia was reappointed as Delhi's education minister and was also Delhi's deputy chief minister and finance minister. This meant that he could marshal the entire government machinery to pursue AAP's vision in education. Within the first few months, the government declared a bold vision: their goal was to make Delhi's government schools better than private ones. Mr Sisodia added, 'The day I feel confident about sending my own child to a government school, I will consider myself a successful education minister'.[3] The biggest hurdle for the government was to achieve this vision working with the same set of 50,000-odd officials, principals and teachers that were part of the capital's failed school education system for decades. Most of them were either deeply cynical of the possibility of any systemic change or were jaded with the many failed attempts by new ministers or bureaucrats who imposed their ideas upon them, without understanding the ground realities.

When Mr Sisodia and his team got to work, they had little idea of how long it would take to transform the government school system as it wasn't something that had been attempted before on this scale in India. There was no playbook. Sure, governments have created model schools or piloted innovative programmes, but turning around a failed government school system to provide better outcomes for every student was unprecedented. Yet, before the end of its first term, the AAP government managed to achieve the impossible—successfully changing the perception of Delhi's government schools and significantly improving the outcomes for students.

A primer on Delhi's school education system first. In 2015, Delhi had 1,007 government schools catering to 15.4 lakh students (36 per cent of all students), mainly at secondary and senior secondary levels, i.e. classes VI to XII. The Municipal Corporation of Delhi (MCD), ruled by the BJP between 2007 and 2022, ran nearly 1,700 MCD primary schools catering to around 7.5 lakh students (16 per cent) and acting as feeder schools to Delhi government schools at the class VI level. Over 2,600 private schools catered to the remaining students.

Now let's look at the impact of Delhi's education reforms initiated under AAP's tenure. The most visible impact for any school system in India is the class X and XII board results. Since Delhi does not have a state board, all Delhi government schools are affiliated with the Central Board of Secondary Education (CBSE) and therefore have higher standards than other state boards. The pass percentage in class XII board results have risen steadily from 88 per cent in the academic year 2014–15 to 97 per cent in 2023–24.[4] In 2015–16, for the first time in Delhi's history, Delhi's government schools outperformed Delhi's private schools in the class XII board results. This trend continued for the subsequent nine years barring 2022–23 (Figure 6). The class X board results tell a similar story. From a low pass percentage of 69 in 2017–18, which was when CBSE re-introduced the board exams, class X results improved steadily to a pass percentage of 94.2 in 2023–24, beating the all-India average of 93.6 per cent, for the first time in seven decades. Further, the gap in class X pass percentage of government schools and private schools has narrowed from 21 per cent in 2017–18 to just 1.5 per cent in 2023–24.[5]

Figure 6: In Delhi, government schools have consistently
outperformed private schools in Class 12
board results (in pass %)

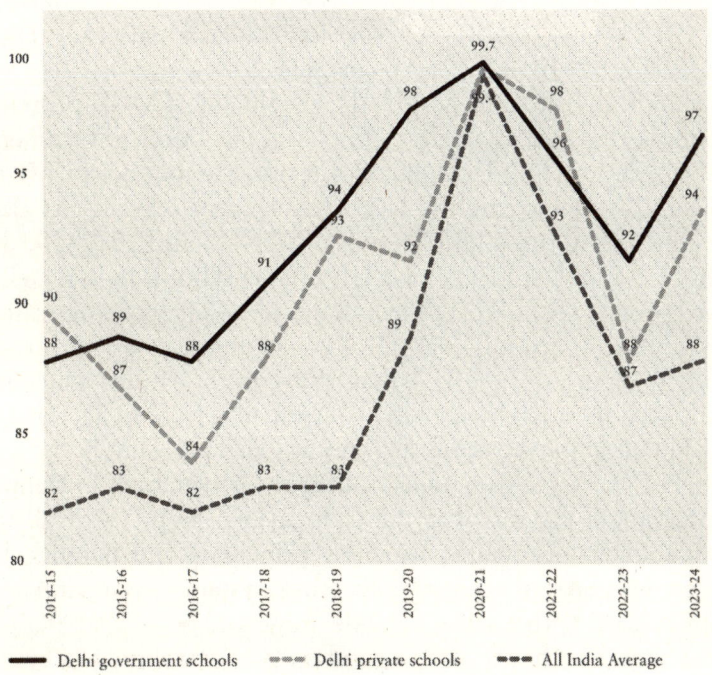

Source: Central Board of Secondary Education (CBSE)

Another important metric of success has been an increasing
number of Delhi government school students clearing the
top engineering and medical entrance tests in the country,
the IIT-JEE and the NEET. The number of government
school students who passed JEE mains has increased from
around 50 in 2015 to 783 in 2024—a fifteen-times jump.
1,414 government school students cleared the NEET-UG
exams in 2024, about two-and-half times higher than the
569 students who had cleared the exam in 2020.[6] Besides
these measures, Delhi government schools have managed to
considerably improve the foundational competencies—i.e.

basic reading and math skills—of its students leading to a
10 per cent to 20 per cent annual improvement in students
from classes VI to VIII.[7]

With improved outcomes, the total student enrolment
in Delhi government schools has risen from 15.4 lakh
in 2014–15 to 17.2 lakh in mid-2024—an increase of
1.8 lakh.[8] In the same period, the enrolment of MCD primary
schools that act as feeder schools to the Delhi government
school system has declined. As a result, the number of MCD
class VI students entering Delhi government schools has also
declined by about 40,000 between 2014–15 and 2023–24.[9] In
effect, 2.2 lakh students have left private schools to join Delhi
government schools over the past decade—a fact corroborated
by several anecdotal examples. For example, the *Hindustan
Times* reported in 2017 that 900 of the 1,200 students
admitted to a newly opened government school in Sector 21,
Rohini, had moved from surrounding private schools.[10]

However, the true impact of the transformation in Delhi's
government schools was the change in perception of all its
stakeholders—students, teachers, principals and parents. In
just five years, the entire education system was revitalized
and infused with a sense of pride, hope and belief that Delhi's
government schools are as good as private schools in every
respect. In 2020, the Boston Consulting Group (BCG) carried
out an independent assessment of Delhi's school education
reforms over the period 2015–20.[11] The study included
surveys with 577 parents and 7,096 teachers apart from focus
group discussions with principals, students, district officials
and other stakeholders. The study found that 95 per cent of
parents and teachers believed that Delhi's education reforms
had a significant positive impact. The BCG study stated, 'The
degree to which this has happened in Delhi is not something
that we have seen in any other seemingly similar education
transformation efforts across the country.'[12]

So, what is the Delhi education model? The Delhi
education model can be broken down into two overarching
goals and seven key levers that made it successful.

The first goal is that every child must have access to quality education, regardless of their ability to pay. Inequality in the quality of education is a defining feature of India's school education system. Barring a few elite private schools or model government schools, the vast majority of Indian children receive poor quality education. The tragedy of our education system is that most teachers and principals have internalized the belief that underprivileged children, often first-generation learners, cannot excel so there's no point trying. 'Our education model is only breaking the mindset and system where 5 per cent get the best education and 95 per cent the worst kind,' writes Mr Sisodia in his book *Siksha: My Experiments as an Education Minister*.[13] Over the past decade, Delhi's government schools have strived to set a minimum benchmark of infrastructural facilities and quality of education that every child gets that is comparable to the top private schools.

The second goal is to broaden the purpose of education beyond employment to build a more humane society with happy, public-spirited citizens. India's entire education system is geared towards preparing human resources to contribute to the nation's economy. 'The current system aims to teach children everything from science to grammar, in the hope they find employment. But there is no stress on ensuring that the child does not participate in any kind of violence, does not contribute to pollution and does not spread hatred or corruption. Good grammar is assured but not courteous conduct,' writes Mr Sisodia.[14] The Delhi education model aims to use education as a means to raise the consciousness of the country and its society. In Mr Sisodia's words, 'we are imagining, planning and creating a system where on seeing an increase in violence in a city, the chief minister not only directs his chief of police to end the violence in two days but also directs his chief of education to make a plan for ending violent tendencies in people in two years.'[15]

Over the past decade, the AAP government has worked towards realizing these goals through the following seven levers. First and foremost, a strong and sustained political will. It was because Chief Minister Kejriwal made education the topmost agenda of his government for not just one to two years, but for a decade by allocating about 25 per cent of his budget; it was because the education minister, Mr Sisodia, personally led the design and delivery of every single initiative in Delhi that made it possible. Few education ministers get up at 6 a.m. at least thrice a week, year-after-year, to carry out surprise inspections of government schools. Mr Sisodia did so as a signal to the entire system that for this government, education was the top priority. Mr Sisodia also built an excellent team of experts from outside the system to work alongside him to deliver this vision, notably, Ms Atishi, the advisor to the education minister who later succeeded him in 2023 as Delhi's education minister, and Shailendra Sharma, principal advisor to director education.

The first big signal of the AAP government's commitment to education went out through Mr Sisodia's maiden budget speech in 2015 when he announced the historic decision of doubling Delhi's education budget, specifically the plan or the discretionary component of the budget that is invested into new schemes and initiatives.[16] Through its two terms, the AAP government achieved the unique distinction of being the only government in India to allocate the highest share of its budget to education—nearly 25 per cent in some years, and consistently over 20 per cent each year. In comparison, the national average for share of education spending among all states/UTs has declined steadily over the past decade from 16.5 per cent in 2013–14 to 13.3 per cent in 2023–24 (Figure 7).[17] In absolute terms, the AAP government has spent a staggering amount of over ₹1 lakh crore on education in the past nine years with the annual spending increasing by two-and-half-times from around ₹6,500 crore in 2014–15 to ₹15,700 crore in 2023–24.

The second lever was creating a shared vision for transformation and communicating the same continuously to all stakeholders in the system. In April 2015, Mr Sisodia spent eight days to attend a full-time Jeevan Vidya Shivir workshop in Raipur with fifty top officials to build a mission-aligned team committed to the agenda of transforming education. Over time, all 1,000 principals and thousands of teachers were exposed to this workshop. In addition, Mr Kejriwal and Mr Sisodia consistently communicated their vision for education to all stakeholders in the system through school visits, conferences, public speeches, press conferences, social media posts etc. Mr Sisodia was directly connected to senior officials, principals and school management committee (SMC) members over WhatsApp reinforcing the larger vision as often as possible.

Figure 7: Allocation to education in Delhi's budget vs all states/UTs (in %)

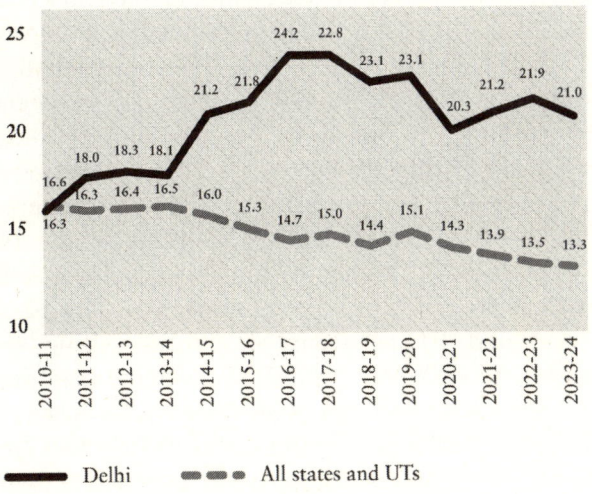

Source: State Finances: A Study of Budgets, RBI

The third lever was building world-class infrastructure as a means to restore human dignity. Until 2015, much of Delhi's government school system had come to be defined by dilapidated buildings and stinking toilets, just like anywhere else in India. Over the past decade, all government schools in

Delhi were renovated with tiled flooring, clean and functional toilets, modern libraries, science laboratories, air-conditioned auditoriums, well-lit classrooms with designer desks and in some cases, swimming pools and hockey turf grounds. Over its two terms, the AAP government built over 22,700 new classrooms as compared to only 24,100 classrooms built in 1,007 schools in the preceding seven decades—the equivalent to adding 613 new schools apart from the construction of sixty completely new schools bringing the total to 1,067 schools by mid-2024.

The fourth lever was empowering and investing in the capacity building of principals and teachers. They were made an integral part of the design and delivery of every single education reform. The teacher-training budget was increased by eleven times in the first year itself and top universities globally were roped in to provide training to Delhi's principals and teachers. In the past decade, government school principals have received leadership training at IIM Ahmedabad, United Kingdom and Finland. Similarly, over 900 teachers have received training in Singapore, apart from thousands of teachers participating in exposure visits to leading school systems nationally. The government also invested heavily in reducing vacancies, recruiting over 30,000 regular teachers in the past decade. Teacher vacancies in Delhi government schools were around 5 per cent in mid-2024. The assessment by BCG found 91 per cent of teachers citing renewed motivation and enthusiasm towards teaching after five years of Delhi's education reforms, with improved teacher training and an overall positive environment, as the top two factors.[18]

The fifth lever was making parents take active ownership of education in government schools through the school management committees (SMCs). For the first time in Delhi, the SMC members were elected among parents. SMCs were empowered to supervise all activities of the school with the principal as its chair, and an annual fund of ₹5–7 lakh was allocated to each SMC—making this the largest experiment in decentralizing government school administration in India. Starting 2016, the government also started organizing regular mega parent-teacher meetings (PTM) to bridge the divide between schools and parents and make parents equal stakeholders in the vision of providing quality education to every child. The assessment by BCG found 55 per cent of parents citing increased academic performance and 42 per cent citing regular attendance as the biggest changes in their children due to the Delhi's education reforms.[19]

The sixth lever was introducing pedagogical and curriculum reforms to provide holistic education to children that is relevant to the contemporary world. Between 2018 and 2021, the government introduced three mindset curricula—happiness curriculum, entrepreneurship mindset curriculum and *deshbhakti* curriculum—to help students become emotionally and professionally sound while also being responsible and empathetic citizens. In 2021, the government created its own state board—the Delhi Board of School Education (DBSE)—replacing a system plagued with rote learning and high-stakes final exams with one that promoted inquiry-based and experiential learning with competency-based assessments. The AAP government also launched a network of Dr B.R. Ambedkar Schools of Specialised Excellence (ASOSE) that were choice-based schools for classes IX to XII, allowing students to specialise on the basis of their aptitude and interest. Such has been the demand for ASOSEs that over 1,44,000 applications were received for admission to around 6,000 seats in 2024—a selection rate of 4 per cent for a government school system![20]

The seventh lever was effectively regulating Delhi's private schools to ensure they serve the needs of about 40 per cent students studying in them. Till 2015, the most frequent complaint of parents sending their children to private schools was arbitrary annual fee hikes of between 8 to 15 per cent.[21] Acting on these complaints, the AAP government used its statutory powers to get the accounts of hundreds of private schools examined by CAG-empanelled auditors. Many schools were found violating laws and indulging in profiteering. For the first time in India, private schools had to reverse their fee hike and refund excess money taken from parents. A total of ₹32 crore was refunded to parents until 2020. Furthermore, the AAP government completely overhauled the process for admissions to private schools for underprivileged children under the 25 per cent quota mandated by Section 12(1)(c) of the Right to Education Act (RTE), 2009. A manual process that was left to individual schools and riddled with corruption was replaced with a centralized and fully transparent online process with a computerized lottery for admissions. Since 2015, the number of private schools declining admission under the RTE act has fallen sharply from 61 per cent to 1 per cent and total admissions have increased by two-and-half times to over 31,000 each year.[22]

The bulk of the AAP government's education reforms and spending has been in school education for the simple reason that schools are the weakest link in India's education system denying lifelong opportunities to millions of underprivileged students even before they move to higher education. There is no denying that there is a dearth of quality higher education institutions too, especially those that can command a skill premium in the market and offer well-paying jobs ex-campus. While the bulk of the higher education institutions in Delhi are governed by the Central government, the capacity of higher and technical education institutions falling under the Delhi government has increased significantly in the last decade too from nearly 84,000 in 2014–15 to 1.6 lakh in 2023–24—a 90 per cent rise.[23]

The launch of the Delhi Skills and Entrepreneurship University (DSEU) in 2020 marked a significant milestone in the AAP government's efforts to reimagine skills education in India through a job-targeted curriculum, designed and delivered in collaboration with industry partners to ensure graduates are employable. Within three years, the university has expanded to over 15,000 students and forty multidisciplinary programs with an impressive placement record of over 80 per cent in degree courses in 2023–24.[24] Another landmark initiative in higher education was the launch of the Delhi Teachers University in 2022.[25] The University was envisioned as India's first institute of global eminence in teacher education—like the IITs and IIMs in their fields—at both pre-service and in-service stages of the school education system, and in the areas of education studies, leadership and policy.

This is not to suggest that the Delhi education model is perfect. Systematic efforts towards early childhood care and education (ages three to six) are still at a nascent stage with nursery classes started in over 300 Delhi government schools and the education curriculum being delivered in existing *anganwadis* with the help of external partners. The goal of assuring a minimal benchmark in foundational competencies for all children is still a few years away, although Delhi has made more progress than most states and is moving in the right direction. More worryingly, a substantial number of children fail in class IX every year, with over one lakh failing in 2023–24 alone. The main reason for this is the no-detention policy under the RTE act that automatically promoted children till class IX, effectively taking the accountability off the school system to ensure basic learning outcomes are achieved at each level. The AAP government dropped the no-detention policy in 2023 and is taking several other steps to address this issue.[26]

Besides lighting up the future of lakhs of underprivileged children, a significant impact of the Delhi education model has been that it has created space for education in India's political discourse. Seven decades after independence, no political party in India ever campaigned on its track record of turning around a government school system, delivering better board results than private schools and getting lakhs of students from private schools to migrate to government schools. Mr Kejriwal did so in the 2020 Delhi elections and won handsomely. Ever since, the AAP has religiously included the promise of replicating the Delhi education model in all its election manifestos in state elections around India, partially contributing to its rise as a national party in 2022. If there is one party today that has become synonymous with high-quality public education, it is the AAP.

Restoring Dignity to Government Schools

Dilapidated buildings, leaky ceilings, broken windows and stinking toilets have long defined how government school buildings look anywhere in India. When the AAP government came to power in 2015, it expected the condition of government schools in the national capital to be slightly better. Unlike government schools in the remote interiors of Jharkhand or Odisha that are difficult to reach for high-ranking officials, these Delhi schools existed in plain sight in those very streets and colonies where India's most powerful lived. Yet, these school buildings looked no different. 'Ceilings threatening to come crashing down any minute, a few tattered durries to sit on and broken blackboards hanging precariously from the walls were common sights,' recalled Mr Sisodia.[27] Owing to inadequate classrooms, instances of children being taught in corridors or even under a tree weren't uncommon.

It wasn't just that Delhi's government schools suffered due to lack of investment. It was in fact a lack of concern for human dignity that had condemned lakhs of underprivileged children to study in a living hell. The same government that built a world-class metro rail system in Delhi with squeaky clean stations for the rich and the middle classes couldn't find the money or the resolve to build similar school infrastructure for the children of the poor. The impact of this neglect on the psyche of the students and teachers was deep. Teachers were demotivated to teach or innovate when the entire system didn't even bother to have toilets fixed. For the students, it manifested in the form of a deep-seated inferiority complex and lack of confidence in body language. What one child in class VI said to Mr Sisodia during one of his school visits in 2015 sums up the sentiment: '*Desh ka bhavishya hum thode hi hai; woh toh private schools mein padhne waale bacche hai.*' (We aren't the future of this country; those children who study in private schools are).

Such was the physical state of Delhi's government schools that Mr Sisodia and his team struggled to figure where to begin implementing their dreams of transforming them. He realized that any conversation on achieving academic excellence or implementing world-class pedagogical interventions in the current system wouldn't just be big talk but a cruel joke on a system broken for decades. The immediate task at hand was to fix the malaise afflicting the physical infrastructure of Delhi's government schools to restore the sense of dignity across the school education system.

In April 2015, Mr Kejriwal addressed over a 1,000 government school principals at the Thygaraj Stadium making a public commitment to make available all the necessary resources provided the principals led the effort of making government schools so strong that parents would choose them over private schools.[28] He asked each of them to prepare a vision document for their schools outlining their needs. Only 200 of the 1,000 principals submitted a response, of which only fifty-four prepared detailed vision documents outlining a future roadmap with their expectations from the government. The rest merely asked for minor repairs and furniture replacements.

Perturbed by the indifference, Mr Sisodia met many principals in small groups over long dinner meetings at his home. He learned that most of the principals hadn't bothered to respond as they had no trust in political leaders who said all the right things about education in public forums but then took commissions from mid-day meals of government school children. Some principals were so disillusioned that they thought even if the minister meant well, their vision would be lost in the dusty files of bureaucracy.[29]

The AAP government first decided to take up the task of turning the fifty-four schools into model schools. It was an important first step to signal change to a moribund system. Some of the best engineers from the Public Works Department (PWD) were selected and tasked with turning the proposals of the principals to reality. Many governments routinely build new school buildings, but the AAP government took care to infuse these buildings with soul—each of them sporting unique aesthetics, murals and architectural designs. The project teams were constantly pushed to deliver on the vision of building world-class infrastructure that was better than Delhi's private schools. The classroom furniture, water coolers, toilet accessories, electrical fittings, tiling—everything had to be of the best quality. Plans for each new school building and the designs of rooms, labs, libraries etc., were personally overseen and approved by Mr Sisodia and Delhi's then PWD Minister, Satyendar Jain, a professional architect turned politician. 'It felt like we were getting our own houses built, which was the sentiment behind this initiative,' recalled Sisodia.[30] The visible progress in these model schools within a year injected a shot of enthusiasm in the entire system.

Soon after the fifty-four model schools were renovated, the AAP government initiated a complete makeover of all remaining schools. In the past decade, as record capital budgets were allocated to the education department, every single Delhi government school has seen a radical physical transformation. The revamped school buildings bore an altogether different look with mosaic flooring, clean and functional toilets, modern libraries, science laboratories, air-conditioned auditoriums, well-lit classrooms with smart boards and colourful, designer desks that were an instant hit with the children. Once constructed, systems were created to maintain this infrastructure and carry out annual whitewashing of all schools during the summer holidays.

None of this came easy. Former advisor to the education minister, Ms Atishi, recalls working for nearly nine months to fix the issue of toilets alone. The first thing she would notice entering any school building was the smell from the toilets. She figured the issue was poorly drafted government tenders. Sanitation services were outsourced on lowest rate (L1) basis without specifying the minimum quantity of cleaning supplies to be procured for each school or penalties to be applied in case of failure in performance. After several months of back and forth with the department, a new tender was drafted to fix these gaps. This is just one example. For any new infrastructure procurement that was a departure from the past, Mr Sisodia had to spend endless hours convincing the bureaucracy why it was needed. For instance, the file for approving designer desks that cost more than twice the older desks took about two years to pass.[31]

The most immediate impact of these efforts was the increase in the number of classrooms. In nearly seven decades since Independence, Delhi's previous governments had managed to build around 24,100 classrooms in government schools till 2015.[32] With over 15 lakh students to accommodate, many schools had eighty to 100 students per classroom with the highest at 174 students in a classroom.[33] From 2015 to mid-2024, the AAP government added over 22,700 new classrooms—almost doubling the stock of classrooms in just nine years.[34] Achieving this was no easy task since the Central government agency—the Delhi Development Authority (DDA)—that controls all land allotments in the national capital, refused to give necessary land for the construction of new schools. In the first four years, the DDA allotted only one new plot to construct government schools.[35] The AAP government worked around this challenge by going vertical, adding new floors and additional buildings within existing schools to optimally utilize the available space. This was equivalent to adding 613 new schools apart from the construction of sixty completely new schools bringing the total to 1,067 schools by mid-2024.

The government took special care to renovate staffrooms, turning shabby storeroom-like spaces to clean, comfortable rooms with coffee machines and a fridge. This small intervention went a long way in restoring the trust and the dignity of teachers and telling them that this new government cared. Like every single small change that was initiated, the bureaucracy resisted even the decision to install coffee machines and fridges in staffrooms, deeming it as an unnecessary expense.[36] An officer commented that the coffee machines can be installed but the teachers should bring their own coffee powder—an idea Mr Sisodia shot down immediately. After two years of files moving back and forth, this proposal too saw the light of day—another instance that shows how political will and persistent effort were critical in bringing about the smallest changes in the government school system.

Apart from building the academic infrastructure of classrooms, labs and libraries, the AAP government also laid emphasis on building world-class sports facilities in Delhi government schools that had the necessary space. For the first time in Delhi or perhaps any government school system in India, modern Olympic-sized swimming pools, turf hockey grounds, football grounds and basketball courts were built—that was straight out of a dream for the students. The government opened these sports facilities to any school student studying in Delhi, in any government or private school, providing free coaching too. By March 2024, twenty-six government schools in Delhi had swimming pools, seven had football grounds and three had hockey turfs that were used for training and competitions by all school students in Delhi.[37]

An important aspect of the physical transformation was that it wasn't limited to a few pilots or model schools, but touched each and every Delhi government school within five years. An independent assessment by the BCG in 2020 on Delhi's education reforms brought out the deep impact of this structural overhaul with 87 per cent parents and 76 per cent teachers attesting to significant infrastructure upgrades. Principals, teachers, parents and students reiterated that the fact that they now have access to a school that feels like a private school; that they are in an environment which is comfortable and appealing; and that small amenities, such as cushioned chairs, coffee machines in staffrooms and high-quality lighting and ventilation in classrooms has been made available, has been a big driver in generating commitment and momentum.[38]

Decentralizing and Empowering Frontline Actors

When the AAP government first articulated its vision of providing world-class education in government schools in 2015, most of those well versed with the system laughed it off. Even if they appreciated the intent, they held it impossible to change the attitude of school principals and teachers who have little incentive or motivation to do their jobs well. The stereotype was that government teachers preferred to loiter around or sit under a tree knitting sweaters than teach in classrooms. Many, including some principals and teachers, blamed the students and their parents as being disinterested in education. The government knew that its toughest job would be to instil a sense of purpose and align all frontline stakeholders towards its vision of transforming the school education system.

The education department is often the largest department in a state government. Delhi's education department housed over 60,000 teachers, principals and officials. A defining feature of the Indian state is centralization in decision-making; the frontline workers are expected only to follow orders taken several levels above them. For instance, principals of Delhi government schools were never envisioned as school leaders having sufficient autonomy in running their schools. They had been largely reduced to paper pushers— implementing directives passed by district or state officials for compliance or seeking approval and waiting for months to make the smallest expenditures in their schools. Meanwhile, broken windows continued to remain broken.

Teachers, the last cog in the wheel, were treated as free labour to do all kinds of field work like conducting surveys, filling family health registers, doing election duty etc., and then teach in whatever time remained. Even within the classrooms, they had no freedom to make their weekly lesson plans or introduce innovative ways of teaching. Most of them were resigned to viewing their role as completing the syllabus irrespective of what the students learnt. Teacher trainings had become a punishment, designed in a top-down rigid manner that added little value to classroom practices. Parents were completely cut-off from the school system, often prevented by security guards from entering the school premises—their role perceived as limited to taking care of their children at home.

In the first few months, Mr Sisodia and his team spoke at length with several groups of principals and teachers to understand what could be done to make them own up and implement the government's vision. While several grievances surfaced, the overwhelming feeling that emerged was that of being disempowered and voiceless in a system that had, for decades, cared little for them. It became clear that no change could be brought about in the current system without entrusting dignity and autonomy to the frontline actors. Throughout the first few years, both the chief minister and education minister publicly announced on multiple occasions to school principals and teachers, a guarantee to solve every grievance; in return, they were asked to give their absolute best to teach the students well. Based on this understanding, a number of reforms were rolled out in government schools.

Envisioning Principals as School Leaders

The past decade has seen a radical shift in the role of principals and teachers in Delhi's government schools. The role of school principals was recast as school leaders empowered to take everyday decisions. Their financial powers were enhanced from ₹5,000 to ₹50,000 to meet the school's immediate needs—printing a magazine, organizing an annual sports day function or undertaking urgent repairs. To reduce their burden of maintaining school infrastructure, an 'estate manager' was appointed from retired defence personnel and given the charge of supervising cleanliness and repairs. Another major devolution was authorising principals to hire contractual staff and experts as per the school's requirements. This allowed schools to hire estate managers, cleaning staff, expert teachers for subjects like arts, sports, music, etc., with minimal effort and procedural complications.[39] To strengthen their authority over teaching staff, principals were allowed to recommend transfers of two teachers annually—which worked best as a deterrent against errant teachers.

The most critical intervention to instil confidence and change the mindset of school principals was leadership training. For the first time, a custom leadership course was designed in partnership with IIM Ahmedabad for government school principals. All those who attended this training in Ahmedabad came back with the inspiration and the toolkit required to be better leaders. In addition, a special partnership was struck with the University of Cambridge and Finland's education department to provide leadership training and exposure to their best schools. In April 2016, Delhi became the first state to send a batch of ninety government school principals to Cambridge, UK, to receive leadership training from one of the world's best education systems.[40] So far, the practice was for ministers and senior IAS officers to make foreign visits and then relay the information back to mid-level officers. The AAP government flipped this practice, directly sending the frontline leaders to learn first-hand what they were expected to deliver. Till early 2024, 1,694 principals from Delhi government schools attended leadership training at IIM Ahmedabad and 471 visited UK and Finland.[41]

Winning the Trust of Teachers

The task of re-establishing the trust of teachers was going to be far more difficult given their sheer numbers—over 50,000 teachers. To begin with, the AAP government sent a clear signal that it valued the role of the teacher within the classroom by banning all non-academic duties assigned to them except election duty. Initially, much of the bureaucracy protested this decision as they had become used to thinking of teaching staff as government workers, easily available for any random field work. To reduce their paperwork, all teachers were given tablets, which helped with attendance and preparing results online—another move the bureaucracy resisted for two years since it was used to minimal spends on teachers. The added benefit of introducing tablets was instant data access to the education minister and senior officers of the department—an exercise that would take weeks earlier.

Another key grievance that was voiced in discussions with teachers was the disparity between pay scales of permanent teachers and guest teachers, who comprised one-third of all teachers but were hired on short contracts at very low salaries. The AAP government first attempted to regularize guest teachers, but these efforts were blocked by Delhi's L-G.[42] Eventually, the government increased the salaries of guest teachers by 80 to 90 per cent and granted them the provision of casual leave to win their trust and give them a shot at a dignified life.[43] From the academic standpoint, in the first year itself, the government reduced the syllabus by 25 per cent till class VIII so that the teachers could focus more on developing competencies rather than finishing the syllabus. Inputs were taken from teachers on what topics were not so important and could be omitted.[44] The government also did away with the stifling schedule for weekly lessons, binding on all teachers. Instead, teachers were now given the freedom to draw up their own monthly schedules and follow it through. This move inspired many capable and diligent teachers to take initiative.[45] All these efforts, combined with a major infrastructure overhaul, including upgradation of staffrooms, played a critical role in bridging the trust deficit with teachers.

The following example highlights how small, deliberate actions were critical in winning over the trust of teachers. Earlier, teachers attending annual teacher-training sessions were made to sit on wooden desks in regular classrooms of a government school and given a simple tea-samosa as refreshments. In 2016, when the same teachers came for the annual teacher-training sessions, they were received in a larger hall with round tables and cushioned chairs. They were given spiral-bound notebooks and pens for the session, and special packed lunch *thali*s were ordered for them. This small gesture meant a lot to the teachers. There is no reason why previous governments couldn't have done this; the problem was that nobody cared for the teachers enough. Over the years, the practice of doing all teacher trainings within Delhi has also been done away with. Every year, Delhi's teachers visit leading schools and educational organizations within India such as Dream a Dream (Bengaluru), Gyan Shala (Ahmedabad), Rishi Valley School and Agastya Foundation (Andhra Pradesh), SECMOL (Ladakh), Auroville (Puducherry) among many others, to learn from the best in their field.

The intervention that had the biggest impact on the quality of teaching practices in Delhi government schools was the mentor-teacher programme. A special cadre of 200 mentor-teachers—one for every five schools—was created from among the brightest, most motivated teachers to provide day-to-day mentorship and academic support. The mentor-teachers received special training nationally and internationally and were consulted during the design of any new academic intervention so that they could help other teachers translate them to reality inside the classroom. For the first time, the government teachers now had a dedicated person who would sit in the classrooms to observe their teaching, hone their skills and provide feedback on newer, better methods of teaching.

Delhi's mentor-teachers have made myriad contributions to the success of Delhi's education model over the past decade, significantly improving the academic environment in schools.[46] To provide world-class mentoring and leadership training to the mentor-teachers, the AAP government inked a partnership with the National Institute of Education, Singapore. Till early 2024, over 930 mentor-teachers have been trained there, making it the first such international training programme for government school teachers in India.[47] The sheer scale of Delhi's investment in providing world-class training to its teachers and principals is reflected in the eleven-time increase in the training budget from ₹9 crore to ₹102 crore in the first year itself.[48]

The government further amplified the environment of positivity and respect among teachers by publicly celebrating top performers. Starting 2017, the state teachers' awards were given out by the chief minister and education minister, at a glamorous award function in Thyagaraj Stadium that was no less than a rock concert with famous bands such as Indian Ocean invited to perform. Profiles of these teachers were displayed prominently at metro stations, while a collage of their photos were displayed inside trains as well as in public hoardings all over Delhi. Being recognized in this manner publicly was unimaginable for government schoolteachers who were, until then, voiceless and invisible cogs in a giant machine.

To ensure sustained change in teaching-learning practices in Delhi's schools, the AAP government in 2021 restructured the two key institutions responsible for teacher training and academic innovations in government schools—the state council of education research and training (SCERT) and district institutes of education and training (DIETs). For the first time, a common teacher-educator cadre was created, their pay scales enhanced to UGC-scale and the number of academic faculty posts in SCERT and DIET enhanced from 240 to over 700. While announcing this landmark reform, Mr Sisodia said, 'We have increased the posts and salaries in SCERT/DIET to instil a sense of respect for the talent that comes into the system. Delhi is the only state in this country where SCERT/DIET faculty are given this scale and honour.'[49] SCERT and DIET faculty have played a key role in anchoring all academic reforms initiated in Delhi in the past decade including the mentor-teacher programme, happiness curriculum etc.

Decentralizing Government School Administration through School Management Committees (SMCs)

One of the biggest successes of the Delhi education model has been the establishment of an institutional platform to involve parents in the administration of government schools i.e. SMCs. Until 2015, there was no communication between the parents of students in government schools and their teachers or principals. The AAP government addressed this gap by activating the SMCs that were formed under the RTE act but existed only on paper. Each committee had sixteen members including the principal, who acted as the chair, while twelve members were chosen among parents of the students from the school. For the first time in Delhi's history, in 2015, and every two to three years thereafter, except during the Covid-19 period, elections were held to democratically elect parents to the SMCs. Pamphlets were distributed to the parents of over 15 lakh children to generate interest and participation in SMC elections. The government invested heavily in capacity building of the newly elected members and devolved substantial administrative and financial powers to them. The SMCs have played two important roles in improving the environment of Delhi government schools.

First, they provided a strong layer of supervision in every school, rectifying many of the small issues that arose in their day-to-day administration that the bureaucracy had struggled to resolve. For example, an SMC cleared up the garbage and debris left behind by a construction contractor by mobilizing youth from the vicinity.[50] Another SMC in an evening school shift in East Delhi adopted an innovative approach to stop the persistent issue of teachers leaving two hours before the school ended to reach home early. The SMC members installed a big lock on the main gate of the school premises for the last two hours of the school every day, taking duties to sit with the security guards, and refusing to open the lock for any teachers attempting to scoot off early!

In 2017, interacting with over 16,000 SMC members at the Indira Gandhi Stadium, Mr Kejriwal announced a historic decision to further empower SMCs by allocating an annual fund of up to ₹4 lakh per school, later increased to ₹5–7 lakh.[51] The funds were to be managed solely on the basis of decisions taken by the SMC and could be used for hiring temporary teachers, carrying out repairs or for any education-related activity. No government in India has given its SMCs such powers, making Delhi's SMCs the largest experiment in decentralizing government school administration in India. SMCs have used this fund in innovative ways over the years, including beautifying school buildings, creating a reading corner under the staircase, setting up a botanical garden, undertaking urgent repair works, hiring resources persons to teach extra-curricular subjects like arts and sports, among others.

The second crucial role the SMCs played is that they acted as the eyes and ears of the education minister in every school. Each SMC had an MLA representative as a member, chosen from among the most dedicated volunteers from the area. An informal network of seventy SMC assembly coordinators and thirteen SMC district coordinators was formed for smooth coordination with all the schools. A WhatsApp group was created to connect them directly with the education minister to exchange any information pertaining to schools or for escalating urgent issues. This informal information network was crucial in ensuring the education minister's office had the pulse of every single school at his fingertips. 'What was lacking in a school? Which principal or teacher was performing well and who wasn't? If I needed information on any project or plan quickly, I would get in touch with the SMC and get it within an hour or so while it usually took a week to ten days for the department to collect the same information,' recalls Mr Sisodia from the initial years of forming the SMCs.[52]

Fostering empathy and connection between parents and teachers through mega PTMs

Yet another initiative that proved to be a milestone in bridging the divide between schools and parents was the mega Parent Teacher Meeting (PTM). Starting July 2016, a day was set aside for a mega PTM to be held every three to four months in all government schools. All parents were invited to come along with their children to interact with teachers. To increase awareness among parents, a publicity blitz was launched with paper ads, SMS messages and an intense week-long radio campaign with multiple advertisements recorded in the voice of children, the education minister and the chief minister. The outreach strategy proved to be effective with hordes of parents showing up at the very first mega PTM. The government made the event festive—schools were decorated with flowers and balloons and NCC cadets welcomed parents with folded hands and offered them a cup of tea upon arrival.

'The objective of the mega PTM wasn't just to discuss the students' report cards but to make parents familiar with the other aspects of their child's personality as well—what were his/her interests other than studies; what were their health challenges; what was the environment at home, etc.,' recalls Mr Sisodia.[53] The experience of the first mega PTM had a deep emotional impact on parents as well as teachers and broke the wall separating them. A young teacher who had thought of the parents of a child struggling in studies as negligent learned that they were uneducated labourers who left home at 5 a.m. to wash cars and sell vegetables for the rest of the day, to feed their family. She realized how difficult it was for the parents to pay attention to their child's education given their circumstances. In another instance, a mother, when told by the teacher that her daughter was a bright student, stopped assigning her household work so she could focus on studies.[54] Over the years, many such anecdotes attest to the impact of mega PTM in fundamentally altering the relationship between teachers and parents of government school students.

The success of Delhi's education model over the past decade has been in large measure due to multitudes of initiatives taken to decentralize and empower the frontline actors in the education system—principals, teachers and parents. Effectively, they have turned each Delhi government school into an autonomous learning institution with the SMC at the heart of it. Mr Sisodia captured this sentiment succinctly in 2020, saying, 'Every school in itself is a government, headed by the principal, supported by the SMC members as its cabinet. It is our endeavour that the SMCs should take the entire responsibility of the schools so that the state government can limit its role to framing policies and providing resources.'[55]

Changing Mindsets Through Curriculum Reforms

The existing education system has largely limited itself to the narrow goals of learning outcomes, academic achievements and job placements. While important by themselves, they have ended up subjecting students to severe stress and judgement at all times. In addition, students are burdened with other stresses like family conflicts, peer pressure and physical or mental health issues, which can over time severely hinder a child's learning and development. From the very beginning, the AAP leadership had envisioned the need for providing holistic education to students that doesn't just prepare better human resources for the economy but also happier human beings contributing to a harmonious society.

The first challenge in reimagining the approach towards education was going to be changing the mindset of principals, teachers and education department officials and reversing their many biases of what the education system can and cannot achieve. For example, many teachers and principals in India's public education system believe, to this date, that a majority of underprivileged children coming to government schools are academically weak and cannot be taught. The first step to change this mindset was taken by Mr Sisodia in April 2015, when he took a team of fifty senior officials and principals for an eight-day Jeevan Vidya Shivir workshop in Raipur founded on a *co-existence* model of education inspired by education philosopher, A. Nagraj.

At the core of this vision is a critique of a model of education that is based on competition rather than collaboration and that aims to create resources that can be deployed as little more than tools in a market economy. The *co-existence* model of education, on the other hand, places equal value on developing children's emotional quotient and personalities, so that they learn to prosper through collaboration and sharing of resources.[56] Eight days of nonstop discussion and reflection on education at the Jeevan Vidya Shivir workshop, the first such experience for most government officials, played the most important role in building a new understanding of education and inspired the principals to take leadership roles in this transformation. In the first term of the AAP government, all 1,000 school principals, SCERT and DIET faculty and thousands of teachers were exposed to this workshop, effectively creating a mission-aligned cadre of senior functionaries who subscribe to the same philosophy and have a common agenda to transform education in Delhi.[57]

Before the AAP government could attempt any major reforms to change the mindset of students, it had to attend to the more immediate challenges of fixing infrastructure and empowering teachers and principals to effectively perform their day-to-day roles. Another big challenge was the deep learning deficits that existed, particularly in classes VI to VIII, with a large proportion of students lacking basic reading and math skills. This was due to the fact that most Delhi government schools catered only to secondary and higher secondary education (class VI onwards) for students completing their primary education from poorly run municipal schools. Every year, nearly 1.7 lakh students from municipal schools enter class VI of Delhi government schools with an accumulated learning deficit over five years. An internal survey in 2016 revealed the shocking reality that nearly half of the students in class VI of Delhi government schools couldn't read at all, three-fourths couldn't read their Hindi textbooks and two-thirds couldn't do a simple division.[58]

To address this problem, the AAP government collaborated with Pratham, one of India's most respected education non-profits, to launch a remedial learning programme based on its globally acclaimed 'teaching at the right level' model. The model had been studied extensively by researchers, including Nobel Prize winning economists Abhijit Banerjee and Esther Duflo, and proven to be the most cost-effective intervention to improve basic learning outcomes.[59] The approach works by assessing children's learning levels, grouping them based on learning levels rather than age or class and restructuring classroom instruction to the level and pace of the student rather than anchoring it in a rigid class-wise curriculum. The goal was to help students attain grade-appropriate learning levels as quickly as possible. Launched as Chunauti in 2016, the programme faced a lot of resistance initially from teachers and parents, but was accepted once they saw it was effective. From 2018 onwards, the programme was modified to Mission Buniyaad and implemented for classes III to VIII as a focused campaign in the first half of every academic year with impressive gains in basic reading and math skills of students. After running Mission Buniyaad in 2023, the share of class VI students who could read Hindi stories increased from 40 per cent to 72 per cent and those who could do a simple division increased from 33 per cent to 64 per cent.[60]

By 2018, once many of the basic issues in government schools were addressed, the AAP government moved its attention to introducing three big-bang curriculum reforms aimed at holistic development of all students. Referred to as the 'mindset curricula', they were an attempt to build an individual's capacity to think critically about the true nature of progress and happiness.[61] First to be introduced, and perhaps the most celebrated reform of the Delhi education model, was the happiness curriculum. Launched by His Holiness the Dalia Lama in July 2018, this was the first time in the world that a curriculum was introduced to teach happiness by inculcating mindfulness and social-emotional learning as an everyday practice in a formal education system.[62] The content for the curriculum was created by a joint team of Delhi government teachers, principals and some of the most reputed organisations working in child psychology such as the non-profit, Dream a Dream. Over 8 lakh students and 20,000 teachers from nursery to class VIII in over 1,000 Delhi government schools today start their day by spending one period of forty minutes in a happiness class. A unique feature about the curriculum is that it has no books for students, no homework and no examination. Instead, there is a teacher's handbook for each grade whose major components are guided mindfulness practice, sharing views and expressing emotions with the help of games, stories and role-playing activities. The curriculum design has a strong child-centric pedagogy. Half the time is allocated for reflective discussions where students are encouraged to discuss their views and reflect on their emotions.

Though the education system took some time to adjust to this radically new curriculum, within one year, teachers and principals credited it for changing the behaviour of students, especially of classes VI to VIII.[63] The Brookings Institution conducted a pilot study in 2019 covering 218 teachers and 1,155 students that validated positive effects of the happiness curriculum.[64] Overall, students' relationships with their teachers improved, their participation in classes increased and they were more focussed and mindful. The teachers too were able to prioritize values over academic success, change their orientation for designing classes and displayed increased collaboration with other teachers. Here are some interesting anecdotes from the field on the impact of happiness classes:

'When we are feeling hot and really tired, we bring air-conditioning to our homes, and we feel happy and relaxed about it. The Happiness Curriculum is doing exactly the same thing. If I am feeling tired and stressed in other classes, the Happiness Curriculum is like an air-conditioner to me.'

—A class V student in
a Delhi government school[65]

'I have seen tremendous change in my grandchild in the last one year. Earlier, the child used to fight with the other children in the neighbourhood. This has changed now and he shows them a lot of love and respect.'

—A grandmother of a Delhi government
school student[66]

'I am noticing a lot of change in my daughter since she started attending the happiness class. Earlier she rarely spent time with me and was glued to the phone and TV. But now she not only spends time with me but also helps me with housework. She shares all the stories told to her in the happiness class. It feels good to connect with her and share her happiness.'

—Geeta, a Delhi government
school parent[67]

Delhi's happiness curriculum attracted curiosity and attention from the day it was introduced. The curriculum innovation has been appreciated by several national and international media like BBC, CNN, NPR and *Le Monde*, and was also featured in Harvard International Education Week and the World Economic Forum.[68] Delhi's happiness classes came into the global spotlight in February 2020, when the then US First Lady Melania Trump visited a Delhi government school to participate in a happiness class and said she found it 'very inspiring'.[69] Netherlands King Willem-Alexander and Queen Maxima have also visited Delhi's happiness class. In 2021, the happiness curriculum was recognized by the international WISE Awards for Educational Innovative Project in partnership with Dream a Dream. The success of the curriculum has motivated over 200 private schools in Delhi to voluntarily implement the programme. It has also informed the design of the Government of Uttarkhand's Anandam Pathyacharya curriculum that was rolled out in 2019 for nursery to class VIII students in over 20,000 government schools.[70]

In 2019, the AAP government introduced the second major curriculum reform—the entrepreneurship mindset curriculum (EMC)—with the aim of helping students in classes IX to XII develop a problem-solving mindset that can prepare them for professional success. Mr Sisodia realized that India's education system was creating a generation of youngsters with certificates in their hands standing in queues to become jobseekers and not job providers. He argued that it was the failure of the current education system that 'equipped our children with knowledge and qualifications but didn't give them the self-confidence or ability to apply these skills independently—the entrepreneurship mindset.'[71] The aim of the EMC was, irrespective of what careers students pursue, to infuse confidence in them to attempt new, bigger things, to make courageous decisions and to erase the fear of failure and make them pioneers in their work.[72]

This too was a radical experiment in the Indian and probably global education system with no precedents for developing a four-year curriculum for students from classes IX to XII. A team of teachers, SCERT faculty and experts in this field like Udhyam Foundation, was created that worked non-stop for six months to come up with the first draft of EMC. After multiple rounds of piloting and testing, the EMC was rolled out for over 6 lakh students and 20,000 teachers in all Delhi government schools in July 2019. Besides mindfulness practice, students learn through individual and group activities and get the opportunity to interact with established entrepreneurs in their classrooms.

The most coveted component of the EMC was 'Business Blasters'—a practical component that enables students in classes XI and XII to develop their own start-up with the government providing seed capital of ₹2,000 per student along with business coaching and mentorship. Students are encouraged to make teams of five to ten members and implement a real-world start-up idea with the pool of seed money provided to them. If they lose the seed capital, no questions are asked and if they make profits, they keep them. After several rounds of selection, the top 100 teams participate in an investment expo for real-life pitching to investors from across the country—a kind of 'shark tank' for school students. Business Blasters became the world's largest startup programme for school students when it was launched in 2021, with a budget of ₹60 crore for 3 lakh students, in over a 1,000 government schools.

The programme proved to be a huge hit among the students, sparking off tens of thousands of promising startup ideas every year. In 2023–24, a total 2.43 lakh students of classes XI and XII conceived and developed 37,983 business ideas with their seed money.[73] An interesting feature of these ideas is that they often tried solving the problems of the lower socio-economic strata through affordable solutions. Here are a few examples of successful startups from the Business Blasters programme, as profiled by the *Indian Express* in 2023:[74]

'In 2021, Divyanshi Chitransh (18) and her classmate pitched an idea for a startup, called 'Divine Creations', where they made and sold traditional paintings online and offline. In just a year, the Class XI students made a whopping ₹10 lakh—helping Divyanshi support her family after her father lost his job during the pandemic. What gave Divyanshi, then a Delhi government student, a leg-up was the ₹2,000 seed money given under the Business Blasters Programme.'

'For Aryan Jaimini, art is everything. 'Government school students like me from middle-class families were encouraged to study, not pursue extra-curricular activities. But I wanted to prove one can make a life out of Art,' said the twenty-year-old, who runs a startup called 'Metal Mate' that turns junk into decorative art which he sells on social media and markets at exhibitions. Aryan and his team of five got the seed money in 2021 while he was studying in class XII at Rajkiya Pratibha Vikas Vidyalaya in Rohini Sector 21. Today, the startup has made about ₹85,000 in a year.'

In September 2021, the AAP government introduced the third mindset curriculum that built on the previous two curricula to create a society where individuals live in harmony with fellow citizens and with renewed faith in the power of the Indian Constitution to ensure justice and dignity for all citizens. Called 'deshbhakti curriculum' (deshbhakti is Hindi for patriotism), the initiative promotes active citizenship from nursery to class XII by exploring themes of love and respect for the country, identifying the strengths and challenges of the country and reflecting on what each student can contribute to the country's progress.

An underlying essence throughout the curriculum is on bridging the gap between values and actions, and making each child realize that every small act of theirs has an impact on the country—be it offering bribes to public servants, breaking a traffic red light, disrespecting women or a person from a different caste or religion or abusing the environment. Launching the curriculum, Chief Minister Kejriwal defined the concept of patriotism that the initiative hoped to instil as, 'patriotism in its true sense is a feeling of empathy and connection to each and every citizen. A deep-rooted belief that the constitutional values of justice, liberty, equality and fraternity must be lived in even the smallest of acts.'[75]

The deshbhakti curriculum was integrated in the academic structure as a daily period for nursery to class VIII students, and for two periods a week for class IX to XII students. Like the previous two curricula, a child-centric pedagogy was adopted that was activity and discussion-based without any preaching. At the end of each lesson, students were expected to reflect and introspect on their learning. Homework was a crucial part of the curriculum where students till class VIII were expected to discuss key questions in each chapter with their family and neighbours to broaden their perspective, such as: 'what is the true meaning of being a deshbhakt? What are the reasons that make us proud of being an Indian? What factors have kept India from being a developed country even after seventy-five years of Independence? What is an individual's role in creating the India of one's dream?' For students of class IX to XII, the curriculum's practical component emphasized collective action to solve issues around them. Over the past few years, inspired by the deshbhakti curriculum, students have taken the initiative to stop wastage of food from mid-day meals, initiated plastic segregation and recycling in their schools and taken care of injured birds and animals, among many other such efforts.

A few testimonials from students attest to how the deshbhakti curriculum has impacted them:[76]

> 'I had a friend who was from a different caste. My parents convinced me not to be friends with her due to this reason. So I reduced my interaction with her. Then during the deshbhakti classes, when my teachers spoke about how it's wrong to discriminate based on caste and I realized the error of my ways. How can I be a deshbhakt, if I do this? I went back to her, apologized and we started speaking again.'

> —Vanshika, a class X student in Delhi government school

> 'I understood through these classes that deshbhakts are not just the freedom fighters or the soldiers protecting the country but that we can also become a deshbhakt by our small deeds. Now I consider myself a deshbhakt because I have started acting in the interest of the country like keeping my surroundings clean, motivating other people to keep the country clean and using cloth/ paper bags instead of plastic bags.'

> —Kanishka, a class IX student in Delhi government school

Delhi's three mindset curricula represent the most concerted effort by any public education system in India so far and perhaps among a select few globally, to reimagine the education system and help students become emotionally and professionally sound while also being responsible and empathetic citizens.

Delhi Education Reforms 2.0

By the end of the first term of the AAP government, the Delhi education model addressed the many gaps in Delhi's government schools, a legacy of several decades, emerging as among the best government school systems in India. School infrastructure had significantly improved; principals, teachers and parents felt empowered; enrolment was rising and students were outperforming their peers in private schools. But the goal of providing world-class education to the children in Delhi was still distant. Setting the agenda for the second-generation of Delhi education reforms in 2021, Mr Sisodia declared, 'We are not stopping at this; we now aspire to be the best-in-the-world. Our vision is to create government schools in Delhi that would be at par with the international schools in the coming years.'[77]

Despite launching three innovative mindset curricula, Mr Sisodia knew that the structural challenges at the core of the traditional education system still persisted in Delhi's government schools. Unlike most state governments, the capital didn't have a state education board until 2020 and all its government schools were affiliated with CBSE, which had many drawbacks. First, the core curriculum and examination system was heavily textbook-centred and rote-based, inflexible in its choice of subjects and heavily reliant on the end-term examination as the defining indicator of student performance. Second, the high-stake board examinations had become stressful for students, adversely impacting their mental well-being. Third, the curriculum failed to connect education with the contemporary needs of society or prepare students for top national competitive exams like JEE or NEET. As a result, a massive coaching class industry had mushroomed all over India.

Towards the end of its first term, the AAP government started drawing up plans to give Delhi its own education board that would be comparable to the best in the world. In March 2021, the Delhi cabinet cleared the proposal to

establish the Delhi board of school education (DBSE) that
was a huge departure from all central or state education
boards in India. The DBSE was designed in collaboration
with the international baccalaureate (IB) board to adopt the
best practices globally in the field of curriculum, pedagogy
and assessment, after carrying out an in-depth review of
competencies adopted by the world's best education systems
in Finland, Singapore, Canada, Australia and Korea.[78]

Unlike the existing system that promoted rote-learning
through a teacher-led instructional approach, DBSE promoted
critical thinking and conceptual understanding through an
inquiry-based and experiential learning approach. It laid
emphasis on student-led discussions, with teachers playing the
role of facilitators. DBSE also replaced high stakes end-term
examinations with competency-based assessments through
the year that judges students' ability to apply acquired
knowledge, skills and attitudes to perform tasks in real life.
Among the biggest strengths of DBSE was its flexibility, for
it caters to diverse student aspirations by providing options
for specialized learning. The DBSE was rolled out in 2021
with thirty government schools with the hope that over time,
all government schools and private schools in Delhi would
migrate to it. In May 2023, DBSE set a new benchmark when
it announced the results of its first board exams with 99.5
per cent students clearing class X and 99.3 per cent clearing
class XII exams.[79]

To bring the promise of DBSE to life, the AAP government
established a network of Dr B.R. Ambedkar Schools of
Specialised Excellence (ASOSEs) in 2021. The idea was born
out of a realization that the current education system provides
students with a standardised, one-size-fits-all education. This
leaves little scope for students who have early awareness of
and interest in specific fields, to pursue specializations of their
choice or to develop specialized curriculum that is in-tune
with the requirements of industry and competitive exams.
A Delhi government survey in 2020–21 of 3,200 students
and parents revealed that 83 per cent students from class

VIII to XII expressed an interest in early specialization in their subjects of interest and 75 per cent parents believed early specialization would be beneficial for their child.[80] The ASOSEs were established as choice-based schools for classes IX to XII that allow students to specialize in their chosen fields of study. All ASOSEs feature world-class infrastructure, partnerships with globally reputed organizations and increased exposure to various career pathways through master classes, expert interactions and field visits.

As of March 2024, a total of fifty-five ASOSEs had been established in Delhi, catering to over 12,000 students across five specializations; science, technology, engineering and mathematics (STEM)—to prepare students to get into leading Indian and global institutes for engineering, medical, pure and applied sciences; high-end twenty-first century skills that focuses on skill and entrepreneurship development; performing and visual arts; humanities and the armed forces preparatory school to prepare students for entry to the Indian defence services. Each specialization offers a combination of foundational and specialized subjects at each grade level. Students get exposure to different disciplines through a bouquet of specialized subjects in classes IX and X, after which they choose one discipline for a deep dive in classes XI and XII. The AAP government has roped in some of India's best and most experienced institutes as knowledge partners to support the design and delivery of the new curriculum, such as Ashoka University, Tata Institute of Social Sciences (TISS), IIT Delhi, National Institute of Fashion Technology (NIFT) Delhi and Lend a Hand India.

In just three years, Delhi's ASOSEs have set a new hallmark for secondary education in India by achieving stellar results. Of the 395 students who appeared for IIT-JEE examinations in 2024, 70 per cent cleared JEE (Mains) and 21 per cent cleared JEE (Advanced) to secure admission into the IITs.[81] Of the 255 students who appeared for NEET in 2024, 95 per cent cleared the test, rivalling the success rate of renowned schools and coaching institutes across the country.[82] In 2023, thirty-two out of seventy-six students, including nine girls from the first batch of the armed forces preparatory school cleared the written NDA examination—a success rate of 42 per cent that was among the highest from any school across the country.[83] In 2023, students from Delhi's ASOSE in Rohini, Sector 11, won the first edition of Delhi Robotics League, India's first state-wide school-level robotics competition, beating top private schools. With rising awareness, the demand for admissions to ASOSEs have risen significantly with over 1,44,000 applications received for 6,000 seats in academic year 2024–25—a selection rate of 4 per cent for a government school system!

Another innovation under the Delhi education reforms 2.0 deserves mention here—the Delhi model virtual school (DMVS). Launched in August 2022 by Mr Kejriwal, DMVS is a full-time regular online school that runs on a cutting-edge technology platform created by Google and Schoolnet India to make quality education accessible remotely to every child.[84] DMVS is affiliated to DBSE and carries all the hallmarks of a regular Delhi government school, viz. full-time students and teachers, regular teaching-learning activities, assessments—providing a comprehensive and interactive virtual environment to its students. Conceived in the wake of the Covid-19 pandemic, DMVS is expected to cater to those students who have constraints attending a physical school, such as those working eight to ten hours a day, those pursuing other passions (art/sports), or having familial responsibilities or a serious illness and wish to experience the Delhi model of education. A total of 430 students, 95 per cent from Delhi and the rest from thirteen states, were enrolled in DMVS as of mid-2024.

The diversity of initiatives under Delhi education reforms 2.0 have challenged all pre-existing notions of how far state governments in India can go to raise the bar on innovation and redefine benchmarks in public education. It has also brought the AAP government much closer to realizing its vision of providing world-class education to every child in Delhi.

Transforming India's Government Schools

India stands at the precipice of an education crisis. It is probably the only big economy in the world, the fifth largest in 2024, to rank among the bottom fifty countries in terms of mean years of schooling—6.6 years as per the 2023–24 UN Human Development Report.[85] This is lower than many countries in South Asia like Bangladesh and Sri Lanka and in Sub-Saharan Africa like Kenya, Congo and Nigeria. While this is just a measure of access to schooling, the quality of school education is a bigger concern. The Annual Status of Education Report (ASER) 2023 finds that 25 per cent of teens between ages fourteen and eighteen can't read class II-level text fluently and more than half are unable to do a simple division.[86]

Those who are fortunate to complete higher education and graduate, struggle to find jobs. Years of poor schooling followed by a higher education system obsessed with granting degree certificates rather than imparting skills, has contributed to making half of all our graduates unemployable.[87] The International Labour Organization (ILO) has estimated that among all young Indians under twenty-five years of age, unemployment is the highest among graduates at around 30 per cent.[88] A sharp division in the quality of education that an elite few get versus the rest, is perhaps the biggest contributing factor to India's spiralling income inequality. In 2022, for the first time since independence, India's income inequality was worse than it was under the British rule and higher than all G20 nations, including the US.[89]

For the past seven decades, governments in India have waxed eloquent about the importance of education to building a strong economy and a developed country—'Viksit Bharat' being the latest catchphrase—but few have shown the appetite to put money where their mouth is. India's obsession with high talk, no walk on education began from the days of drafting the Constitution, when many members of the Constituent Assembly objected to placing the right to free and compulsory education up to the age of fourteen under Article 46 of the directive principles of state policy rather than as a fundamental right to avoid committing a budget. A disturbed member of the Constituent Assembly from Bihar, Professor K.T. Shah, said in 1948:

> 'Even this right to compulsory primary education has been provided for in such a clumsy, half-hearted and hesitating manner that one wonders whether the framers of this Draft were at all anxious that the curse of ignorance that has rested upon us all these years should be removed at all. The provision made here just permits the State, even within the period of ten years, only to 'endeavour' to give effect to this aspiration. Even there it is not compulsory.'[90]

It was only in 1968 that the first National Policy on Education, based on the Kothari Commission report of the Central government, advocated a specific share of public expenditure in India (by central and state governments) be allocated to education every year—6 per cent of the GDP. For the next five decades, every major education policy document of the Government of India and several election manifestos of political parties of all shades reiterated this promise with no real action. Most recently, the much-celebrated National Education Policy 2020 (NEP 2020) once again advocated this demand, raising hopes that India's education sector will finally turn a page. The reality has been quite the opposite.

Over the past decade, the Central government's budgetary spending on education has declined consistently from 4.6 per cent in 2013–14 to 2.9 per cent in 2023–24.[91] The average budgetary spending on education by all states and UTs has also declined steadily from 16.5 per cent in 2013–14 to 13.3 per cent in 2023–24.[92] As a result, the total public expenditure on education in India as a share of its GDP has ranged between 2.4 per cent to 2.9 per cent throughout the past decade—a far cry from the promised 6 per cent.[93]

This steady withdrawal of the Indian state from the education sector has had grave consequences for the government schooling system. The total number of government schools in India have reduced from 11.1 lakh in 2014–15 to 10.2 lakh in 2020–21. Enrolments too have declined over the past decade although government schools still cater to 55 per cent of all students. Private schools have stepped in to fill this gap, increasing from 2.9 lakh to 3.4 lakh in this period.[94] There is an acute shortage of teachers in government schools with over 8 lakh vacancies remaining to be filled in December 2023. Backward states, such as UP, Bihar and Jharkhand that need well-performing public schools the most, reported over half of these vacancies.[95]

To its credit, the NEP 2020 is a commendable policy document for it sets right many policy priorities for the first time in India's school education system. It sets the goal of the education system as one that builds character, enabling learners to be ethical, rational, compassionate and caring, while at the same time preparing them for gainful, fulfilling employment. It emphasizes the need for universalizing quality early childhood care and education for ages three to six years by 2030. It accords the highest priority to achieving foundational literacy and numeracy skills in all class III students by 2025. It highlights the urgency to fill the huge vacancies for teachers and fix the severely deficient infrastructure in government schools. It talks about empowering and providing continuous professional development to teachers and principals. At the pedagogy level too, it talks about moving away from rote learning to a more inquiry-driven and experiential learning that promotes critical thinking.

The NEP 2020, however, is a highly flawed policy document, as it fails to connect any of these noble intentions with actions. It describes the 'what' but provides no roadmap as to 'how' states can go about implementing these ideas and, most importantly, 'where' the funds will come from. A beautiful policy without a credible implementation plan is like watching a pretty science fiction film and imagining yourself living in a different world for a few hours, only to discover later that nothing really has changed around you. For this very reason, the NEP 2020 risks being condemned to the dustbin of history just as all other well-meaning education policy documents, beginning 1968, have been.

Those who have read the preceding chapters must have noted the many similarities between the prescriptions under the NEP 2020 for the school education system, and the reforms designed and successfully piloted under the Delhi education model over the past decade—with one major difference. The Delhi education model is no science fiction; it is a real-world policy-cum-implementation model that arguably provides the most realistic roadmap for any Indian state keen on realizing the vision of NEP 2020. Providing an elaborate roadmap for scaling-up the Delhi education model elsewhere is beyond the scope of this book. It may not even be wise to scale it as is. However, Indian policymakers keen to do so will have to set four key priorities which the AAP government did when it began conceptualizing the Delhi education model and working towards the impossible task of turning around a state-level government school system.

First, there cannot be any conversation about transforming India's government schools without setting aside sizeable budgets. No amount of drafting new policies or giving inspiring speeches will help until our governments marshal the political will to put the required money on the table first. Until that happens, any talk of *viksit bharat* or making India a *vishwaguru* is akin to fooling the people of the nation. Delhi's experience shows that, even in the national capital, fixing the accumulated deficiencies in our government schools over the past several decades—i.e. building state-of-the-art infrastructure, hiring sufficient teachers, investing in world-class teacher training—required setting aside nearly 25 per cent of the budget consistently for a decade. Many states may not be in a position to set aside huge budgets immediately, but there has to be a commitment to start phasing towards that within two to three years. There are two potential pathways to mobilize these funds.

One, by imposing new taxes like the Central government did, through a 2 per cent education cess in 2004 to fund the Sarva Siksha Abhiyan (SSA). The SSA succeeded in considerably expanding the government school infrastructure across India and improving the access to primary education. Under the present GST regime though, states have no powers to raise additional taxes and therefore, the onus is on the Centre to find the solutions. For instance, the Centre relaxed the fiscal deficit limit under Fiscal Responsibility and Budget Management (FRBM) Act to fund vaccination expenses during the Covid-19 pandemic. Perhaps it's time to treat the crisis afflicting our government schools with a similar urgency. Second, is to take the path Delhi did. The AAP government did not raise any new taxes; rather it prioritized the needs of the education department above all else. Our state governments need to start budgeting for education the way a lower middle class or a middle-class family does: set aside the budget to provide the best quality education for the children first and meet all other needs from what's left. A bullet train, a coastal expressway, a grand statue, a metro rail for a tier two or three city, can all wait until government schools get their due. The fact that the AAP government managed to considerably increase the state budget at the same time meant that other departments didn't really have to sacrifice much, making it a true win-win option.

The second priority should be to introduce only those policies that can be implemented at scale. Governments across India love to create islands of excellence and celebrate them endlessly. Kendriya Vidyalayas are one example. The most recent example is the PM-SHRI (PM Schools for Rising India) scheme launched in 2022 by the Narendra Modi government. The scheme aims to develop 14,500 schools across India as model schools at a cost of ₹27,000 core in five years showcasing NEP 2020 in action with no plans for the remaining 99 per cent government schools.[96] In contrast, every intervention under the Delhi education model was introduced with the clear vision of scaling them across all schools in a time-bound manner with the requisite resources aligned for the same—be it infrastructure upgrade or strengthening the SMCs or the business blasters programme.

Building capacity to implement at scale can be a huge challenge. The AAP government addressed this by staggering different initiatives over the years, bringing multiple external experts to work full-time with the government and engaging many of India's leading education nonprofits to co-design and implement reforms at scale. This is again where the Central government can play an important role. It can create a dedicated support unit at the Ministry of Education that documents successful at-scale initiatives being implemented by any state government in line with NEP 2020 and provides free technical assistance and handholding to any other state committing financial resources to implement these initiatives at scale.

Till date, over 20 state governments have sent their delegations to study the interventions under the Delhi education model, including BJP-ruled states such as Madhya Pradesh, Assam and Gujarat. The AAP government has provided them all the assistance possible, but any one state can go only so far. The Central government is best placed to act as a clearing house of ideas that help realize the vision of NEP—be it Delhi's happiness curriculum, Uttarakhand's Anandam Pathyacharya curriculum or Tamil Nadu's activity-based learning model. Progressive ideas being implemented at scale should become the motto for this unit. It's time our governments realize that India can no longer afford slow-moving pilots while millions of underprivileged children continue to suffer a dysfunctional government school system every day.

The third priority should be keeping teachers and principals at the heart of every reform. Inspired and capable teachers are the most important agents of change in any system-wide effort for education reform. Unfortunately, government school systems are too large and bureaucratic and often devalue the role and knowledge of these frontline workers. The AAP government empowered Delhi's teachers and principals in multiple ways, treating them with dignity, care and respect. It has made lasting investments in training them in leadership and behaviour change besides cutting-edge teaching methods. They were closely involved from the design stage of every major reform—be it designing the happiness curriculum or entrepreneurship mindset curriculum or Mission Buniyaad. In addition, pre-service teacher training also needs reform to ensure new teachers coming into the system come with the right set of tools and attitude—something that the Delhi Teachers University is attempting to do.

The fourth priority, often the most ignored one, is actively involving parents in providing holistic education to their children. If the goal of the education system is not just to produce skilled human resources but also to make compassionate, caring and public-spirited citizens, then the role of parents cannot be ignored. Children may spend four to five hours a day in the school, but the remaining time is spent at home. Delhi's mega PTM had a huge impact in breaking the silos between the two most important stakeholders in a student's life—teachers and parents—who helped each other understand what they can do better. A series of parent workshops have also been held in Delhi's schools to reinforce behaviours at home that can provide the right environment for a child's holistic development. In addition, activating the SMCs to make parents take active ownership in the education of their children—the way Delhi has done—is perhaps the only scalable way to make over 10 lakh government schools across India accountable in their day-to-day administration.

The discussion thus far has traced the evolution of the Delhi education model over the past decade and how it could guide similar efforts across India. Needless to say, the starting point of any such reform effort is strong political will. Reforming state-wide government systems is more complex than any other public institution for the sheer variety of stakeholders involved. Unfortunately, decades of abject neglect has taken the soul out of this very institution that determines the future of half of our children. Bureaucracy alone cannot fix this problem; in fact, they are part of the problem. Inspired political leadership that makes education its topmost priority and engages deeply and honestly with the reform process is the only one that can do this, as Delhi has shown. Most traditional parties are averse to doing this for two simple reasons. Public funds invested in run-of-the-mill infrastructure projects like roads, flyovers etc. lend themselves to easy commissions than hiring more teachers and fixing toilets in government schools. Second, rising demand for private schools benefits political bosses too, who often run these institutions themselves. The ultimate responsibility, therefore, rests with the Indian voter. Only when they start demanding and voting for parties that place education at the top of their political agenda, will things really change.

Chapter 3

Health

Birth of India's First Health Guarantee Model

Picture a government clinic or hospital in India. The first image most of us are likely to evoke is that of an inefficient, chaotic and crowded space, dehumanizing in its care, and providing no guarantee of quality or timely service. For more than seven decades, this has remained the enduring legacy of India's chronically underfunded and overstressed public health system. This was the case in Delhi too until 2015, when Mr Kejriwal and his new cabinet decided that providing free and quality healthcare to every resident of Delhi, rich or poor, was among the foremost duties of any democratically elected government.

This principle seems almost radical in a nation with a crumbling public health infrastructure. Government-funded primary healthcare is, by and large, non-existent in most parts of India, especially urban areas. Even where primary health centres (PHCs) exist, the absenteeism of doctors and health workers is rampant. An independent survey of over 1,400 PHCs across 19 Indian states in 2003 revealed a 39 per cent average absence rate for health workers and 43 per cent for doctors.[1] Crowding in government hospitals is thus unavoidable. For the poor, availing care in itself

101

entails travelling long distances, forsaking daily earnings and queuing up for hours to see a doctor who is often rude and dismissive. Diagnosis and treatment demand more resolve: most prescribed medicines and tests are unlikely to be available in the government hospital, and major surgical procedures have long waiting periods, often running into years. It is no wonder the rich and the middle class have completely exited the public health system. Those left behind are also increasingly seeking private healthcare. The National Sample Survey data of 2017–18 showed less than one-third of Indian citizens visit government health facilities for any treatment; the share among the poorest quintile too was alarming low at 36 per cent.[2]

Until 2015, this systemic neglect was evident across Delhi's crumbling public health infrastructure as well. Primary healthcare was inadequate and largely dysfunctional; it comprised 260 dispensaries run by the Delhi government, less than one per municipal ward; provided few medicines or diagnostic tests and was ridden with chronic absenteeism of government staff. These dispensaries, typically run in a multi-floor concrete structure built at a cost of ₹5 crore each with more than a dozen government staff, weren't delivering much value to the people. Tertiary care was fragmented across hospitals run by the Central government, the Municipal Corporation of Delhi (MCD) and the Delhi government—the latter had the largest share in this network. The missing layer of primary care flooded the 37 Delhi government hospitals with the healthcare needs of almost 20 million residents, severely impacting the quality of service. Medicines, procured and distributed centrally in a top-down system, were perpetually out of stock. The backlog was such that an average citizen would have to wait for more than two years to undergo a high-end diagnostic test or a surgical procedure.

The Delhi Model sought to dismantle this sordid state of affairs. AAP in February 2015 declared education and health as its top two priorities, and both received substantial budgetary allocation from the first year itself. This wasn't empty election rhetoric: the AAP government, through its two terms, has consistently allocated over 10 per cent of its budget to the health sector, and between 12 and 15 per cent since 2021. Over the past decade, Delhi has allocated the highest share of its budget to the health sector among all Indian states and UTs; Delhi's allocation is almost two-and-half times the national average of 5 to 6 per cent.[3]

In absolute terms, the national capital's health budget has tripled from approximately ₹3,000 crore in 2014–15 to ₹9,000 crore in 2023–24. The biggest jump has been in capital spending that rose to over ₹1,700 crore in 2022–23, nearly eight times higher than what the Congress government invested in Delhi in 2012–13. In per capita terms, Delhi's health spending increased from ₹1,718 per capita in 2014–15 to ₹4,440 per capita in 2022–23—the highest in India and more than twice the average for all other states/UTs of ₹2,200 per capita.[4]

After crossing the first hurdle of apportioning money, AAP turned its focus to figuring a systemic solution to the underlying issues grappling Delhi's ailing public health system. One thing was for sure: merely throwing more money at a derelict and dysfunctional system wasn't going to suffice. Mr Kejriwal decided to entrust this responsibility of fixing Delhi's public health system, and delivering a key election promise, to his enterprising health minister, Satyendar Jain. In a lighter vein, Mr Jain was often referred to by his colleagues as the idea minister of the AAP government, for he held a reputation of coming up with out-of-the-box solutions to any governance problem.

Few health ministers get a carte blanche to reimagine and redesign the entire healthcare system with no budget constraint. Even fewer health ministers enter office with a wish to even do so: like education, health is not a sought-after ministry at either the state and central government level. That, however, wasn't the case with Satyendar Jain. Once the vision and ambition to reform Delhi's public health system were set and the budgets allocated, Mr Jain led his team of officials to go about upturning possibly every status quo element of Delhi's healthcare system. Over the next few years, Delhi's health minister—a professional architect before entering politics to join AAP—became the unlikely architect of a healthcare guarantee model unheard of in India.

Delhi's unique health model was designed based on three guiding principles. First, public health services should be efficiently provided to citizens, and in a way that is dignified and respectful. Second, all citizens should, irrespective of income or any eligibility criteria, be able to access healthcare facilities and schemes. If the right to free and quality healthcare is to be equated with the right to life, the government should not act as a gatekeeper to decide who deserves to live the most—an idea consistent with the United Nation's vision of universal health coverage. Third, governments should leverage multi-stakeholder partnerships to deliver the best health outcomes to its citizens at the lowest possible cost. Instead of pitting private health providers against the government health system, both should collaborate to provide high-quality care to citizens.

These principles informed the AAP government's comprehensive three-tier healthcare system in Delhi. The mohalla clinics would offer universal primary care, polyclinics ensured availability of specialised treatment at the secondary level, and speciality and super-speciality government hospitals provided the tertiary level of care.

At the primary level, the innovative concept of mohalla clinics introduced the idea of universal primary care at walking distance from every neighbourhood for the first time in India. These air-conditioned clinics were built in prefabricated structures at a minimal cost of ₹20 lakhs per unit. Each clinic provided consultation with a MBBS doctor, 164 essential medicines with a tech-enabled supply chain system to eliminate stock-outs, and 90 diagnostic tests through empanelled private labs—all free of cost to every citizen. As of early 2024, 540 mohalla clinics are operational in Delhi, conducting over 2 crore out-patient visits and 10 lakh tests every year.

Over the past decade, no healthcare innovation in India has been nationally and globally celebrated as much as Delhi's frugal mohalla clinics. They were an instant hit with the people of Delhi for their convenience, efficiency and quality of care, registering over 7 crore out-patient visits since 2015. Internationally, the intervention has received accolades from the world's leading health journal, the *Lancet*, and the *Stanford Social Innovation Review*. Two former United Nations Secretary-Generals, Kofi Annan and Ban Ki-Moon, have visited and applauded these facilities; Mr Annan called the mohalla clinics 'a model for all Indian states embarking on the journey to Universal Health Care'. Inspired by the success story, seven Indian states have introduced similar models providing free primary healthcare in urban areas till 2024, including Jharkhand (Atal mohalla clinics), Telangana (Basthi dawakhana), Madhya Pradesh (Sanjeevani clinics), Karnataka (Namma clinics), Rajasthan (Janta clinics), Maharashtra (Aapla davakhana) and Chhattisgarh (Hamar clinics).

At the secondary level, polyclinics were introduced to provide quality secondary care through specialist doctors, in a dignified and respectful environment quite unlike the chaos that engulfed government hospitals. These polyclinics were administered by the nearest Delhi government hospitals and functioned as community outposts of the hospital's out-patient department, thereby reducing travel time and cost for patients seeking secondary care. By early 2024, thirty of the planned 100 polyclinics are functional, catering to nearly 15,00,000 out-patient visits every year.

AAP's response to the demand and backlog at the tertiary level was to expand the capacity of the government hospital system. During AAP's nine years, the infrastructure has seen a massive expansion in scale and size, going from 37 hospitals and 9,523 beds in 2015 to 40 hospitals and 13,708 beds in early 2024.[5] The 44 per cent increase in beds is only a fraction of new hospital beds being added: 25 projects with a cumulative total of over 16,000 beds are currently at different stages of construction, all expected to be commissioned by 2026. This would lift the total capacity in public hospitals under the Delhi government to over 30,000 beds—a threefold increase since 2015. Efforts were simultaneously made to ensure the availability of medicines at the hospital itself, and a dedicated helpline monitored directly by the health minister's office was launched for patients to seek immediate resolution in case of non-availability of medicines or any services at hospitals.

The three-tier action plan, as meticulously as it was designed, wasn't a quick fix—it would take time and tenacity to see it through. AAP thought an interim solution necessary to deliver upon its promise of free and quality healthcare to all. In March 2017, the government announced a unique initiative wherein any Delhi voter could get a referral for over 100 high-end radiological tests (including MRI, CT scan etc.) or over 800 treatment packages (including critical care like cancer care, heart bypass surgeries etc.) in any of the empanelled private health facilities of their choice if the waiting period extended beyond 24 hours and 30 days respectively at any Delhi government hospital. Any such treatment would be completely free of cost, cashless and paid for by the Delhi government. The initiative allowed the residents of Delhi to avail 2.4 lakh high-end diagnostic tests and 7,036 surgeries free of cost at private facilities in 2023–24. Only a few developed countries, such as Sweden and Finland, have a health guarantee policy in place with assured waiting times; Delhi in 2017 became the first state or UT in India to assure free treatment to every citizen for any ailment, irrespective of the cost, within a guaranteed time frame.

The final piece needed to complete AAP's health guarantee model was introduced in February 2018. With the launch of Farishtey Dilli Ke initiative, the government guaranteed free and timely emergency medical care for all road accident victims in Delhi. Irrespective of their residential status, any road accident victim in Delhi will be eligible for cashless treatment at any private hospital of their choice, with the cost borne by the Delhi government. Private hospitals were issued strict instructions not to decline any road accident victim for lack of payment. The government also announced a reward of ₹2,000 and a certificate of appreciation for the good samaritans—*farishtey*—who bring accident victims to hospitals. Till March 2024, more than 28,500 road accident survivors have availed free treatment in private hospitals under the initiative.

Collectively, Delhi's health reforms have substantially expanded the coverage of Delhi's public health system from 3.2 crore outpatient visits in 2014–15 to 5.1 crore outpatient visits in 2022–23—a 62 per cent rise in eight years.[6] The number of free tests availed by patients has also nearly doubled from 2.8 crore in 2014–15 to 5.1 crore in 2022–23.[7] The reforms have also brought significant improvements in some of the most staunch long-term health indicators, such as the Infant Mortality Rate (IMR)—measured as the death of infants before reaching the age of one per 1,000 live births— and Under-5 Mortality Rate (UMR)—the death of children before reaching the age of five per 1,000 live births. Sample registration system data shows that Delhi's IMR dropped by 40 per cent between 2014–20, positioning Delhi next only to Kerala among regions with the lowest IMR.[8] Delhi's UMR also dropped by 33 per cent from 21 to 14 against the all-India average of 32 in 2020.[9]

With continued investments to improve both quality and reach, AAP's publicly funded health guarantee model has infused new life into Delhi's public health system.

Mohalla Clinics: the ATMs of Primary Healthcare

On a cold winter morning in January 2014, a few days into office, Chief Minister Arvind Kejriwal and Health Minister Satyendar Jain decided to visit the inundated outpatient wards of a few government hospitals. Talking to patients and doctors for nearly half a day, the ministers stumbled upon a glaring fact: over 90 per cent of the patients were visiting the hospitals for minor ailments, such as fever and infections, instead of visiting government dispensaries. The 260 dispensaries set up by previous governments over seven decades were ineffective, besides being too few in number, in providing primary care to Delhi's burgeoning population. Medicines and diagnostic services were rarely available, health staff were absent and the poor were left with the choice of either seeking paid care from local private clinics, many of them run by unqualified practitioners or 'quacks', or to flood Delhi's far-flung government hospitals. The doctors bemoaned that much of their time was spent on treating minor ailments rather than attending to patients with major diseases, thus compromising the quality of care.

To Mr Kejriwal and Mr Jain, the writing was on the peeling wall—Delhi's primary healthcare system needed a major overhaul to support both patients and providers of care.

They searched for a solution within the current ecosystem. Apart from the physical dispensaries, Delhi government had a fleet of 85 mobile van dispensaries stationed for two hours every day in low-income neighbourhoods to provide basic care, consultation and medicines. Perhaps scaling this initiative would solve the fundamental gap in Delhi's public health system, Mr Kejriwal and Mr Jain hoped, but further scrutiny revealed the mobile van dispensaries had severe limitations. While they resolved the accessibility question, high levels of patient dissatisfaction remained because of inconvenient timings (people hate to change their schedules to visit a clinic), long queues owing to the restrictive two-hour windows and unavailability of most medicines or tests.

It became clear that a lasting solution would need to adopt a 'patient first' approach—one that would provide primary care at a convenient distance, at a time suitable to the patient and with all the attendant facilities. While the first AAP government fell after 49 days in February 2014, it had diagnosed the nature of the primary care problem. Mr Jain in a 2017 interview said:

'The idea of mohalla clinics struck me when I was hearing about what ATMs did to the banking system. It decluttered the banks and made basic banking services accessible at walking distance for everyone. I knew this is exactly what is needed in primary care.'[10]

The typical family doctor-compounder setup, which generations of Indian middle-class families relied upon for accessible primary healthcare, was the solution that needed scaling up. When AAP came back to power in February 2015, it lost no time in launching the mohalla clinics—the ATMs of its primary healthcare system—that provided free consultation, tests and medicines within walking distance of every neighbourhood.

On 19 July 2015, AAP launched the first mohalla clinic in the middle of a slum cluster in Peeragarhi village, located in the western region of Paschim Vihar. The original plan was to open 1,000 clinics that would cater to 10,000 people each; as of March 2024, there are 540 mohalla clinics catering to every social stratum, from the previously unserved and underserved areas such as unauthorized colonies of outer Delhi to the posh colonies of south Delhi. Each clinic is typically a three-room structure staffed by four health workers: an MBBS doctor, a pharmacist, a nurse/midwife and a helper. All essential primary health services are covered under the clinics, including treatment for chronic diseases such as diabetes, asthma and hypertension. For more serious cases, the mohalla clinics act as referral centres to polyclinics or Delhi government hospitals. The clinics remain open for six hours a day, from 8 a.m. to

2 p.m., six days a week, typically catering to 100–120 patients every day. If the demand spills over to 150 patients, the clinic operates in two shifts from 8 a.m. to 8 p.m.

At the clinic's core are six innovative features that offers AAP's simple and straightforward solution a unique appeal and makes it a breakthrough healthcare innovation globally. First, the clinics epitomize frugal innovation by delivering last-mile, affordable and quality primary healthcare. These air-conditioned clinics are compactly built inside porta cabins, occupying only 600 sq. ft. space, making it possible to place them in the densest urban areas, which is typically the case with the low-income neighbourhoods. They would provide all the comforts of a private facility at a capital cost of ₹20 lakhs per clinic. In contrast, the pre-existing government dispensaries took years to be constructed, were non-air-conditioned, multi-storey concrete structures spread over a wider area and were built at a cost of ₹5 crore each.

Second, by virtue of being embedded in the heart of the community, the clinics redefined the doctor-patient relationship. The doctors at mohalla clinics familiarized themselves with individual patients and the community's unique characteristics that impact its well-being, such as the supply of drinking water and sanitation facilities. This has had a huge qualitative impact on the quality of care offered. In many ways, this model was inspired by the idea of a family physician who caters to a community and develops a care-giving bond with the patients over time. There are reports of doctors at mohalla clinics mediating social issues of domestic violence and the problem of alcoholism.[11]

Third, the intervention creates a unique public-private partnership model to deliver quality primary healthcare by roping in private MBBS doctors and health workers. This innovation allowed the government to quickly achieve the scale it did. The mohalla clinics witnessed low absenteeism since they operated only for six hours a day, allowing private doctors to continue with their private practice outside clinic hours. The AAP government also created a unique outcome-based compensation structure, paying doctors a fixed amount for each patient served, which in turn created direct accountability that was missing in the existing public health system. Staff misbehaving with patients, for instance, would result in lower compensation over time as repeat visits by patients dropped. The incentives of the clinic staff and patient outcomes were thus directly aligned, popularizing the clinics with the people of Delhi who could now access professional care with dignity and respect.

Fourth, the well-stocked clinics provide 165 essential medicines and 90 tests free of cost to patients, addressing all their health needs at one go. The government was aware that adding diagnostic services to the patient care offering was an important citizen expectation. Since setting up a laboratory for each test at each clinic was infeasible, the activity was outsourced by empanelling private labs who agreed to offer tests at a fraction of their retail prices given the bulk volumes involved—a true win-win. Today, a resident can walk into a mohalla clinic, have a nurse-cum-lab technician collect their sample and receive test reports at the clinic the next day. The speedy digital reports reach the patient on WhatsApp on the day of sample collection.

Fifth, the paperless *clinics* functioning on the backbone of cloud technology have drastically lowered costs and raised efficiencies. Each mohalla clinic is equipped with three tablets, one with each key staff member including the doctor. Patient details are keyed in on the tablet and history tracked over time; prescribed tests or medicines are updated for the pharmacist or the lab technician to provide follow-up services. Capturing real time information further ensures smooth supply chain management and minimizes stock outs of any medicines— challenges that ailed the older system.

Sixth, the mohalla clinic reinforces AAP's commitment to free and quality healthcare for all citizens, without imposing any income or eligibility criteria. When the idea of 1,000 mohalla clinics providing completely free services was first mooted, the government faced a massive pushback from the bureaucracy, which insisted on introducing an income criterion to streamline claims and ensure only the poorest benefit. This would have required people to carry a proof of their poverty every time they wished to get tested, purchase medicines or seek care at the clinics. It was only after Mr Kejriwal stood his ground that the original idea passed through unharmed.

Since their inception, Delhi's mohalla clinics have attracted the interest of many independent researchers keen to study its impact on the public health system and the patients. The vignettes below illustrate the impact of the clinics on Delhi's aam aadmi:

'Shanti, 38, a domestic help suffering from diabetes, is the sole bread earner in her family of two children. Earlier, visiting a government facility for measuring her sugar level and collecting medicines used to be a harrowing experience for her. She had no one to accompany her to the doctor and getting the test done and buying medicines burned a hole in her pocket. She therefore avoided visiting the doctor until the glucose levels were too high to go unmonitored. Now with the mohalla clinic in her neighbourhood, she gets her sugar levels measured on a regular basis.' [12]

'Babu Ram, 42, a migrant rickshaw puller from Bihar and resident of Vikasnagar Extension, has high blood pressure and needs regular medication. He earlier visited a government dispensary, but its functioning was sporadic. He was often forced to visit government or private hospitals for checkups and medication. To do this, he had to forego that day's earnings and spend long hours waiting for his turn as well as for purchasing the medicines from the medical stores. But now, Babu Ram says he can visit the mohalla clinic on any day of his choice, consult the doctor and get his medicines free of cost. He does not lose that day's work.' [13]

A study published in the international journal *Health Policy and Planning* in 2023 found these clinics to have substantially reduced patients' out-of-pocket health expenditures while also reducing the average cost of delivering primary care by the government. On average, a patient spent ₹667 to visit and avail primary care in Delhi's public hospitals but would spend merely ₹42 to visit a mohalla clinic, cutting expenses by 94 per cent. At the same time, providing outpatient care in a public hospital costs the government ₹439 per patient while it costs only ₹101 per patient in a mohalla clinic—a 75 per cent cutback.[14]

The economics align with the experiences. A patient exit survey covering 109 clinics and 1,700 people, done by the global research firm IDinsight in 2019, revealed high patient satisfaction with 97 per cent stating they would return to the clinic again for treatment. Nearly 70 per cent patients had to wait less than 10 minutes and 92 per cent were satisfied with the time spent with the doctor.[15] A systematic review of eleven studies in 2020 found patient satisfaction reached around 90 per cent. The doctor-patient relationship in hospital-based systems, the review noted, had become hurried and transactional, with doctors spending less than a minute on average per patient. In contrast, the time spent by mohalla clinic doctors was significantly higher and associated with higher patient satisfaction, better treatment compliance, regular follow-ups and improved clinical outcomes.[16]

The rootedness of mohalla clinics also ensured they could reach the most vulnerable populations, especially women, the elderly and children, and in turn, bridge the gender gap in health care. Women, particularly housewives, constitute two-thirds of all patients visiting mohalla clinics, studies show.[17] Since visiting government hospitals demanded both time and money, usually difficult for women tasked with household responsibilities, they avoided accessing primary healthcare and waited until they fell seriously ill. When the clinics opened in their community, women could avail free health services within minutes and at minimal cost.

Despite global recognition and far-reaching impact on people's lives, the scaling of the mohalla clinic model has battled a persistent non-cooperation by the BJP-ruled Centre. The Delhi L-G, a Central government nominee who approves all policy decisions of the elected government, stalled for several months a proposal to expand the model beyond the first 100 clinics. It was only when forty AAP MLAs protested outside the L-G's residence for six hours that the file was approved.[18]

This was only the beginning of a miasma of repression. The Central government has turned down the AAP government's requests over the years to set aside small land parcels around each community for building these clinics.[19] The government had to eventually resort to utilizing land from its existing departments, including alongside PWD roads and pavements. Over 170 clinics continue to function in rented apartments or rent-free premises offered by generous citizens. In September 2016, the Centre's non-cooperation gave way to active obstruction when the MCD, then governed by the BJP, demolished many newly built mohalla clinics on the pretext that they were obstructing public movement.[20]

Despite these obstacles, the AAP government in Delhi persisted and managed to open 540 clinics in nine years, against its original target of 1,000 clinics, and registered over 7 crore outpatient visits. It took just two years however for AAP to build nearly 800 clinics after it formed a government in Punjab in early 2022—showcasing the possibilities of what could have been possible in Delhi had the Centre not stood in the way.

In 2021, the AAP government initiated a second generation of reforms to make mohalla clinics better serve the primary healthcare needs of all the people of Delhi. A new award-winning design was unveiled that was smaller (roughly 400 sq. ft.), built from upcycled shipping containers and took only three days to assemble at any site.[21] Eight such mohalla clinics have already started functioning in Delhi with several more in the pipeline.

In 2022, the AAP government piloted twenty clinics inside government school premises with the goal to cater to the physical and mental well-being of over 17 lakh students enrolled in Delhi government schools. In what could be a first such initiative in India, the school health clinics were assigned a dedicated psychologist to conduct individual counselling sessions and group life skills sessions with students.[22] There are plans to further extend reach among women by transforming either existing clinics or setting up independent mahila mohalla clinics, staffed only by women doctors and health workers, to offer prenatal and antenatal care services. Five mahila clinics were piloted in 2022.[23]

With a commitment to well-rounded care, the AAP government created polyclinics as a second tier to offer specialized health services. While over 90 per cent of the outpatient needs of Delhi's residents were expected to be resolved at the mohalla clinics, some cases would require consultation with specialists. The polyclinics would save citizens from the hassle of visiting distant hospitals while also reducing the outpatient burden in hospitals. The AAP government converted the largely dysfunctional dispensaries built by previous governments to polyclinics, skirting the issue of land availability. The responsibility of providing specialists and running the polyclinics was given to the nearest Delhi government hospital. In addition to free tests and medicines, each polyclinic had in attendance gynaecology and paediatrics specialists every day, and orthopaedics, eye, ENT, surgery and skin specialists once a week. Mr Kejriwal inaugurated the first such clinic in Gandhi Nagar in East Delhi in November 2015.

Against its original vision of setting up 100 polyclinics, AAP has managed to open only 30 sites as of March 2024. The availability of specialized personnel has reined in expansion. As permanent government staff, specialist doctors at Delhi government hospitals could only be recruited through the Union Public Service Commission (UPSC) examination, conducted by the Central government. However, the Centre was unable to fill vacancies at Delhi government hospitals and polyclinics for several years despite court strictures, hindering their scale-up plans.[24] In early 2024, after considerable internal resistance, a new model for polyclinics was approved wherein, similar to mohalla clinics, specialist doctors could be hired on a contractual basis. All 100 polyclinics are expected to be functional by early 2025.

Together with reforms in primary and secondary care, AAP also undertook innovative measures to strengthen tertiary healthcare, leading up to the creation of India's first healthcare guarantee model.

Revamping Delhi's Government Hospitals

Unlike primary care services, Delhi's tertiary healthcare network was built on sturdier grounds. The thirty-seven government hospitals were the mainstay of the public health system for several decades before giving way to neglect. Chronic underinvestment in capacity by successive governments led to massive overcrowding, poor quality of services and persistent shortage of medicines. To top it, there were long waiting periods, sometimes beyond two years, for many high-end diagnostic tests and life-saving surgeries. By 2015, the ground had begun to crack.

When AAP entered the scene, step one was to improve the quality of outpatient services in hospitals due to an overwhelming and often unmet demand. Patients floundered to register for an out-patient department (OPD) appointment and receive quality consultation during a limited time slot. To address these challenges, AAP added new OPD counters by hiring outsourced workers to complement the government health workers. The limited time slots for OPD consultation, resulting in a huge patient burden for doctors was the next challenge. Previously, studies showed a typical doctor-patient interaction in government hospitals lasts under one minute.[25] This was addressed by increasing the consultation hours from four to six hours in all Delhi government hospitals.[26] Doctors were further instructed to attend to all patients with valid OPD registration cards, even if that required extending consultation hours occasionally. Rigid consultation hours earlier often meant people had to return and spend another half a day to see a doctor.

Step two was to make medicines available and affordable. Medicines, procured and distributed centrally in a top-down system, were perpetually out of stock, forcing even the poorest to buy medicines from private pharmacies. This was perhaps the biggest grievance with Delhi government hospitals. The AAP government deployed a three-fold strategy, starting with ramping up procurement of drugs. Each hospital was asked to review its essential drugs list (EDL), which existed only on paper earlier, and to maintain sufficient stocks of each medicine for three months. The medical superintendents of each hospital were empowered to purchase up to ₹50 lakh of medicines from local stores at pre-approved rates in case of stock-outs.[27] Moreover, stern measures were put in place to ensure hospitals prescribed medicines only from those in the EDL. This would deter doctors prescribing costly medicines available only in private pharmacies when an equivalent or generic version was available in the hospital.

With the necessary measures in place, the AAP government then geared to strengthen monitoring systems to crack down upon errant hospitals. A dedicated helpline number, 1031, was launched to deal exclusively with patient complaints regarding any of the services at government hospitals, including unavailability of medicines. Boards advertising the helpline number were put up prominently in all hospitals with the assurance of immediate help. The aggrieved were asked to wait for a callback from the hospital; nodal officers appointed for this task would then resolve these complaints in real time. The grievance would be marked 'closed' once the 1031 helpline team received confirmation from the patient. Till date, over 1,500 calls are received every day on this helpline. A few examples of the 1031 helpline in action, as reported by the *Indian Express* in November 2019, illustrate its success:[28]

Dharmendra Kumar, a resident of Kalyan Awas in East Delhi, said: 'I was refused medicines at Lal Bahadur Shastri hospital earlier this month. While leaving the premises, I saw the poster about the helpline number and called it to see how it works. Within thirty minutes, I received a call from the hospital's drug store and my problem was resolved.'

Neha Srivastava (27), who was in her last month of pregnancy, had gone to Pt. Madan Mohan Malviya Hospital last month for an ultrasound. Due to give birth on November 22, she was asked to wait till December for the test. After repeated requests to doctors failed, she finally called the Delhi government helpline, 1031. 'Doctors were rude and told me to come back in December for a simple diagnostic test. They did not even refer me to another hospital. I saw a poster of the helpline number at the hospital, made a call and explained the problem. Within 20 minutes, I received a call from the hospital administration. They gave me a referral prescription and my test was immediately done at another hospital,' said Srivastava, who gave birth to a healthy girl two days ago.

In addition to this, Mr Kejriwal and Mr Jain made monthly surprise visits to check the availability of medicines and interact with patients about any gaps in service. Invariably the medical superintendents would be summoned immediately after and handed over a list of deficiencies to be corrected within 24 hours.[29] On one such visit, Mr Kejriwal himself took the prescription from a patient standing in queue for medicines to check if the prescribed medicines were available. When his turn came, the patient was informed that 'the medicine prescribed by the doctor was not part of the hospital's inventory list and therefore unavailable', a clear violation of the government's order, which invited immediate action against the doctor.[30]

The measured and meticulous strategy was instrumental in substantially addressing the issue of unavailability of medicines. For the first time, patients seeking tertiary care were assured they will get all medicines free from the hospital itself. A report by the *Hindustan Times* in early 2016 validated AAP's success: 'Pharmacy stores near Delhi government hospitals have seen a 50 per cent dip in their sales since February as almost all medicines prescribed by the doctors are present in the hospital dispensary, according to store owners.'[31]

It is worth noting these measures foregrounding healthcare were not rocket science. These could have been implemented, indeed should have been, decades earlier. All they demanded was a government that cared enough to understand the challenges of an average patient and marshalled the political will to execute considered solutions. Mr Kejriwal gained a reputation for his frequent surprise visits, signalling to the entire system that health was not an election rhetoric but an abiding priority of this government. This culture of unannounced inspections was carried forward by AAP's next health minister, Saurabh Bhardwaj.[32]

Chronic underinvestment in hospital infrastructure presented another challenge for the AAP government, perhaps its toughest trial so far: there was no capacity to meet the rising demand for tertiary care. Between 2010 and 2015, the Congress government under then-Chief Minister Sheila Dikshit made a capital investment of ₹1,462 crore in Delhi's public health infrastructure—less than the AAP government's capital spending of ₹1,745 crore in just 2022–23. In total, the government in its first nine years has made historic allocations worth ₹6,585 crore. The allocation allowed for a massive capacity expansion drive to build new hospitals and improve existing ones by optimizing space and adding more beds. As of early 2024, there are approximately 13,708 beds across 40 hospitals—a 44 per cent increase in the public health system's capacity over 2015. Further, eleven new hospitals with over 10,000 beds are under construction and fourteen existing hospitals are being remodelled to add around 6,000 beds—all to be commissioned by 2026. This would take the total hospital bed capacity to nearly 30,000 beds—a three-fold rise in just over a decade.

The government hospital system was being nurtured at last. This historic expansion was achieved not solely by higher budget allocations, but by challenging and undoing the assumptions dictating how projects are designed and budgeted. Satyendar Jain, the architect-turned politician, turned the economics of public hospitals on its head: he questioned the benchmark construction cost of ₹1 crore per new hospital bed based on which all projects in India were budgeted. His arithmetic yielded 70 per cent savings, as the capital costs of new projects under the AAP government came down to ₹30 lakh per bed. The 16,000 beds in the construction pipeline will cost the Delhi government approximately ₹4,900 crore instead of ₹16,000 crore if one were to follow the benchmark costing. What was Mr Jain's magic mantra?

'The current system has created illogical benchmarks for adding new hospitals,' Mr Jain said in a 2017 interview. He further explained:

'. . . if an AIIMS has to be built, it is costed at ₹1.5 crore per bed, if a regular non air-conditioned government hospital is to be built, it is costed at ₹1 crore per bed. So a 200-bedded hospital was costed at ₹200 crore. This didn't make any sense to me. Even a three-bedroom flat in Delhi including land is available for ₹70–80 lakh. Why should then the construction cost of a single government hospital bed, which doesn't include land cost, come to ₹1 crore? I even checked the construction cost of Medanta hospital—a five-star air-conditioned hospital—and that too was ₹70 lakh per bed. I figured something was seriously wrong. Extra money was being budgeted so that everyone with a vested interest could benefit.

'Being an architect, I reviewed all the designs and figured that the area set aside for patients was less while unnecessary large areas were allotted to offices of the medical superintendent, other senior officers and even for stores. I cut down all these unnecessary elements, reduced construction cost per bed while adding value to the patient experience.'[33]

During its second term, the AAP government attempted an ambitious plan that leveraged technology to further enhance efficiency and patient experience. It sought to bring all health facilities—hospitals, polyclinics and mohalla clinics—

under a cloud-based health information management system (HIMS). All services related to patient care, from hospital administration and budgeting to supply chain management, would now exist on a single platform. The HIMS would enable better management of the patient load, reduce crowding in hospitals and waiting time and improve the transparency and accountability of Delhi's medical facilities.

In practice, the system would assist patients with scheduling appointments, accessing medical reports on their phones and also avail of telemedicine from their homes. The government also plans to issue QR code-based e-health cards to each resident; the IDs would contain the patient's medical history, which could be accessed by the doctors only with the patient's consent and would help patients schedule a visit or treatment at any health facility connected to the HIMS system. There is also a proposed mobile app and a 24/7 call centre to function as the first port of call for a resident seeking care. The Covid-19 pandemic and subsequent procurement delays interrupted this mega health reform, but once implemented, the initiative is expected to take Delhi's public health system to global standards.

Despite its audacious plan to triple the capacity of Delhi's hospital infrastructure, AAP realized that it will take several years before this vision is translated to reality. Impediments, such as huge delays in recruitment of government doctors and health workers, especially specialists, bogged down its plans. As of early 2024, 39 per cent posts of specialists, 33 per cent posts of pharmacists and 20 per cent posts of nurses were vacant, affecting the regular functioning of Delhi government hospitals as well as the polyclinics under them.[34] All recruitments in Delhi are controlled by the Central government and Delhi's Lt. Governor, a personnel conundrum we will revisit in the final chapter.

An interim solution was urgently needed if the Kejriwal government wanted to keep its word of providing to every citizen of Delhi free and quality healthcare as a basic human right.

Guaranteeing Tertiary Care by Leveraging the Private Sector

In the last three decades, India's healthcare market has seen two opposing trends—a rapidly shrinking share of public healthcare providers corresponding with a rising share of private providers, with the latter booming in tier 1 and tier 2 cities. About 70 per cent of all outpatient visits and 58 per cent of all hospitalizations occurred in private facilities in 2017–18, per official figures.[35] The private sector in 2020 accounted for 62 per cent of the 19 lakh hospital beds available across India.[36] The glaring demand–supply gap existed in Delhi's public health infrastructure too and would take years to resolve. The AAP government realised the need for an interim solution to cater to the rising demand for free tertiary care among Delhi's residents.

That is when it struck upon a model that no government in India had ever tried, and which would become the linchpin of Delhi's health guarantee model. The AAP government in February 2017 launched the 'Quality Healthcare for All' scheme, which leveraged private sector infrastructure to provide guaranteed treatment—cashless and free of cost to all Delhi residents. The scheme had two main components.

Under the first component, all Delhi voters could avail high-end radiological tests (e.g. MRI, CT scan, PET-CT etc.) from a list of empanelled private diagnostic labs in case the waiting time in any government hospital shot beyond twenty-four hours. Starting with 13 tests and 22 diagnostic labs in 2017, the list has gradually expanded to cover 137 tests and 36 diagnostic labs as of early 2024. To avail free test at an empanelled private lab, the patient visiting a Delhi government hospital, or a polyclinic attached to it, would simply need to obtain a referral for the test from a government doctor confirming the long waiting period or unavailability of the test. The government in 2022 got rid of the 24-hour clause after it became the chief cause behind aggrieved patients being harried by doctors for referrals.

The number of beneficiaries availing free, cashless tests at private labs annually has climbed from 52,000 in 2017 to nearly 2.5 lakh people in 2023–24.[37]

The second component made life-saving surgeries and treatments attainable for all: Delhi voters could now avail a range of costly procedures, including heart bypass surgery or cancer treatments, completely free from a list of empanelled private hospitals (certified by the National Accreditation Board of Hospitals) if the wait time exceeded thirty days in any Delhi government hospital. Included in this scheme was one month of post-operative care to be provided by the same private hospital. The list, which in 2017 included fifty-two surgeries across sixty private hospitals, has expanded to cover 872 treatment packages (including non-critical procedures like knee/hip replacement) in 115 certified private hospitals as of 2024. Around 23,000 residents have availed free surgeries under this scheme so far, with their number steadily rising every year from 1,508 in 2017 to 7,036 in 2023–24.[38]

The 'Quality Healthcare for All' scheme was unique in ensuring that there was no discrimination: all Delhi voters, regardless of income or social demographic, would be eligible to avail free care. This became the chief bone of contention for Anil Baijal, Delhi's L-G at the time, who stalled approval and insisted upon retaining the income criteria, as was the approach followed by all government health schemes across India.[39] Yet, Mr Kejriwal remained undeterred. Quality healthcare for all, just like quality education, was a basic human right, he argued. The Delhi L-G relented eventually.

The economics of the AAP government's interim solution worried many. How could any government afford free treatment for its citizens in private hospitals with no caps? The AAP had a well thought out strategy. It extended the Central Government Health Scheme (CGHS) to Delhi's people with cooperation from the private sector. The boom in the private healthcare industry had left many hospitals with excess capacity; most of them had already negotiated under the CGHS to provide government employees with free healthcare at a fraction of the cost. Empanelment under the Delhi government scheme was optional, so only those facilities with excess capacity, which included many top private hospitals, registered under it. Since they already incurred the fixed costs of land, staff and equipment, treating patients referred from government hospitals meant offsetting their high running costs. It made sense to the government too since the CGHS rates were often less than what it would cost to treat in its own hospitals. Moreover, the government mandated a physical visit and a referral by a government doctor to avail free treatments in private facilities—thereby curbing misuse. The innovation by the AAP government created a unique win-win-win situation for the government, private hospitals and the patients. By partnering with the private sector, Delhi became the first Indian state to establish a model that assured free and quality treatment for every Delhi resident for any ailment, irrespective of the costs, within a guaranteed time period.

An interesting outcome of the scheme was that for the first time, accountability was indirectly imposed on government hospitals. Hospitals could previously shirk off their responsibility by citing low demand for surgeries or test. Now, the health minister and his team would review every month the number of free surgeries recommended and compare it with those conducted in-house by each government hospital. This in-built accountability mechanism pushed several government hospitals to optimally utilize their in-house capacity. For example, Baba Saheb Ambedkar Hospital, a 500-bedded hospital under the Delhi government, performed over 95,000 surgeries in 2022–23 as compared to 57,500 surgeries in 2014–15. Similarly, the 640-bedded Deen Dayal Upadhyay Hospital, which carried out 48,000 surgeries in 2014–15, performed nearly 73,000 surgeries in 2022–23 with the same resources.[40]

Thus, the AAP government was able to change the story of government hospitals in Delhi: it turned the enduring crisis of capacity in government hospitals into an opportunity to introduce a radical initiative that was unprecedented across India.

Universalizing Emergency Medical Care

Countless lives are lost every day in India because road accident victims fail to get the necessary help within one hour of the accident, in what trauma experts call the 'golden hour'. Such is the scale of the crisis that India, with just 1 per cent of the world's vehicles, accounts for 11 per cent of road accident fatalities in the world.[41] Over 1,68,000 deaths were reported in 2022—the highest in the world—and this number is only rising every year.[42] Apart from human errors and faulty road engineering, the absence of a prompt emergency medical care system is a big driver of these stark numbers.

In 2016, the Supreme Court delivered a national milestone in providing timely emergency medical care to road accident victims through the Good Samaritan Law that provided legal protection to bystanders assisting road accident victims in getting medical help. The mandate, tirelessly advocated by a leading non-profit organization, SaveLIFE Foundation, remedied a social reluctance among people to offer help for the fear of being embroiled in legal hassles. Yet, this was only half the problem solved. What also deterred bystanders was private hospitals' refusal to admit accident victims without a surety of payment. Hospitals were mandated under the Supreme Court directions and Section 357C of the erstwhile Code of Criminal Procedure to provide free treatment to any road accident victim—a legal responsibility they dodged for the fear of incurring losses. This imposed a moral dilemma: many were willing to help, but didn't want to shoulder the medical cost or risk the victim's life by traveling to a public hospital further away to seek free treatment.

The AAP government addressed the conundrum at the heart of this exploding crisis in February 2018. It introduced financial (a cash reward of ₹2,000) and non-financial incentives to motivate good samaritans, a pilot project later christened as the 'Farishte Dilli Ke' scheme. This gesture also signalled to the people of Delhi that the government was going to stand with them, as they support those in need.

Significantly, the AAP government also decided to bear the entire medical expenditure in any private or public hospital for any road accident victim, irrespective of whether the person was a Delhi resident or not. This provision was extended to include victims with acid attack and thermal burn injuries. To ensure immediate care and safe recovery, accident victims could opt to be admitted in a private hospital within seventy-two hours of the incident. This would allow victims, first admitted to a smaller private or government hospital, to get stabilized and later opt for a more advanced medical treatment should they need it.

Private hospitals were compensated based on CGHS rates, akin to the free surgeries initiative, but participation in the Farishte scheme wasn't optional. Missives were issued to each private hospital informing them of the government's decision and warning them of the regulatory baton that the AAP government would wield in case a hospital was found to have declined treatment. The scheme was widely advertised: all private hospitals were directed to prominently install boards publicising the scheme along with the helpline number (1031) for people to get in touch with to register concerns and complaints.

With this, the Farishte scheme removed the biggest bottleneck, and the subsequent hurdles, that prevented accident victims from getting life-saving care within the golden hour. When launching the Farishte scheme, Mr Kejriwal explained the motivation behind the initiative:

'We value the life of every Delhi resident. If the government is in a position to save the life of even a single Delhi resident, we are willing to bear whatever the costs be. For the first time, a person in Delhi has the confidence that if they become victim of a road accident, the Delhi government will stand with them.'

Measured in numbers, the Farishte scheme has benefitted more than 28,500 road accident victims as of March 2024. The number of victims availing free treatment has steadily risen from 1,540 in 2018–19 to 7,314 in 2023–24, echoing the initiative's resounding success.

Another important aspect of making timely emergency care available within the golden hour is a responsive city ambulance system. Until 2015, Delhi's round-the-clock free ambulance system was severely stretched and underfunded with a fleet of 150 ambulances to service a city of 2,00,00,000 people. The fleet was managed by an autonomous body under the Delhi government called Centralised Accident and Trauma Services (CATS) and had a response time (call to patient pick-up) of around fifty-five minutes. It is no wonder that during May 2020, when the first Covid-19 wave put pressure on the overstretched ambulance system, the response times sky-rocketed, peaking as high as 14 hours. At a time of crisis, Delhi government's think-tank DDC brought on board SaveLIFE Foundation to overhaul and modernize Delhi's ambulance system.

Within a short span of time, gaps in the system were identified and a three-pronged strategy put into implementation. First, a technological interface was developed that used real-time data and predictive algorithms for optimal deployment of ambulances; patient call volumes and traffic conditions were factored in instead of fixed district-wise allocations based on population. Second, a performance monitoring system was put in place to rigorously monitor over 68,000 data points every day covering the call patterns and response times of each ambulance. Third, private ambulances hired contractually were formally added to the system to meet the high patient demand, and their deployment was integrated through a common full-time control room.[43] Mr Kejriwal oversaw these improvements and monitored the average response times every day.

This new, integrated and optimized emergency medical response system was created to adapt to the changing needs of Delhi. Within three months of the first Covid-19 wave, the capacity of Delhi's ambulance system tripled to nearly 600 and the response times were reduced to eighteen minutes.[44] Requests for ambulances have increased—from 734 per day in 2019–20 to 1,843 in 2023–24—reflecting the increasing confidence of the people of Delhi in the city ambulance system. As of March 2024, even as the ambulance fleet shrunk to 380 after the removal of private ambulances, the average response time remained well under twenty minutes.[45]

The AAP government's provision of free medical treatment to road accident victims and the overhaul of Delhi's city ambulance system has further strengthened the health guarantee model that became a defining aspect of the Delhi Model.

Moving Away from Health Insurance to Health Guarantee Model Nationally

The Covid-19 pandemic brought to light the crippling realities of India's public health system. Arguably, several countries struggled to cope with the health and economic consequences of the new pandemic, but India earned a distinct disrepute. Apart from an overrun hospital and diagnostic capacity, even the crematoriums flooded with bodies at the peak of the second wave in 2021. The haunting imagery of the River Ganga swollen with bodies will remain etched in public memory as a symbol of how the country's health systems failed the people exactly when they needed it the most. This reality was a stark reflection of the abject neglect that India's public health systems have been subject to for decades.

Indian policymakers have long extolled the virtues of a robust and well-funded system. The National Rural Health Mission (later renamed the National Health Mission) was launched in the early 2000s to provide equitable, affordable and quality healthcare to the poor. This was supplemented with a slew of health insurance schemes by state and central governments, such as the Rashtriya Swasthya Bima Yojna, to support vulnerable populations. While each initiative was an improvement to the ailing health system, India was nowhere close to providing Universal Health Coverage (UHC). The WHO defines UHC as a system that ensures *all people* have access to the full range of quality health services they need, when and where they need them, without financial hardship.[46]

In 2011, a High-Level Expert Group on UHC under the Planning Commission recommended governments to move beyond 'health insurance' by providing 'health assurance' through the continuum of healthcare services—primary, secondary and tertiary—to all citizens.[47] The expert group, chaired by leading expert and Padma Bhushan awardee Dr K. Srinath Reddy, reaffirmed the central role the public sector ought to play in providing UHC in India. The private sector could offer contractual services where necessary, but direct provision of services by the public sector was imperative. The committee emphasized the importance of a robust primary healthcare, suggesting 70 per cent of all health expenditures be dedicated towards it. The National Health Policy 2017 paid heed and committed to achieving UHC in India through a range of measures, including increasing the public health spending to 2.5 per cent of GDP by 2025.[48]

Regrettably, most of these recommendations continue to remain only on paper.

Over the past three decades, even as the Indian economy has boomed and government budgets expanded, governments irrespective of political allegiance have failed to make adequate investments in India's public health system. Globally, India ranked 179 among 189 countries in terms of its public health spending, per the Economic Survey of India 2021. The Central government's health spending has steadily declined from 2.6 per cent in 2017–18 to 2.3 per cent in 2021–22 and slipped to 1.9 per cent in 2022–23—making India one of the few countries globally to slash healthcare budgets after the ravaging Covid-19 pandemic.[49] At the state level, health spending has averaged a meagre 4 to 6 per cent of annual budgets over the past decade.[50]

The total public health spending in India was only 1.3 per cent of GDP in 2023–24—about half of the 2.5 per cent target set by the National Health Policy 2017, and a fraction of the 5 per cent target set by WHO. All other BRICS nations currently outspend India on public health; South Africa allocates 5.3 per cent of its GDP to health, Brazil 4.6 per cent and China 3.1 per cent. Dr Reddy aptly remarked that India is yet to learn the most revealing lesson from Covid-19 pandemic: 'that a sub-optimally resourced and underperforming health system is a banana peel on which the national economy can keep slipping'.[51]

A state of chronic underfunding has contributed to catastrophic health expenditures. Contrasted with the global average of 18 per cent, Indian citizens were forced to bear nearly 50 per cent of expenses out of their pockets, with

Uttar Pradesh recording the highest share at 71 per cent, as per National Health Accounts 2019–20.[52] It is estimated that extortionate health costs push over 10 crore Indians into poverty every year.[53] Overall, India ranks 161 among 188 countries in terms of out-of-pocket expenditure on health.[54]

In the midst of these concerning trends, Prime Minister Narendra Modi in 2018 launched his most ambitious initiative for the health sector—the Ayushman Bharat scheme. Touted as a game changer, the scheme did little to alleviate this stress. It had two main components covering insurance and infrastructure. One, the Pradhan Mantri Jan Arogya Yojna (PM-JAY) targeted the bottom 40 per cent of the Indian population, offering a ₹5 lakh hospitalization cover across several public and private hospitals all over India. Under the second component, 1.5 lakh Health and Wellness Centres (HWCs) were to be established by upgrading existing sub-health centers and primary health centres (PHCs) to offer comprehensive primary care. Echoing the story of initiatives past and present, the outcome of the Ayushman Bharat scheme is a far cry from the goal of achieving UHC for it overlooks the healthcare needs of 60 per cent of Indians. Even for the poor, the scheme fails to cover hospitalization costs exceeding ₹5 lakhs, or outpatient care, including tests and medicines that constitute the largest portion of out-of-pocket health expenditure.

This is not to say that establishing UHC in India is impossible. The AAP government's health guarantee model in Delhi, established over the last decade, comes closest to the idea of universal healthcare in the Indian context.

India is large and diverse, but Delhi's tryst with universal healthcare holds material lessons for the entire country. The first and the most glaring is the urgent need to increase India's public health spending. Decades of being the country that spends the least on public health globally has taken a toll on India's public health infrastructure. As of March 2022, there was a shortfall of 25 per cent sub-centres, 31 per cent primary health centres and 36 per cent community health centres in rural India, whereas the shortfall in urban PHCs was

40 per cent, per government data.[55] The Delhi government's health spending stands in stark contrast, beating national and state trends over the past decade, and even surpassing the Central government's budget for flagship health schemes. The entire spending under the Ayushman Bharat scheme, pan India, was ₹6,800 crore during 2023–24; the Delhi government allocated nearly ₹9,000 crore to its health sector in this period. It's clear that unless governments start putting money where their mouths are, progress will be slow and sore.

Second, any work towards universal coverage has to start by building a free and reliable primary healthcare system. Government data reveals that 48 per cent of all spending on healthcare in India happens at the primary level, while only 13.5 per cent happens at the tertiary level, which the current insurance-led approach seeks to tackle.[56] An effective primary health system, which covers preventive care services, can go a long way in reducing the overall disease burden, improving the health of the nation and nurturing people's larger well-being.

Unfortunately, the Ayushman Bharat scheme's attempts to improve India's primary health system has proven to be largely cosmetic: it rebranded existing sub-centers and PHCs as health and wellness centers without fundamentally addressing underlying issues, such as high staff absenteeism and unavailability of tests and medicines. Of the 1,60,000 HWCs opened by early 2024, 85 per cent were sub-centers that run without an MBBS doctor. They were attended instead by a community health officer, who lacked training to provide all primary health services. An RTI response from the Ministry of Health revealed that only 26 per cent of the HWCs have a nurse. Ground reports further exposed the presence of ghost centres that existed only on paper.[57] Delhi's mohalla clinics, in contrast, demonstrated the possibility of providing free and quality primary healthcare to all citizens—a feat that has evaded India for seven decades. Take the shortage of trained staff, an issue that continues to plague the Ayushman Bharat scheme and hinders scaling up of quality primary care across India. Delhi's (and later Punjab's) mohalla clinics experimented with leveraging trained staff from the private sector and offering performance-based incentives to encourage them to work in the remotest corners of the country. In the long-term, India must work towards increasing the capacity of medical colleges to produce skilled personnel across levels, but AAP's alternative presents an interim solution that can work swiftly, successfully and at scale.

The third principle of an effective UHC model is to meet the outpatient treatment needs of citizens, a missing element across almost all national initiatives. An independent study shows that the reason why 69 per cent of patients are impoverished in India due to health emergencies were due to out-of-pocket expenditure on medicines alone.[58] Research shows even patients hospitalized under the PM-JAY end up paying substantial outpatient costs.[59] Here again, Delhi's health model that offers free consultations, tests and medicines for all outpatient needs, while relying on the private sector to provide free high-end diagnostic tests, provides a replicable model for the rest of the country.

Fourth, the public health sector will have to play a central role in delivering UHC. Even in 2024, the state of India's public health infrastructure continues to stay dismal. A government survey in June 2024 showed nearly 80 per cent of India's public health facilities failed to meet minimum standards for infrastructure, manpower and equipment.[60] The private sector has emerged as a dominant force in India not by design but due to the failure of the public sector in providing reliable and cost-effective health services. Further, driven by profit, much of the private health sector is concentrated in urban areas with far-flung rural areas left at the mercy of public health facilities. A health insurance card under PM-JAY means little if there is no nearby hospital to go to at times of emergency.

The Covid-19 pandemic showed the perils of over-reliance on the private sector. An analysis based on RTI data by Scroll. in shows that between March 2020 and December 2021, less than 12 per cent of patients hospitalized during the pandemic were treated for free under PM-JAY.[61] Multiple ground reports reveal that when the demand outstripped supply for hospital beds, most private hospitals turned their back on free PM-JAY beneficiaries, preferring patients making direct payments at higher rates.[62] Unhappy with the low schedule of rates and payment delays running into six months (as against the promised 15 days), a large number of private hospitals have started exiting PM-JAY. As on March 2024, of the 12,631 private hospitals empanelled under PM-JAY, 3,543 hospitals had not admitted any patient under the scheme in the last six months and another 6,551 hospitals had been inactive since their empanelment—leaving only 20 per cent private hospitals participating in the PM-JAY.[63]

In contrast, the AAP government's approach in Delhi differed radically. It has sought to expand the public health system's capacity at all levels, including tripling the capacity of hospital beds, while strategically leveraging the private sector to provide timely tertiary care and make up for the public sector's deficiencies. Further, the Delhi health model has partnered to scale private sector innovations that can offer higher quality of care at lower costs, for example by outsourcing all tests conducted in mohalla clinics and polyclinics.

Fifth, and most critically, is a vision to achieve UHC that is inclusive of all Indian citizens. It is unfortunate that while UHC was the driving goal for the National Health Policy 2017, Centre's most ambitious scheme for the health sector launched in 2018 covers only 40 per cent of the population and that too for their hospitalization needs, which accounts for only 13.5 per cent of an average citizen's out-of-pocket health expenditure. This 40 per cent isn't even spread evenly across all Indian states. For urban areas, all those with a two-wheeler or an income above ₹20,000 per month are automatically excluded. For Delhi, where the AAP government has raised the minimum wage to the highest in the country at ₹17,494 per month, only a small fraction of residents would qualify.

This exclusion of India's middle classes from most public health sector initiatives is not without damage: it ensures solutions and systems will be designed for under-resourced groups and will continue to remain sub-standard in quality and experience. The participation of India's middle classes has the power of effectively shaping the public health system into a functional, efficient one. Delhi's health model is aware of this force and has designed its initiatives to cater to all citizens of Delhi from the very beginning. The air-conditioned mohalla clinics catering to two crore outpatient visits every year are a shining example of the quality that public health facilities can deliver, if solutions are designed for all, not just one section of the society. To do so at a pan India level will mean substantial investments over years, but a beginning must be made now. An interim solution could be devised by providing differential subsidies based on income levels so that even the middle and upper classes get the benefit of a quality public health system and don't have to rely entirely on private care.

India's excruciatingly slow progress at achieving UHC over the past few decades shows that an insurance-led approach is going to take us nowhere. Instead, Delhi's health guarantee model that prioritizes public health spending, free outpatient care, leveraging private sector and catering to all citizens provides the most definite template for achieving UHC in India.

Chapter 4

Air Pollution

Cutting Through the Smog

To those experiencing Delhi's winter pollution at its peak for the first time, the scene is straight out of an apocalyptic film. As soon as November approaches, a thick blanket of smog descends upon Delhi and its surroundings, leading to a national outcry. It was only a matter of time when, in December 2015, the Delhi High Court said: 'It seems like we are living in a gas chamber.'

If there is one issue in Delhi that has consistently attracted global attention, or rather notoriety, for the past decade, it is air pollution. Every winter brings its share of media furore and stern orders from courts demanding action. By now, there should have been greater clarity on what causes Delhi's toxic winter air pollution, and the measures needed to fix it. But the state of our politics, supported by a media that values slanging matches over intelligent debates, has ensured that at the end of every winter, citizens are left with more questions than answers, more noise than light.

'Wicked problems' have been defined by planners as problems with many interdependent factors making them seemingly impossible to solve. Because the factors are often in flux, and difficult to define, solving wicked problems requires a deep understanding of the stakeholders involved, and an innovative approach.[1] In Delhi's context, the problem of air pollution, more than any other, would qualify to be called a wicked problem.

The easiest way to begin cutting through the smog hovering over discussions of Delhi's air pollution is by understanding the science behind it. Back in 2014, much of north India had a rudimentary set-up to monitor air pollution with only six manual monitors in Delhi measuring PM2.5 levels and none in the rest of the NCR.[2] Fortunately, a lot has changed since. The term Air Quality Index (AQI) was defined by the Union environment ministry in October 2014.[3] A series of subsequent investments by governments in advanced air pollution monitoring systems as well as excellent work done by several academic and research institutes over the last decade have done much to further our understanding.

Let us therefore base the discussion on Delhi's air pollution problem in a few irrefutable facts borne out by data and science. First is the role that adverse meteorological factors play in causing Delhi's excessive winter pollution, in particular the phenomenon of thermal inversion. Delhi's pollution in summers is far less due to constant dispersion and movement of air horizontally, due to high wind speeds, as well as vertically. The latter happens due to air's natural circulation pattern—air close to the ground heats up during the day and moves up, to be replaced by colder air that sinks from above.

In winters, the natural flow of hot and cold air gets reversed as the ground cools down more rapidly than the sky, causing the air near it to become cold and dense. This season coincides with people lighting bonfires to stay warm and farmers lighting farm fires to clear crop stubble, releasing a lot of smoke. The next day, when the sun is out, the thick haze blocks the sunlight from penetrating the air and warming the ground. As a result, the layer above the haze, where the sky is clearer, becomes warm and sits atop the cold air underneath—a thermal inversion—acting as an invisible lid over the pollutants. In addition, the sudden drop in wind speed in Delhi's winters limits horizontal mixing and dispersion of pollutants—a double whammy.

Second, we need to stop thinking of this phenomenon as Delhi's air pollution problem and call it for what it is— north India's air pollution problem. A total of forty-two Indian cities featured on the list of world's fifty most polluted cities in 2023, prepared by the international agency IQAir, based on the annual average level of the pollutant PM2.5 in air.[4] Eighteen of these forty-two cities are located in the Delhi National Capital Region (Delhi- NCR)—the larger metropolitan region of 55,000 sq km surrounding Delhi and comprising twenty-four districts from the states of Haryana, Uttar Pradesh and Rajasthan in addition to the eleven districts of Delhi. It is noteworthy that the national capital itself occupies only 1,480 sq km or 2.7 per cent of the landmass of Delhi-NCR.

Third, several studies have now shown that only a third of Delhi's air pollution is contributed by local sources, with the remainder coming from sources outside Delhi. The first scientific study to estimate the contribution of local and external sources in Delhi's air pollution was carried out in 2016–17 by The Energy and Resources Institute (TERI) and the Automotive Research Association of India (ARAI), and funded by the Central government.[5] The TERI-ARAI study physically gathered air-quality samples from twenty identified locations in Delhi-NCR over three months of summer and winter each to determine the contribution of different polluting sources in Delhi's air. The study concluded that local sources contributed to only 36 per cent of Delhi's winter PM2.5 pollution, sources from Delhi-NCR region contributed 34 per cent with the rest coming from outside NCR (Figure 8).

One big limitation of this study, however, is that it dissects Delhi's pollution at a fixed point in time i.e. 2016–17. A lot can change in Delhi-NCR within a few years. To address this, the Indian Institute of Tropical Meteorology (IITM), Pune, a Government of India funded body, launched a decision support system (DSS) in the winter of 2021. The DSS does not do any real-time physical sampling of air quality. Instead, it relies on the static data of emissions from different NCR districts captured by the TERI-ARAI study and combines it with real-time data of PM2.5 levels, wind and other meteorological data from forty-three air quality monitoring stations, to predict the real-time contribution of various sources to Delhi's pollution. 'The DSS can tell us how much of the pollution is coming from Delhi and how much from nearby districts,' said Gaurav Govardhan, scientist, IITM, speaking to the *Indian Express*.[6] The result was similar to the trend seen in the TERI-ARAI study.

Figure 8: Local and external contributions to winter PM2.5 pollution in Delhi (in %)

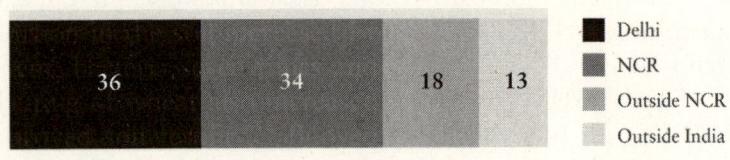

Source: TERI-ARAI study on source apportionment of PM2.5 and PM10 in Delhi NCR, 2018[5]

On 4 November 2022, when Delhi's AQI hit a peak 450, the DSS revealed that local pollution sources contributed between 20–30 per cent of the total PM2.5 volume, while 70 per cent of the pollution came from NCR cities and beyond.[7] A similar peak pollution episode was repeated on 2 November 2023, when the PM2.5 levels crossed 300 micrograms per cubic metre ($\mu g/m^3$), twenty times above the WHO safe limit of 15 $\mu g/m^3$ a day.[8] Once again, the DSS revealed that local sources contributed to only 25 per cent of Delhi's pollution.[9]

The TERI-ARAI study also estimates the contribution of different sources to Delhi's PM2.5 pollution—in summer and in winter (Figure 9).[10] These estimates include the combined share of sources located inside and outside Delhi. For example, there is hardly any polluting industry inside Delhi, but industrialization is rampant in the belts of Jhajjar, Sonipat and Panipat in Haryana, which ends up contributing as much as 30 per cent to Delhi's PM2.5 pollution in winter.

Put together, these facts point to an important, even if an inconvenient, truth—Delhi's air pollution problem cannot be solved only by obsessing about the local sources of pollution situated within Delhi's boundaries. Even if these local sources were reduced to an impossible zero i.e. if the national capital was locked down, PM2.5 levels will still be about 70 per cent of its levels otherwise. Clearly, polluted air sees no boundaries. What this points towards is the need for a regional approach and a coordinated action plan among all stakeholders and governments of Delhi-NCR, if not north India.

Figure 9: Summer and winter contributions of different sources to Delhi's PM2.5 pollution (in %)

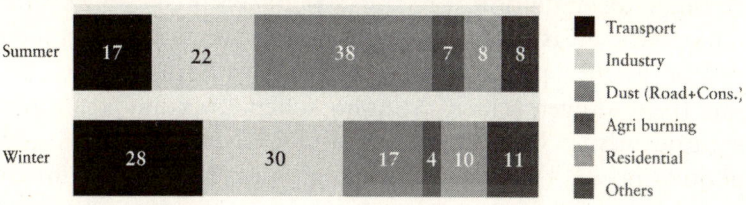

Source: TERI-ARAI study on source apportionment of PM2.5 and PM10 in Delhi NCR, 2018[10]

Bending the Pollution Curve

Given that Delhi's local sources contribute to only about a third of Delhi's air pollution, it would have been easy for the AAP government to do little but express outrage at surrounding states for causing Delhi's pollution. Yet, driven by the health impact of air pollution on citizens, and the desire to set a benchmark for Indian states battling pollution, the AAP government initiated an ambitious set of reforms. In Chief Minister Kejriwal's words, AAP took a bet which no other political party in India was or still is willing to take: 'good green policies can make for good politics'.[11]

The AAP government embraced a two-pronged strategy to fight air pollution. First, it strictly enforced short-term emergency measures during the winters, such as the graded response action plan (GRAP) mandated by the Supreme Court and the odd-even vehicle rationing scheme. Second, and more significantly, it launched a series of long-term reforms and actions on all the major polluting sources within Delhi to reduce round-the-year pollution levels.

A framework for Delhi government's long-term action plan on air pollution was defined and presented first in March 2018 as part of the budget speech given by the then finance minister and deputy chief minister of Delhi, Manish Sisodia. Coined as 'green budget', Delhi's long-term plan to fight air pollution listed twenty-six initiatives aimed at reducing pollution and carbon emissions from sources within Delhi. Working with experts, the AAP government estimated that these twenty-six initiatives would lead to an annual reduction in 503 tonnes of PM2.5, 4,540 tonnes of Nitrogen Oxides (NOX), 9,364 tonnes of Sulphur Oxides (SOX) and 2.1 million tonnes of Carbon Dioxide (CO_2).[12] Thanks to persistent action on these long-term measures, today Delhi stands out among all Indian states for taking the most aggressive action on air pollution. Sample the milestones achieved in the past nine years.

First, the AAP government is the only one in India to shut all thermal power plants within state boundaries. Second, it drastically increased wind and solar power installations in Delhi's energy mix from virtually nil to over 2,000 MW, bringing the total share of renewable energy to 34 per cent—the highest in Delhi's history.[13] Third, from a baseline of four to five hour power cuts in the summer of 2014, the AAP government ensured 24/7 power supply drastically, reducing reliance on polluting diesel generator (DG) sets. Fourth, all the 1,627 industrial units in Delhi have transitioned from polluting fuels such as coal, diesel etc., to clean fuel—piped natural gas (PNG). Fifth, the AAP government managed to increase Delhi's green cover by 44 sq km despite the pressures of a growing economy and the challenge of shrinking space for planting trees. Sixth, the AAP government implemented an ambitious EV policy that has seen Delhi emerge as the EV capital of India with a 12 per cent registration rate among new vehicles—the highest in India. Seventh, it modernized and increased the fleet of Delhi's public bus system to a highest ever 7,683 buses, 25 per cent of which were electric buses—again the highest in India.

The net result of these actions is an unprecedented decline in Delhi's air pollution levels over the past decade, quite contrary to the gloomy picture usually painted about Delhi. The three-year average trend for PM2.5 levels in Delhi dropped from 189 µg/m3 in 2012–14 to 104 µg/m3 in 2021–23—a staggering decline by 45 per cent—per a Centre for Science and Environment study based on Central Pollution Control Board's (CPCB) real-time air quality data in the five oldest monitoring stations in Delhi (Figure 10).[14] CPCB's data for annual average PM10 and PM2.5 levels reveals a similar downward trend with a 36 per cent and 32 per cent decline respectively between 2014 and 2023 (Figure 11).[15]

Correspondingly, the number of 'good', 'satisfactory', and 'moderate' air quality days (i.e. AQI under 200) in Delhi increased from 108 in 2016 to 206 in 2023—a rise by 91 per cent.[16] At the other end, while the number of 'severe plus' air quality days (i.e. AQI above 500) in 2023 was similar to 2019, 2020 and 2021, the peak PM2.5 concentration has reduced substantially from 546 µg/m^3 in 2019 to an all-time low of 349 µg/m^3 in 2023.[17]

Figure 10: Three-year trend in 5 oldest real-time air quality
monitoring stations in Delhi show a 45 per cent decline in
PM2.5 levels from 2012–14 to 2021–23 (in µg/m³)

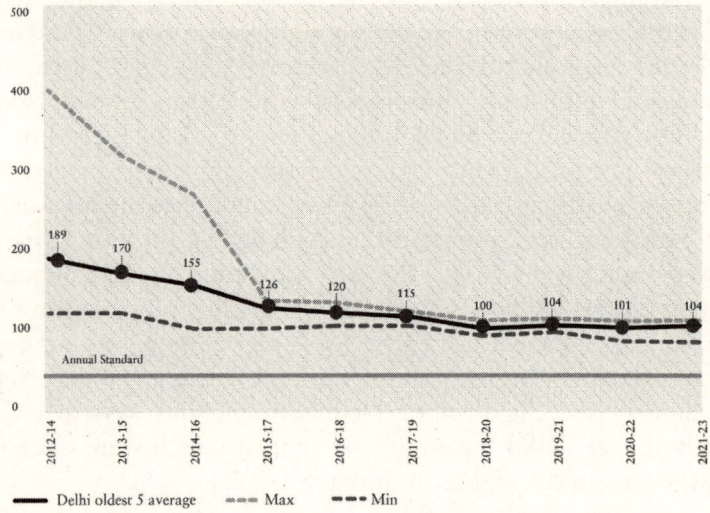

Source: CSE analysis based on Central Pollution Control Board
(CPCB) data[14]

Figure 11: Annual average PM2.5 and PM10 levels in
Delhi from 2014 to 2023 (in µg/m³)

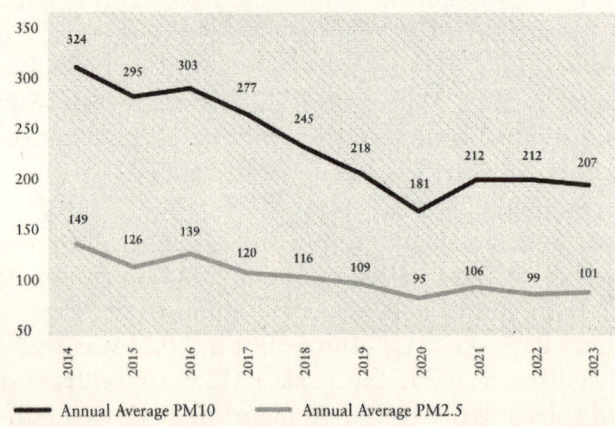

Source: CPCB and Delhi Pollution Control Committee (DPCC) data

Delhi's progress throws up another interesting fact—the period between January to October is progressively getting better year-on-year with 2023 recording the least polluted ten months in six years, barring the Covid-19 year of 2020. The period during January–October in 2023 recorded a daily average PM2.5 concentration of 75 µg/m^3 as against a range of 81–95 µg/m^3 during the corresponding periods from 2017 to 2022.[18]

So, what made this progress possible in Delhi? And why is similar progress not being replicated at the regional level?

Reducing Vehicular Pollution

The multitude of sources behind Delhi's air pollution makes it difficult to pick any one as a silver bullet. But a good place to start would be vehicular emissions. Studies have consistently shown that vehicular emissions are among the most significant local sources of pollution in Delhi, contributing to a third of all PM2.5 emissions and over 80 per cent of Carbon Monoxide (CO) and Nitrous Oxide (NOx) emissions.[19]

Delhi's tryst with reducing vehicular pollution began at the turn of the century when the Supreme Court ordered a shift of all commercial vehicles including buses, auto rickshaws and taxis from diesel to CNG fuel. By early 2005, over 10,500 CNG private and public buses were plying in Delhi making it the largest CNG fleet in the world.

Next was the adoption of progressively stringent fuel standards beginning with BS-IV grade fuel in April 2010 followed by BS-VI grade fuel in April 2018, both a result of Supreme Court direction. The gains from adopting the latter were particularly huge: 70 to 90 per cent less particulate matter, sulphur and nitrogen oxide, per kilometre. In both these cases, Delhi was the first city in the country to shift to these standards, two years ahead of the rest of the country. Another significant court mandated move came in April 2015 when the National Green Tribunal (NGT), seeking a check on grossly polluting older vehicles, imposed a ban on all diesel vehicles older than ten years and petrol vehicles older than fifteen years from plying anywhere in the NCR. In October 2015, the NGT and the Supreme Court both approved the levy of a green cess, also called environment compensation charge, on all commercial vehicles entering Delhi with the objective of discouraging vehicles not headed for Delhi from entering it, a move that was supported by the newly formed AAP government.[20]

But all these gains over the past two decades were nullified by the sheer increase in the number of motor vehicles in Delhi. The number of registered vehicles has increased four times: from 34 lakh in 2000 to 1.4 crore in 2023. It became clear that any further reduction in Delhi's vehicular emissions will require a mass shift to zero-emissions electric vehicles, apart from a greater adoption of public and non-motorized transport i.e. cycling and walking.

The first nine years of the AAP government have seen a significant expansion in the public transport infrastructure of Delhi, which includes both Delhi's public bus system and the Delhi metro. Unlike the Delhi metro, the public bus fleet inherited by the AAP government in 2015, was obsolete, polluting and unsafe. What transpired thereafter is a story of the remarkable transformation and modernization of Delhi's public bus system. The most significant element is the transition of Delhi's CNG-powered buses to one of the largest electric bus (e-bus) fleets in the world.

In overall numbers, Delhi's public bus fleet under the AAP government has transitioned from an ageing all-CNG fleet of 6,118 buses in March 2015, to a largely new, modern fleet of 7,683 buses by mid-2024. Of the new fleet, 25 per cent (1,970) were zero emissions e-buses. Accounting for 2,637 retiring buses that were scrapped between 2015–24, around 4,200 buses were inducted by the AAP government in this period i.e. 70 per cent of the capacity in 2015. As a result, Delhi today has the largest fleet of public buses as well as e-buses across India. With orders to manufacturers already placed, Delhi's e-bus fleet will witness a massive 4X expansion to 8,280 buses by end 2025, taking Delhi's total bus fleet size to around 10,500. This will catapult Delhi to become the city with the largest e-bus fleet in the world outside China, significantly cutting down on air pollution and carbon emissions. A fleet of 8,280 e-buses will eliminate 4.7 lakh tonnes of CO_2 emissions annually, and 56 lakh tonnes of CO_2 emissions in their lifetime of twelve years.

The transformation of Delhi's public buses has also resulted in one of the most advanced and modern bus fleets in India equipped with air-conditioning, CCTV cameras, panic buttons and disabled-friendly features. In a bid to keep bus travel affordable for the masses, the AAP government ensured there was no hike in fares in its two terms besides making bus rides completely free for women 2019 onwards—the first Indian state to do so. Consequently, the ridership of Delhi's buses has bucked the declining trend of bus ridership across major Indian cities, maintaining the average daily ridership at 42 lakhs between 2016–17 and 2023–24. Several initiatives underway aimed at improving the accessibility and convenience of Delhi's public bus network promise to further increase ridership in coming years (details in chapter 5).

The other critical pillar of Delhi's public transport system, the Delhi metro—a 50:50 joint venture between the Centre and the Delhi government—has been widely perceived as a world-class venture ever since it began operations in 1998. Building upon its strong legacy, the AAP government doubled the rate of expansion of the Delhi metro, adding 200 km of metro lines in nine years i.e. 22.2 km per year as compared to 193 km added between 1998 and 2015 i.e. 11.4 km per year. The number of metro stations have also doubled from 143 to 288 during AAP's tenure. As a result, the daily ridership of Delhi metro has risen substantially from 24 lakh in 2014 to 60 lakh in 2024.[21] In 2020–21, the AAP government approved Phase IV of the Delhi metro expansion that will cover six new corridors with an additional network length of 109 km and eighty-two stations within Delhi. The total cost of the Phase IV corridors is estimated at approximately ₹25,000 crore with the Centre's and the Delhi's share pegged at ₹5,900 crore each and the rest to be financed by debt. As of March 2024, the Central government had approved only the first two priority corridors.

Apart from contributing to the expansion of the Delhi metro, the Central government has offered little financial support to Delhi or other cities investing in clean public transport. The Centre's Faster Adoption and Manufacturing of Electric Vehicles (FAME) India scheme to promote electric vehicles, provided a small subsidy to only 7,000 e-buses nationally over five years (2019–24), only half of which were deployed by early 2024. In Delhi's case, the Centre's financial support was limited to only 1,320 of the targeted 8,200 e-buses—covering 10 per cent of their capital and operating costs, the rest borne by the Delhi government. A rare exception to the Centre's attitude towards Delhi's fight against pollution has been by way of constructing the eastern and western peripheral expressways. Standing at a length of 135 km each, the two six-lane expressways were inaugurated in 2018 to divert about 50,000 heavy diesel vehicles (approximately 30 per cent of commercial traffic) not destined for Delhi away from the heart of the city.

With the plan to overhaul Delhi's public transport system well under way by the end of its first term, the next big challenge for the AAP government was to tackle the pollution from Delhi's burgeoning fleet of over 1 crore private and commercial vehicles by transitioning them to zero-emission electric vehicles (EVs).

In 2019–20, EVs accounted for only 3.9 per cent of new vehicle registrations in Delhi, of which e-rickshaws accounted for 94 per cent. The share of other electric vehicles, particularly two-wheelers or cars that accounted for 92 per cent of all new vehicles registered, was negligible. In August 2020, the AAP government rolled out what was perhaps the most ambitious EV policy by any Indian state/UT. Framed with the singular goal of reducing air pollution in the national capital, the Delhi EV Policy 2020 became the first policy nationally to declare an upfront target of ensuring 25 per cent of all newly registered vehicles to be electric by the end of 2024. The policy provided generous, yet targeted, subsidies for purchase of electric vehicles in the most polluting vehicle segments and laid out a comprehensive strategy for creation of public charging infrastructure.

Within three years of the policy's implementation, Delhi emerged as the undisputed EV capital of India. In 2023–24, the share of EVs among newly registered vehicles in Delhi reached 12 per cent—the highest for any Indian state and twice that of the national average of 6 per cent.[22] In total, over 1,35,000 electric vehicles were sold in Delhi in the first three years of the policy. The impact was most pronounced on commercial vehicles that have far more daily mileage than private vehicles. In 2023–24, EVs constituted over 70 per cent of all three-wheeler freight vehicles and 38 per cent of all taxis sold in Delhi. Delhi also managed to exponentially grow its charging infrastructure in this period with over 4,600 EV charging points and battery swapping stations set up by mid-2023. This wasn't just the highest for any Indian state but also constituted 30 per cent of all charging points in India. We will further unpack the Delhi EV Policy and the many innovations that made it a success in chapter 5.

The AAP government's efforts in reducing vehicular pollution by rapidly expanding and modernizing Delhi's public transport system and by successfully implementing the most progressive EV policy in India shows that there is hope beyond the usual gloom and doom scenarios that animate conversations on air pollution in Indian cities. Provided, of course, there is a political will to fight it.

Curbing Industrial Emissions

Delhi's air pollution first caught the attention of the Supreme Court in 1990s, leading to the first generation of reforms starting with the shifting of Delhi's commercial vehicles to CNG fuel. The Supreme Court then took yet another significant decision to tackle the other major pollutant in Delhi's air—industrial emissions. In 1996, after hearing a plea by environmentalist and lawyer M.C. Mehta on Delhi's polluting industries, the Supreme Court ordered the closure and relocation of over 1300 highly polluting industries from Delhi to the surrounding NCR areas in a phased manner. Little did it anticipate that this was at best a temporary fix to the problem.

The TERI-ARAI source apportionment study of Delhi's air pollution revealed that industrial emissions accounted for between 22–30 per cent of PM2.5 and PM10 pollution levels in Delhi all through the year.[23] This category, 'industrial emissions', includes emissions from industrial units, thermal power plants as well as diesel generators, both within Delhi and from adjoining areas. Let's take stock of emissions from industrial units first.

From the beginning, it was clear to the AAP government that the gains from shifting the most heavily polluting industries out of Delhi to adjoining areas had plateaued. A second generation of reforms targeting industrial air pollution would need to target not just these heavily polluting industries in NCR districts, but also the large number of relatively less polluting industries that had opened up in and around Delhi, using polluting fuels such as coal. Delhi had already banned the use of two cheap but highly polluting industrial fuels, furnace oil and petroleum coke (or pet coke), in 1996. In June 2018, the AAP government went a step further by banning the most popular industrial fuel in Delhi, coal. All industrial units and commercial establishments were granted a period of ninety days to switch over from their existing fuels to any of the clean, approved fuels.

To ensure an effective switchover, the government promoted the use of a clean fuel—piped natural gas (PNG)—in its fifty industrial clusters. This involved laying PNG pipelines in all of Delhi's industrial areas, as well as expenditure by each industrial unit to make provision to use a new fuel. To assist the industrial units in switching to the clean PNG fuel, the AAP government, as part of its 2018 green budget plan, announced an incentive of ₹1 lakh per industrial unit. Slowly but steadily, all fifty industrial clusters of Delhi were connected with PNG lines by January 2021. Soon after, Delhi earned the distinction of becoming the first Indian state with all its industrial units using clean PNG fuel.[24]

In contrast, the remaining NCR areas have severely lagged behind in mandating the use of clean industrial fuels. While Delhi banned the two most heavily polluting fuels—furnace oil and pet coke—back in 1996, the rest of the NCR states implemented this ban only when forced to do so by a Supreme Court order twenty-one years later in October 2017. Samples of furnace oil collected from industries in NCR had 350 times the sulphur content as diesel; and samples of pet coke had 1,400 times the sulphur content as diesel.[25] One can only imagine the harm this delayed action must have caused to the health of those living in the Delhi-NCR region.

Similarly, the remaining NCR areas lagged behind Delhi in banning the use of other polluting fuels such as coal. What Delhi did in June 2018, the remaining NCR states of Haryana, Uttar Pradesh and Rajasthan could have done immediately after. But they did not until January 2023, when the Commission for Air Quality Management in NCR and Adjoining Areas (CAQM), a bureaucratic body set up by the Central government in 2021 to coordinate clean air action plans of all NCR states, banned the use of coal and other polluting industrial fuels in NCR states.[26] The progress on the ground though is a different story. As of March 2023, of the total 7,760 fuel-based industries operating in the NCR, only 4,082 (just over 50 per cent) had opted for running their operations with PNG while the rest were running on biomass-based fuels or other fuels including coal.[27] Further, CAQM's ban on coal doesn't apply to thermal power plants—the other major source of industrial emissions in Delhi. Here again, Delhi has set a benchmark that is yet to be emulated by any other state.

When the AAP government took charge in early 2015, two state-owned thermal power plants were operating within Delhi, generating close to 1,000 MW power. Responding to the air pollution crisis, the AAP government shut down the Rajghat thermal power plant in May 2015, and the Badarpur thermal power plant in October 2018. These were not easy decisions, since the government had to source cheap, alternate power as well as invest in increasing its out-of-state transmission capacity. Yet it chose to do so, making Delhi the first state in India to shut down all its thermal power plants in a bid to curb pollution levels. Simultaneously, the AAP government has rapidly expanded Delhi's share of renewable energy to 34 per cent by mid-2024 by adding over 2,000 MW of wind and solar power. With several green projects in the pipeline, Delhi is expected to hit a 50 per cent share of renewable energy in its total installed capacity by 2027— among the highest in India (details in chapter 6).

The actions of the remaining NCR states, however, stand in stark contrast. There are eleven thermal power plants operating in the 300-km radius surrounding Delhi, most of them in brazen non-compliance of emission norms, accounting for 8 per cent of the PM2.5 pollution in Delhi-NCR, per a study conducted by CSE in 2017.[28] The study found that except one, all other plants reported SO_2 emissions up to three times more than that of the prescribed limits. Similarly, three out of eleven plants were found exceeding emissions norms for particulate matter, and four were exceeding nitrogen oxide (NOx) emission norms.

On multiple occasions, the Delhi government urged the Central government to take legal action and levy hefty fines on these thermal plants for non-compliance of emission norms.[29] But instead of doing so, time and again, the Centre has condoned their actions by granting continuous extension of deadlines to meet emission norms. The story of how these highly polluting thermal power plants surrounding Delhi evaded accountability deserves to be told in greater detail.

Back in December 2015, the Union environment ministry introduced strict emission norms for coal-based power plants across India—to be complied within two years. Non-compliant power plants were required to install pollution-controlling technologies. When the first deadline lapsed, a five-year extension was granted to all thermal power plants except the ones in Delhi-NCR. Because of high levels of pollution in the region, the plants in NCR were tasked to comply by 2019. When the 2019 deadline elapsed, instead of taking action against the errant power plants, the Union environment ministry again extended the deadline to 2022. In September 2022, the ministry once again revised the timelines for meeting emission norms to varying deadlines between 31 December 2024 and 31 December 2026 based on the proximity of the power plants to critically polluted areas. Such constant dilly-dallying shows that when the battle is between a citizen's right to breathe clean air versus polluting industries violating laws with impunity, the Centre has often sided with the latter.

Another significant component of industrial emissions in Delhi-NCR are DG sets, a common fix in industrial, commercial as well as residential areas due to the problem of chronic power cuts that plague almost the whole of India. Back in the summer of 2014, before the AAP government came to power, four to five-hour power cuts were normal even in the national capital.[30] Consequently, the use of DG sets in residential buildings and markets was rampant.

The first five years of the AAP government witnessed a massive investment in Delhi's power distribution infrastructure with the goal of making it robust and capable of providing 24/7 power supply even at the peak of summers (details in chapter 6). As a result, load-shedding in Delhi has reduced drastically from 117 million units (MU) in 2014–15 to 10 MU in 2022–23, a drop by 92 per cent. Today, the sight of inverters or DG sets in Delhi is rare and limited to emergency operations only, such as in hospitals. The India Residential Energy Survey 2020 conducted among twenty-two states corroborated Delhi's progress, rating it as the top performing state providing 24/7 power supply to its residents. The other NCR states—Uttar Pradesh, Haryana and Rajasthan—were rated as the worst, third-worst and seventh-worst states respectively.[31]

Findings from this survey confirm what is only too well known to anyone living in the high-rise societies of Gurugram, Faridabad or Noida, where not a single society operates without full DG back-up. If this wasn't shocking, an official report by Haryana's state-run power distribution company in October 2020 made a disturbing revelation that eighty-two housing societies in Gurugram and Faridabad, home to at least 2 lakh residents, are fully dependent on DG sets. This because the developers had not fulfilled certain norms for setting up permanent power connections.[32] Shouldn't then the respective government authorities be held accountable for even allowing such societies to come up?

The callous attitude of the UP, Haryana and Rajasthan governments is matched only by the unwillingness of the Central government or regulatory bodies like CAQM to impose any penalties on these governments for failure to supply 24/7 electricity. In what can only be called as a 'too little, too late' approach, the CAQM's action on this matter came as late as June 2023 when it passed an order to restrict harmful emissions from DG sets by mandating dual-fuel operation (natural gas and diesel) for all DG sets with capacity above 19KW in NCR areas starting October 2023.[33] In effect, while the CAQM (and by extension the Central government) gave a free pass to the NCR state governments for failing in their duty to provide 24/7 electricity to their residents, it passed on the cost to the consumers by mandating a retrofit of their existing DG sets at an average cost of ₹6 to ₹12 lakh each, without any government incentive. Expectedly, three months after the ban took effect, a survey revealed that over

85 per cent of the NCR residents were reluctant to incur the expenditure to meet the CAQM's mandate.[34]

To summarize, the AAP government in Delhi has taken tough and decisive actions to combat all three major sources of industrial emissions viz. pollution from industrial units, thermal power plants and DG sets. In contrast, the surrounding NCR states have moved reluctantly and belatedly on all fronts, lagging far behind the progress Delhi has made so far.

Greening Delhi

Delhi has been blessed with large green tracts for a long time. The Delhi ridge, often referred to as the 'lungs of Delhi', spans over 8,000 hectares, parts of which were declared as reserve forest as long back as 1915. Commendable work by previous governments ensured Delhi's green cover reached 20 per cent in 2013, higher than most Indian cities. As the AAP government took office in 2015, the challenge was twofold. With almost all the available public land already built upon or covered by plantations, where do you find the extra land to plant more trees and enhance green cover? Moreover, how do you keep the wheels of Delhi's economic engine running, keep all public and private construction projects going, while retaining the existing green cover?

Before we delve into this, it is important to understand the critical role of green cover in fighting air pollution. It is well known that trees act as carbon sinks and are a critical defence against increasing carbon emissions. Trees also help fight air pollution by permanently absorbing toxic pollutants like SO_2, NO_2 and CO. Further, trees act as a barrier—a kind of a giant air filter—for fine particulate matter such as PM2.5, trapping them temporarily through their stems and leaves, and transferring it to the ground during rains.

The AAP government made aggressive afforestation a priority from the very beginning. In the first term of the AAP government, a total of 1.1 crore trees and shrubs were planted—around 23 lakh every year.[35] The pace doubled over the subsequent four years with over 2 crore tree saplings planted i.e. an average of 50 lakh every year.[36] An independent audit by the Forest Research Institute, Dehradun showed that 75–80 per cent saplings planted in Delhi from 2016–2019 survived, attesting to the sincere efforts of the agencies involved. [37] But how did the AAP government find the land to plant these trees?

The traditional approach of meeting annual plantation targets by planting more saplings in existing green areas such as parks and forests had reached its limit in Delhi. To find a way out, Chief Minister Kejriwal and his environment minister for much of AAP's two terms in office, Gopal Rai, held consultations with multiple experts and government agencies. Eventually, the government pursued a three-pronged approach.

First, over twenty large departments of the Delhi government were roped in and told in clear terms—annual tree plantation drives are not just the onus of the environment and forests department, but every government department with a sizeable pool of land. The education department was encouraged to identify land parcels in schools and universities that could be aggressively greened; the transport department was asked to plant trees around all its bus depots and terminals; and most crucially, the public works department was asked to aggressively plant trees and shrubs beside its massive 1400-km-long road network. A system of setting annual department-wise plantation targets was created under the 'green action plan' and rigorously monitored.[38] Each year's plantation drive would typically kick-off with a two-week campaign—'Van Mahotsav'—with all ministers and the chief minister participating with fanfare. Detailed guidelines were drafted to ensure tree plantation in different kinds of land parcels, such as roadsides, was done in a sustainable manner.

Second, the AAP government determined that land measuring over 9,000 hectares in the Yamuna floodplains could be used to systematically increase Delhi's green cover, while also rehabilitating the degraded soil and recharging the groundwater. The only caveat was that the type of plantation had to be carefully chosen to suit the river ecology. This would also take care of the repeated pressure on the Delhi government to dilute its stringent, compensatory plantation norms under the Delhi Preservation of Trees Act, 1994 (DPTA 1994), which require ten saplings to be planted for every tree that is cut.

On two occasions, first in September 2020 and then in May 2022, the Delhi Development Authority (DDA), a Central government agency, wrote to the Delhi government requesting it to bring down the strict compensatory plantation norms in Delhi from ten saplings to two, citing lack of available land to plant more trees.[39] However, the AAP government resisted every such move and recommended the DDA utilize the vast expanse of the Yamuna floodplains for this purpose.[40] This episode also reflects the contrasting commitments of the BJP-ruled Centre and the AAP government to retain Delhi's green cover.

Third, the AAP government actively started promoting the development of 'city forests'—an innovative concept of turning unused land parcels from as small as four acres to over 100 acres, into dense, green spaces accessible to all residents. Where only four such city forests existed in Delhi before 2015, the initiative led to a total of seventeen city forests to be demarcated and developed in Delhi by 2023—the largest two being the Mitraon city forest in south-east Delhi and the Jaunapur city forest in south Delhi, both spanning nearly 100 acres each.[41] The transformation and ecological regeneration of several of these hidden jewels of Delhi is still underway. Once opened to the public, these city forests will provide much-needed recreational space to the residents, besides enhancing Delhi's green cover.

While these measures helped increase green cover, much more was required to preserve Delhi's existing green heritage. There was and still is considerable apathy among the people and government agencies alike, towards the removal of existing trees to create space for construction projects, Delhi's stringent compensatory plantation norms notwithstanding. From an ecological perspective, this was disastrous since it would take decades before ten new saplings would provide benefits similar to a fully-grown tree. An affidavit in the Delhi High Court laid bare the dark truth: between 2019 and 2021, over 1.3 lakh trees were felled in Delhi—an average of five trees every hour.[42]

To address this challenge, Mr Kejriwal announced the Tree Transplantation Policy—the first such policy by any Indian state—in December 2020.[43] Prepared by the DDC after wide-ranging consultations with experts and forest department officials, the policy mandated scientific transplantation of a minimum of 80 per cent of trees affected by a project, apart from carrying out compensatory afforestation. The policy further mandated that tree transplantation shall be carried out only by government-empanelled agencies with proven expertise and experience of carrying out scientific transplantation. The policy linked the payment to these agencies to the tree-survival rate at transplanted sites with a provision of social audit by local citizen groups.

This stringent first-of-its-find policy was an effort by the AAP government to facilitate development projects essential to move Delhi's economy forward, while at the same time raising the economic cost of carrying out ecologically ill-conceived projects. It hoped that this added cost will encourage developers to consider alternatives where minimum trees would be felled.[44] The results of the first two years have been promising: over 15,000 trees were transplanted in Delhi by March 2023 although with an average 60 per cent survival rate.[45] As the science of tree transplantation evolves, the survival rate should hopefully rise further.

As a net result of all these efforts, Delhi has managed to buck the trend seen in most Indian cities by increasing its green cover to 23 per cent in 2021 from 20 per cent in end 2013—an effective increase by 44 sq km or 4,400 hectares in six years.[46] Today, Delhi has the distinction of having the largest per capita forest cover of 9.6 square metres among all the megacities of the country, as per the Forest Survey of India (FSI) data. In comparison, the per capita forest cover in square metres is: Ahmedabad 1.2, Bengaluru 7.2, Chennai 2.1, Hyderabad 8.2, Kolkata 0.1 and Mumbai 5.4.[47]

In mid-2023, Delhi became a signatory to the United Nation's 'Race to Resilience' campaign to catalyse change in the global ambition for climate resilience, pledging to achieve a 25 per cent green cover within the next five years. Welcoming Delhi's commitment, HE Razan Al Mubarak, UN climate change high-level champion for COP28 said, 'Communities must build resilience to climate change, and Delhi's ambitions are exemplary. We can learn from the pragmatic, realistic and just solutions-oriented approach that Delhi is providing.'[48]

Delhi's efforts towards maintaining its existing green heritage while further adding to its green cover, stands in sharp contrast with those of surrounding NCR states, with Uttar Pradesh registering a green cover of 9.2 per cent and Haryana 6.8 per cent in the 2021 State of Forest report.[49] What is even more worrying is that Haryana's green cover reduced drastically by 139 square kilometres between 2019 and 2021, with the districts neighbouring Delhi—Gurugram and Faridabad—registering sharp declines. Amongst the most glaring factors responsible for this decline is that Haryana, unlike Delhi, doesn't have any law that puts restrictions on felling of trees or enforces stringent norms for compensatory plantation. Unfortunately, here again Delhi seems to be lone exception to the trend dominating much of north India.

The Role of Crop Stubble Burning

The sound and the fury of debates on air pollution during Delhi winters peaks every year with the rising intensity of farm fires from Punjab, Haryana and western Uttar Pradesh. As discussed earlier, local sources contribute to only a third of Delhi's winter air pollution, while almost 70 per cent comes from NCR cities and beyond. Of these external sources, pollution from farm fires in north Indian states is probably the most significant contributor for the two months starting late September, touching 50 per cent at its peak.[50]

To the uninitiated, the phenomenon of lakhs of farmers lighting fires on their fields at the beginning of every winter to get rid of the post-harvest paddy straw residue is a peculiar one. The problem arises primarily because of the short time-window between the harvest of paddy and the sowing of wheat. The combine harvesters, the most prevalent agricultural machinery in these parts, cut the paddy stalk a foot above the ground—necessitating either burning or removal by other methods that poor farmers can ill afford. This phenomenon can be traced to fifteen years ago in 2009, when both Punjab and Haryana governments passed acts to conserve their groundwater. These acts delayed the sowing of paddy to June so that when the monsoon began, rainwater could be used for irrigation instead of depleting groundwater. However, this also delayed the harvests of paddy to October instead of August–September, thereby reducing the window between harvests of paddy and sowing of wheat, leaving few alternatives to farmers than burning.

Principally, there are two ways in which the crop stubble could be managed without burning. The first is the in-situ approach, where the stubble is disposed on the farm itself by incorporating or mulching it into the soil through crop residue management (CRM) machines, such as happy seeder, super seeder etc. The second is the ex-situ approach, where the crop residue is collected and supplied for other applications such as boiler fuel in industries and power plants, packaging materials etc. Over the years, scientists and governments have preferred and promoted the in-situ disposal of crop stubble.

For the first few years after the AAP government came to power in Delhi in 2015, it could do little to tackle this problem except plead with the Centre and neighbouring state governments of Punjab, Haryana and UP, to offer cleaner alternatives to farmers. After three years of hue and cry, the Central government decided to act in 2018 by launching its flagship scheme to subsidize the purchase of CRM machines by individual farmers and cooperatives in the states of Punjab, Haryana, UP and Delhi.

Between 2018 and 2022, over 1,20,000 CRM machines were purchased by farmers in Punjab, which sees the highest instances of farm fires every year. However, this did little to arrest instances of farm fires in Punjab, which increased from 45,384 in 2017 to 71,304 in 2021—a staggering 57 per cent rise.[51] Multiple factors inhibited the optimal utilization of these CRM machines, such as the widespread use of long-duration variety rice (Pusa 44), which has a growth cycle of 155–160 days from sowing to harvest, leaving very little time for the use of CRM machines to manage crop stubble. Another factor was that only the rich farmers could afford to buy these partially subsidized machines, hire labour and spend on fuel every year.[52] For small and marginal farmers, setting the stubble on fire was the only economically viable option.

Tired of being a mute spectator, Mr Kejriwal started meeting experts to explore sustainable solutions to this seemingly intractable problem. Soon enough, a breakthrough came from the Indian Agricultural Research Institute (IARI) located at Pusa in Delhi. Presenting to the Chief Minister in mid-2020, the scientists at IARI showcased a fully organic microbial solution, called Pusa biodecomposer, that was capable of rapidly decomposing paddy crop residue into manure within 15–20 days of application, without expensive CRM machines. As it turned out, IARI scientists had been carrying out successful field trials of this solution for three to four years but hadn't found any takers in governments yet. The best part about the Pusa biodecomposer was its affordability—the cost of buying and applying the solution was low enough for the government to fully subsidize it. In October 2020, the AAP government became the first one in India to formally back this intervention to curb farm fires.

In the first year, the AAP government agreed to spray the Pusa biodecomposer free of cost across 1,935 hectares of farm land in outer Delhi, covering thirty-nine villages.[53] An external evaluation by a Central government agency covering seventy-nine farmers in fifteen villages revealed encouraging results. Ninety per cent of the farmers claimed that the solution turned crop stubble into manure in under twenty days. The content of carbon in the soil increased by 40 per cent, nitrogen 24 per cent, bacteria seven times and fungi three times. Further, sprouting of wheat also increased by 17–20 per cent due to improved soil fertility.[54] Buoyed by successful results, the AAP government decided to scale-up free distribution of the Pusa biodecomposer to all Delhi farmers in subsequent years, with the application crossing 5,000 hectares in 2023.

In February 2022, when the AAP government came to power in Punjab, it got cracking on stubble burning right away. While the Pusa biodecomposer proved very effective in Delhi, it was relatively untested in Punjab and could be scaled up only gradually. Further, the districts with highest fire counts had a relatively short window of under ten days to clear crop stubble. In the short term, the AAP government in Punjab inducted an additional 24,000 CRM machines over 2022 and 2023 for in-situ management and targeted them to areas with low penetration of existing machines and high fire counts. The government also promoted ex-situ utilization of paddy straw by significantly increasing the number of compressed biogas plants (from five to forty-three), biomass power plants as well as industrial boilers—approving a dedicated policy in the latter case.

Keeping the long-term picture in mind, in June 2023, Punjab Chief Minister Bhagwant Mann made a personal appeal to farmers in hotspot districts to adopt short-duration rice (PR-126), which has a ninety-to-100-day growth cycle, as a replacement to the long-duration Pusa 44 variety. In the first year itself, the results were encouraging with a 32 per cent shift in acreage from Pusa-44 to PR-126—a shift of 1.8 lakh hectares.[55]

The government also undertook massive awareness campaigns on the ground (wall paintings, hoardings, pamphlet distribution in schools, villages etc.) and educating farmers of the benefits of not burning the crop stubble via mass media. Progressive farmers were recognized and roped in to educate others in the village. As a net impact of these efforts, the AAP government managed to bend the curve of Punjab's rising farm fires and brought them down to the all-time lowest of 36,663 in 2023—a nearly 50 per cent drop in just two years (see Table 2).[56]

Table 2: Farm fire incidents in Punjab (kharif season) have declined by 50 per cent over 2021–2023

Year	Farm fire incidents in Punjab (kharif season)
2017	45,384
2018	50,590
2019	55,210
2020	76,590
2021	71,304
2022	47,922
2023	36,663

Source: Punjab Remote Sensing Centre, Government of Punjab

In the coming years, the AAP government in Punjab plans to permanently address the issue of farm fires through two key measures. First, there is an ambitious crop diversification plan underway to move Punjab away from paddy cultivation altogether to crops that are more suitable to Punjab's ecology such as maize, pulses and oilseeds. This would help its rapidly depleting ground water levels. It also recognizes the fact that the water-guzzling paddy crop was never native to Punjab and was a product of the green revolution era.

Second, the Punjab government plans to provide all farmers—particularly small and marginal farmers—with economically viable choices to manage crop stubble. It is well known that the bulk of the farmers who choose to burn paddy straw do so out of economic compulsion and lack of other cost-effective options. After consulting farmers and agricultural experts in 2022, the Punjab government came up with the most acceptable solution to all: a direct cash incentive of ₹2,500 per acre for farmers to offset the costs of sustainably disposing crop-stubble through in-situ or ex-situ measures of their choice.

Given the substantial financial outlay of nearly ₹1,900 crore per annum to fund this incentive for all farmers in Punjab, it was proposed that the incentive be jointly financed by the Centre, Punjab and Delhi governments since the gains in cleaner air will be felt across the region. While the Punjab and Delhi governments readily agreed to part with their share, the Centre rejected this formulation favoring the existing approach of distributing partially subsidized CRM machines.[57] One hopes that a breakthrough can be achieved soon in financing this ambitious scheme, which could very well put an end to crop stubble burning.

Odd–Even Scheme

While the constantly elevated air pollution levels in Delhi-NCR is an issue that needs to be addressed round the year, the severity of pollution levels in winter months—with peak AQI crossing 500—warrants the introduction of more aggressive, even if temporary, measures to deal with the public health emergency associated with it. In Delhi-NCR, this period begins typically around early October with the onset of the crop stubble burning season. The media, usually quiet through the year on pollution, wakes up to the first sight of hazy, gloomy winter mornings with predictably sensational headlines such as 'airpocalypse in Delhi', 'Delhi turns to a gas chamber' etc., every year.

The first winter after the AAP government assumed office in 2015 was an unsparing one. The smoke from crop stubble burning and firecrackers burnt during Diwali, combined with the phenomenon of temperature inversion, led to a thick blanket of smog engulfing Delhi. For the first time, the Delhi High Court termed Delhi a gas chamber. It was an extraordinary situation, one which deserved an extraordinary response.

After much deliberation, Mr Kejriwal decided to introduce an experiment to drastically reduce private vehicles on Delhi roads for a fortnight in January 2016, which was unheard of in our country till then—the odd-even scheme. Essentially, the government restricted the plying of private vehicles having registration number ending with odd digits (1, 3, 5, 7, 9) on even dates of the month and vice versa.

The decision was anything but easy. Experts had warned that the odd-even scheme had failed wherever it was implemented in any city across the world because people didn't cooperate. There was no template that the government could have borrowed from. The challenge was to drastically reduce the number of private vehicles plying on the roads, while creating as few impediments for smooth movement of people and goods across the city. People had to be able to get to their work, essential commodities had to be delivered to the markets, people had to be able to travel in and out of the city, so on and so forth.

Back in 2016, the capacity of Delhi's public transport system wasn't adequate to absorb the entire load in case the usage of two-wheelers and four-wheelers were restricted. Hence, the government decided to restrict only private cars—approximately 20 lakh. A few exceptions were carved out such as for less polluting CNG-fuelled cars, plying of cars after 8 p.m. or before 8 a.m., emergency vehicles etc.[58] In addition, the trips made by the Delhi metro were increased and over 3,000 private buses hired for the two weeks during the odd-even scheme.

A massive public awareness campaign was launched through newspapers, hoardings, radio-TV, etc., and also in-person through schools, colleges, RWAs etc. A strict penalty of ₹2,000 was announced for any violation of odd-even restrictions. The chief minister and other cabinet ministers set the ball rolling by announcing they will car-pool to work. What worked most effectively though was the personal appeal by nearly 7,000 civil defence volunteers who hit the streets, armed with placards and red roses, standing at all busy traffic signals requesting those violating odd-even restrictions to turn back and do their bit to protect their and their children's health.[59] As an official policy, the government chose 'gandhigiri' to encourage people to make it their movement, rather than punishing them at the first sight of violation.

Mr Kejriwal admitted later, 'I was aware that what we were venturing into was asking the residents of my city to change their way of living. We were asking them to give up their comfort for the collective good of the city. I was apprehensive about how people would respond to the government's decision. But we chose to trust Delhiites and undertook a massive awareness campaign through both the media and personal outreach, which was supported by flawless implementation by different government agencies.'[60]

Eventually, the people of Delhi overwhelmingly welcomed odd-even and made it a huge success. The scheme landed Mr Kejriwal among *Fortune* magazine's 50 greatest leaders in 2016 for his efforts to curb pollution in the national capital. The odd-even scheme was later reintroduced in April 2016 and once again in November 2019, to battle similar peak pollution episodes—every time with an enthusiastic response from Delhi's residents.

The public embraced the odd-even scheme, but did it have any impact on Delhi's pollution levels? The impact of the odd-even scheme on air quality can be estimated only through a scientific evaluation that compares observed air quality during odd-even days with what the levels would have been in the absence of the programme. Meteorological conditions greatly influence how pollution levels vary from one day to the next, and therefore any reasonable evaluation needs to figure out a way to make apple to apple comparisons. Let's look at two independent and scientific evaluations that show the success of odd-even in reducing pollution, but only when implemented in winters.

The first evaluation was conducted by researchers from the University of Chicago and Harvard University and covered both the January and April 2016 rounds of the odd-even scheme.[61] The study compared PM2.5 data in Delhi with neighbouring cities in the NCR—before, during and after the two rounds. The evaluation found that PM2.5 levels were lower by 13 per cent in Delhi during the 8 a.m.– 8 p.m. time zone when the odd-even scheme was implemented in January 2016. No impact was detected at night. No impact was detected when the programme was repeated in April 2016, most likely because the warmer month of April is marked by greater dispersion of particulates. The researchers conclude, 'taken together, this suggests that the main value of an odd-even programme is as an emergency measure during winter months when car emissions play a more prominent role in affecting air quality'.

In another study, researchers from IIT Delhi, IIT Kanpur, IITM Pune, TERI and CSIR-National Physical Laboratory, New Delhi utilized satellite-based estimates of PM2.5 and modelling simulations to examine the potential decrease due to fewer traffic emissions during odd-even. The study concluded that the traffic restriction between January 1–15 in 2016 reduced PM2.5 by 4–6 per cent with a maximum of up to 10 per cent, primarily at three local hotspots in Delhi.[62] Yet another study focused on the impact of the November 2019 odd-even scheme on traffic patterns at ten busy junctions in Delhi. The study found a decrease of about 6 per cent vehicle kilometres travelled during the odd-even scheme implementation resulting in about 15 per cent decrease in daily fuel consumption.[63]

Delhi's odd-even scheme has also spawned off interesting research on public behaviour. One such study by a researcher at Harvard University looked at how the drivers of private cars in Delhi responded to travel restrictions during the odd-even pilot in January 2016.[64] The study repeatedly surveyed 614 car drivers throughout the odd-even scheme duration and found that the use of any motorized vehicle, private or hired, fell by one-third on restricted days of odd-even scheme, with a corresponding increase in share of public transport or cancelled trips.

Taken together, the bulk of the scientific evidence on the impact of Delhi's odd-even scheme on air pollution levels points towards a definite, though modest impact, as an emergency measure to fight peak pollution episodes in winter.

A typical classroom in a Delhi government school before 2015 where students study in a dingy, dilapidated room

Manish Sisodia with Odisha Education Minister Samir Ranjan Dash visiting a modern, revamped Delhi government school at West Vinod Nagar, Delhi on 29 July 2019

US First Lady Melania Trump attends a Happiness Class at Sarvodaya Co-ed Senior Secondary School in Moti Bagh, Delhi on 25 February 2020

Arvind Kejriwal and Manish Sisodia with Tamil Nadu Chief Minister M.K. Stalin visiting a swimming pool at Rajkiya Sarvodaya Bal Vidyalaya, West Vinod Nagar, Delhi on 1 April 2022

Newly constructed school building at Rana Pratap Rajkiya
Sarvodaya Kanya/Bal Vidyalaya, Delhi on 29 May 2023

Education Minister Atishi inaugurating a state-of-the-art
library at Rana Pratap Rajkiya Sarvodaya Kanya/Bal Vidyalaya,
Rithala, Delhi on 29 May 2023

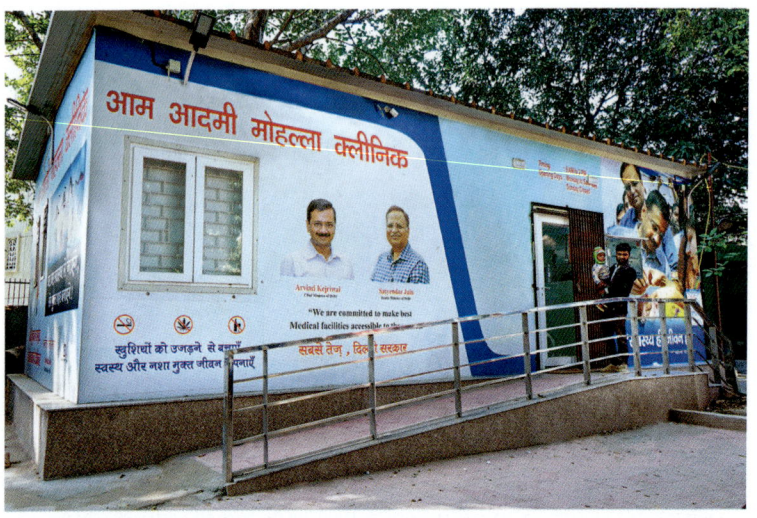

A typical mohalla clinic in Greater Kailash, Delhi. Over 540 of these primary care clinics have been set up in Delhi, catering to over 60,000 patients every day.

Former UN Secretary-General Ban Ki-moon and former Norway Prime Minister and WHO Director-General Gro Harlem Brundtland visited an Aam Aadmi mohalla clinic in Delhi on 7 September 2018

New award-winning design of mohalla clinics set up inside
portable shipping containers in Rani Bagh, Delhi in October 2021

State-of-the-art healthcare infrastructure built as per
international standards at Indira Gandhi Hospital in Dwarka,
Delhi, inaugurated on 10 May 2021

Arvind Kejriwal kick-starts the spraying of the newly developed bio-decomposer solution on the paddy fields in Delhi on October 14 2020, as a sustainable solution to curb farm fires

Arvind Kejriwal and Jasmine Shah at the inauguration of an EV charging station set up under the Delhi EV Policy on 18 October 2022. As of 2023, Delhi had over 4600 charging stations—the highest in the country.

Fifty electric buses flagged off by Arvind Kejriwal and Transport Minister Kailash Gahlot on 2 January 2023. In a landmark step to fight pollution, Delhi has inducted 1970 e-buses—the highest in India.

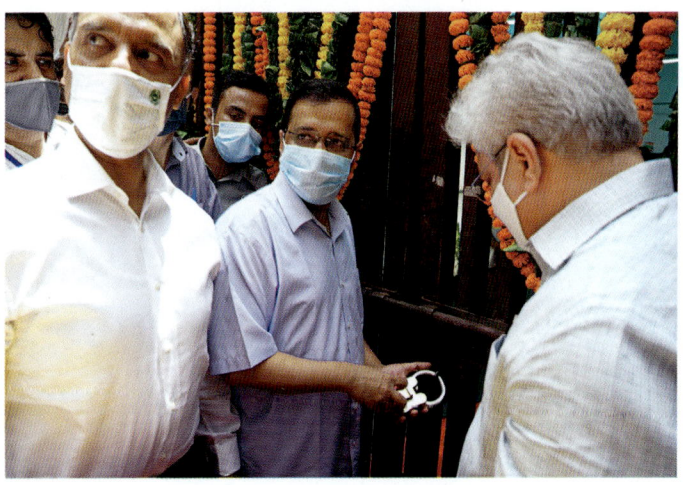

Arvind Kejriwal inaugurated the faceless services initiative of the transport department by putting a lock on the RTO office at IP Estate Zone, Delhi on 11 August 2021

Delhi Solar Policy announced on 30 January 2024 by
Arvind Kejriwal, Atishi and Jasmine Shah, marking a landmark
initiative for providing affordable and sustainable energy

A view of the rejuvenated Rajokri Lake made from a municipal
dump site—the first of fifty such lakes made by the Delhi
government under the 'city of lakes' initiative

SC Mandates an Emergency Action Plan

While the odd-even scheme became the most popular measure taken by the AAP government to fight peak pollution episodes, it was not the only one. Starting the winter of 2016–17, the AAP government started announcing a slew of emergency measures to be implemented in winters. In the first year itself, these included a temporary ban on all construction activities, vacuum cleaning of all roads wider than 100 ft to address road dust, a ban on burning of garbage in the open, etc.

In contrast, all the surrounding cities and NCR states were unwilling to adopt the odd-even scheme or any other emergency measures that would inconvenience people. It was this collective inaction that forced the Supreme Court to take a landmark decision on 2 December 2016 in the matter of M.C. Mehta vs. Union of India to institute the graded response action plan (GRAP).

Simply put, the GRAP is an emergency response mechanism that imposes a mandatory set of actions on all entities operating in NCR in response to worsening air quality levels. Proposed by the CPCB, the Supreme Court-mandated GRAP classifies air quality into four categories: poor, very poor, severe and emergency (severe+), based on the concentration of particulate matter—PM2.5 and PM10. Each category will trigger interventions ranging from ban on burning waste, better pollution control technology for coal power plants/brick kilns to the closure of power plants, ban on the entry of diesel trucks, ban on construction activities etc., across Delhi-NCR.[65] In what can only be seen as an official validation of the odd-even scheme by the Central government, GRAP also mandates the odd-even scheme when AQI reaches emergency levels.

The GRAP was notified by the Union environment ministry in January 2017, effective from the following winter. While the GRAP created a much-needed accountability framework for the measures that all governments and stakeholders in the NCR must adopt to fight peak pollution episodes, its effectiveness has been severely hampered by the indifference of most of the governments outside Delhi.

The reason for this is that the body responsible for implementing GRAP (currently, CAQM) has powers only to issue orders based on changing air quality levels but not to punish or penalize governments for non-compliance. The toughest job of enforcing the stringent measures mandated by GRAP is that of the state governments, whose inaction created the air pollution emergency in the first place! For example, the moment air quality levels dip to very poor category, GRAP mandates shutting down of DG sets and restricting the use of coal in industries across the NCR. By 2018, Delhi had already provided 24/7 electricity and banned the use of coal completely. The GRAP mandate was therefore diligently followed in Delhi. But across NCR, the use of DG sets in residential areas, and coal in industries, is rampant. The result: the GRAP mandated ban on DG sets has been flouted every year since 2017 in all NCR states except Delhi.

The fate of the odd-even scheme has been similar. Even though the entire NCR region has seen several winter episodes of severe+ or emergency air quality levels ever since the GRAP was notified in early 2017, only the Delhi government has implemented it. In contrast, none of the NCR governments have shown any interest in implementing the odd-even scheme despite several episodes of AQI rising beyond emergency levels—a clear violation of GRAP.

In mid-2023, the GRAP was revised by the CAQM to cover even a larger set of stringent actions to fight pollution emergencies.[66] For example, the plying of older BS-III petrol vehicles or BS-IV diesel vehicles (four wheelers) was banned when AQI crossed the 'severe' 400 AQI level. Once again, apart from passing more bureaucratic orders, no mechanism was put in place by CAQM to punish governments that simply do not comply with GRAP mandated measures. The result was the same.

The moment the AQI in Delhi started deteriorating in mid-October 2023 and hit emergency levels in the first week of November 2023, the AAP government imposed progressively stricter measures as mandated under GRAP including a ban of Diwali firecrackers, all construction activities, plying of BS-III petrol vehicles or BS-IV diesel vehicles (four wheelers), ban on all private buses running on diesel etc. In contrast, the governments of UP and Haryana went into hiding, refusing to enforce most of the measures, even allowing thousands of diesel buses to enter Delhi every day from their states.

A visit by Delhi government officials to an inter-state bus terminal at Anand Vihar in east Delhi in early November 2023, when Delhi's AQI hit emergency levels, revealed that the most polluting BS-III and BS-IV diesel buses entering into Delhi were from surrounding states despite CAQM's orders prohibiting them. This prompted Delhi's environment minister, Gopal Rai, to write to the Union environment minister pointing out the futility of GRAP if all other governments except Delhi are brazenly flouting its measures.[67] Predictably, the letter received no response.

In conclusion, while the Supreme Court's order mandating GRAP across NCR was a welcome move, it has had limited impact because of the lack of any real accountability for governments non-compliant with these measures. As a result, GRAP's success has mirrored the commitment with which the governments of the NCR region were already acting on pollution.

Investing in Data

The cliché 'what gets measured gets done' is often true. The converse, 'if you don't want to get anything done, don't measure it' is particularly true in relation to wicked problems like air pollution. Indeed, this has defined the approach of most state governments that have steadfastly refused to invest in adequate air quality monitoring systems to capture the true scale and nature of air pollution plaguing their cities.

The traditional method of monitoring air quality relied on setting up manual stations, which were required to follow the CPCB protocol of a minimum of 104 days of monitoring every year with two twenty-four-hour monitoring sessions every week of the year. But given that they are manual, there is very little discipline at keeping them working. Although the CPCB website shows that over 900 manual monitoring stations are operating across India as on August 2023, less than half of them carried out any monitoring of PM2.5 at all, and just 7 per cent stations met the minimum monitoring requirement of 104 days a year.[68] It would be fair to say much of India is flying blind on the air pollution issue.

In comparison, real-time and automated monitoring stations, also called Continuous Ambient Air Quality Monitoring Stations (CAAQMS) although more expensive are often more reliable and measure more parameters. Only six such monitoring stations were operating in Delhi in 2014. The new AAP government made investing in a modern air quality monitoring network among its first priorities in the battle against pollution. Twenty real-time stations were set up between 2017 and 2018, making Delhi the first state to have a network that captures all eight parameters prescribed by the CPCB. The Central government too set up fourteen additional real-time stations in Delhi, raising the total to forty—the highest in India and among the highest for any city globally.

The rest of the NCR region has, unfortunately, lagged behind in setting up a robust air quality monitoring network.

As of 2022, Delhi with forty monitors accounts for half of all the real-time monitors in Delhi-NCR, with Haryana, Uttar Pradesh and Rajasthan having only twenty-two, seventeen and two real-time stations respectively.[69]

A dense network of forty real-time stations has enabled the AAP government to identify local pollution hotspots, create hotspot action plans and use the rich data to further study the nature of pollution from within and outside Delhi. In 2018, thirteen pollution hotspots were identified in Delhi as these spots have higher air pollution levels in comparison to other areas. Accordingly, special action plans for the winter and round-the-year pollution are implemented for each of these thirteen hotspots.[70]

As the AAP government started seeking systematic and long-term solutions to the issue of air pollution, the biggest hurdle turned out to be unpacking the contribution of various sources that contribute to it. It made sense to direct maximum effort and public funds towards sources that contribute the most. Although, two source apportionment studies on Delhi's air pollution had already been published by 2019—one by IIT Kanpur in 2015 and the other by TERI-ARAI in 2018—both these studies captured source contributions at a fixed point in time. While they offer good reference points in the absence of any other data, relying heavily on them creates two problems.

First, a thriving, constantly growing city like Delhi sees many changes every year that could alter the pollution profile. For example, a major construction project like the central vista or a new metro corridor, could have long-range effects on the composition of Delhi's air pollution. Relying on one-off data taken years ago could hardly be said to be a winning strategy. Second, knowledge of break-up of pollution sources in real-time is essential when pollution levels rise alarmingly, calling for targeted emergency measures.

It was Mr Kejriwal's firm decision to invest in technologies that could unpack in real-time the sources contributing to Delhi's pollution that led to the conception of India's first real-time source apportionment lab for air pollution in 2018.

While the idea principally made sense, turning it to reality was anything but trivial, since neither the hardware nor the software and algorithms for such real-time modelling of pollution sources existed in India. After initial hiccups, a unique joint team was formed between three of India's leading institutions—IIT Kanpur, TERI and IIT Delhi. Credit must go to this team and particularly its lead, Professor Mukesh Sharma of IIT Kanpur, who understood the government's vision and took it up as a challenge to build India's first real-time source apportionment laboratory.

The MoU between the Delhi government and the research team was signed in October 2021 in the midst of the Covid-19 pandemic. A year of relentless efforts ensued. State-of-the-art scientific instruments that made up the physical laboratory at a supersite in Delhi were sourced from Japan, USA, UK, Switzerland, Italy and Australia. Highly sophisticated techniques including a source apportionment algorithm called chemical mass balance and understanding the source-to-receptor linkage were developed for the first time in India. On 31 January 2023, Chief Minister Kejriwal launched India's first supersite to measure real-time break-up of pollution sources in central Delhi.[71]

Within the first year, the data from the supersite started proving to be a milestone in furthering the understanding of ongoing and peak pollution episodes bringing forth hitherto unidentified sources of pollution as important ones. For example, it was identified that the *angeethis* and bonfires used by security guards to keep themselves warm in winters was a significant source of air pollution. Data analysed by the supersite on relative contribution of local and external sources in Delhi's PM2.5 pollution levels in November 2023 revealed a similar picture as presented earlier—only 38 per cent of Delhi's pollution originated from sources within Delhi (Table 3).

Table 3: Relative contribution of local and external sources in Delhi's PM2.5 pollution over five days (18–22 November 2023)

State	Contribution towards Delhi's PM2.5 pollution levels
Delhi	38.3%
Haryana	58.9%
Uttar Pradesh	4.7%
Others	0.01%

Source: Real-time source apportionment lab, Government of NCT of Delhi

One crucial difference between IITM's decision support system (DSS) referred to earlier, and the Delhi government's real-time source apportionment system is that the former doesn't carry out any physical sampling of air quality and uses a modelling-only approach. In contrast, the latter is the first such physical laboratory set up in India that captures air quality samples and uses state-of-the-art instrumentation and algorithms to give a real-time profile of sources behind Delhi's air pollution.

Investments made by the AAP government in setting up the most advanced air quality monitoring framework in Delhi, at par with any city globally, is yet another measure of its commitment to find lasting solutions to Delhi's air pollution. They will also play a crucial role in precisely directing future efforts in cleaning up Delhi's air.

Fixing North India's Air Pollution Crisis

The fact that India's air pollution crisis is a source of only episodic alarm few times every year for its citizens and the media alike, shows how little is understood about this silent killer. A study published in 2023 in the *British Medical Journal* estimated that outdoor air pollution from all sources accounts for over 2 million deaths per year in India.[72] This is about four times more than the assumed leading cause of deaths in India every year—heart attacks.[73]

A report by the Energy Policy Institute of the University of Chicago paints an equally chilling picture of the impact of air pollution in India. It states that nearly 40 per cent of Indians, or over 480 million people from central, east and north India, could lose almost ten years of their life expectancy, if we allow 2019 levels of air pollution to continue. The report's authors call it the greatest global health threat with risks beginning at the foetus stage.[74] In economic terms, a study by Dalberg has estimated air pollution's impact on the Indian economy to be 3 per cent of annual GDP, or 50 per cent of all tax collected annually.[75]

Despite these alarm bells, India has little to show by way of results over the last decade. In 2014, ten of the fifteen most polluted cities in the world were from India.[76] In 2023, this number rose to twelve in the top fifteen and forty-two in the top fifty most polluted cities globally. There's a reason for this dismal result; it is not that we are condemned to living our lives in pollution, it is because other countries that faced similar crises in the past acted far more quickly and decisively than we have.

In 1992, Mexico City was singled out as the world's most polluted city by the United Nations. What ensued in the next twenty-five years offers immense hope to India's mega cities and particularly Delhi. Mexico's population of over 20 million is similar to Delhi. Also, it sits in a valley, which is a geographical disadvantage since it makes polluted air difficult to disperse, just like Delhi. Writing in the *Indian Express*, Mexico's former ambassador to India, Melba Maria Pria

Olavarrieta, explains how their local government responded to the crisis by mandating a series of measures on a war footing. These included, severe curbs on private transport, parking reforms, massive expansion of public transport and bicycle lanes, shutting down a polluting oil refinery within the city and converting its space to an enormous public park and playgrounds. The city also put in place a contingency programme of measures to deal with pollution spikes, much like India's GRAP.[77] As a result, PM10 pollution levels fell from an average of 160 μg/m3 in 1989 to forty in 2014.

Closer to India, Beijing's success in cleaning up its air quality, and the role played by its government, offer valuable lessons too. Beijing's air was more toxic than Delhi's in the late 1990s, which is when it started taking steps to crack down on transport and industrial pollution. But the big shift took place in 2013, after a great smog hit 600 million people in central, northern and eastern China in January 2013, prompting the government to declare a 'war against pollution' and launch a comprehensive five-year action plan to tackle it. The linchpin of the plan was a regional approach to fighting pollution, delineating clusters that were part of the same 'airshed' like Jing-jin-ji (Beijing-Tianjin-Hebei region with twenty-eight towns including Beijing) for taking time-bound action.[78]

Accordingly, Beijing's government as well as those of surrounding provinces coordinated and implemented a joint action plan that included specific targets. Beijing cracked down hard on ownership of private cars, fixing an annual quota for new cars to be given out via lottery—one lakh in 2018. Those wishing to buy an electric car, however, were able to buy one more easily. The flow of trucks within the city was restricted, the use of coal for heating in residential buildings was banned and replaced by natural gas, fuel and engine standards were raised, among other measures. All this came at a substantial cost. Beijing's budget to fight air pollution jumped from just over US$434 million in 2013 to more than US$2.6 billion in 2017. By the end of 2017, cleaner air was visible. The annual average PM2.5 concentration in Beijing had dropped to 58ug/m3, down 35 per cent from 2013.[79]

Delhi's journey over the past decade that resulted in reduction in the three-year average PM2.5 levels by 45 per cent offers important lessons for the rest of north India battling air pollution. Surprisingly, many of the reform measures taken by the AAP government over the past decade (as discussed in this chapter) are yet to be emulated by surrounding states. As of early 2024, Delhi is the only state to have shut all its local thermal power plants, ensured 24/7 power supply thereby eliminating the use of polluting DG sets, transitioned all its industries from polluting fuels to clean natural gas, increased its green cover substantially, invested heavily in expanding public transport and implemented an ambitious EV policy that has seen Delhi emerge as the EV capital of India. In a story of telling contrasts, as of mid-2024, Delhi has inducted nearly 2,000 electric buses, the highest in India, while the rest of the NCR region was yet to induct even a single electric bus.

All these examples show that progress on air pollution across north India is very much within our reach, provided we display the political resolve that countries around the world and the AAP government in Delhi has shown. The pathway to fixing north India's air pollution crisis must have four essential components.

First, the Central government, as well as all the state governments in north India, must acknowledge air pollution as India's biggest public health emergency, rather than living in denial. The fact remains that in the first ten years of his term, Prime Minister Narendra Modi has not once spoken about the gravity of the air pollution crisis facing India or his plans to fight it, within or outside the Parliament. Instead, addressing the Lok Sabha in December 2019, the then Union environment minister, Prakash Javdekar, famously said, 'No Indian study has shown any correlation between pollution and shortening of lifespan. Let us not create a fear psychosis among people.'[80] A similar attitude pervades the BJP-run state governments in Haryana and Uttar Pradesh, whose chief ministers are rarely seen talking about air pollution or their plans to tackle it. A resolute silence or blaming Delhi is their preferred approach, especially during the peak winter pollution episodes.

Second, any search for solutions must begin by accepting the need for a coordinated, regional action plan using the 'airshed' approach, much like what China did in 2013 or what California did in the late 1960s. For far too long, discussion on north India's air pollution crisis has centred on actions taken by the AAP government in Delhi with other governments and stakeholders in the region getting a free pass to pollute with impunity. Two decades after all auto-rickshaws and buses in Delhi switched to CNG, those in neighbouring Gurgaon and Faridabad continue to run on diesel. It's time we recognize that the entire Indo-Gangetic plain spanning 7,00,000 sq km across north India acts as a giant 'airshed'. To begin with, any meaningful action plan to curb pollution will need to impose a time-bound and binding set of measures—a common minimum programme—for the entire NCR region spanning 55,000 sq km, if not a greater region.

A beginning towards this was made in mid-2022 by the Central government's CAQM, which constituted an expert group to prepare a 'Policy to Curb Air Pollution in the National Capital Region' on the directions of the Supreme Court.[81] The impressive 110-page report outlined a number of sector-wise measures to be implemented by all governments in NCR within one to three years. However, like almost all expert committee reports on pollution that came before it, none of the recommendations were binding or backed by a legal mechanism for enforcement.

A year down the line, many of the first-year targets were missed (e.g. provision of 24/7 electricity to avoid usage of DG sets, transition of all industries to clean fuel) with no consequences for non-compliant governments. What is needed therefore is not just any regional action plan, but one that is backed by a strong enforcement mechanism that makes it legally binding on all the public authorities and private stakeholders involved to take time-bound actions. For those who don't, a suitable penalty based on 'polluter pays principle' must be imposed, which at the least should be twice the cost of implementing the recommended measure in the first place.

The third essential component to solving north India's air pollution crisis is backing ambitious plans with ambitious budgets. Beijing alone invested US$2.6 billion (approximately ₹17,000 crore) in 2017 in its war against pollution. Compare this with the fact that Government of India set aside a paltry budget of ₹9,650 crore over five years (2019–24) for its flagship national initiative, the National Clean Air Programme (NCAP), to curb air pollution not just in Delhi, but in 131 of the most polluted cities in India, including Delhi.[82] The share of funds allocated to Delhi was ₹38 crore over five years. The NCAP set a target of 20–30 per cent reduction in PM10 and PM2.5 levels for all the cities over five years. At the end of five years, an independent study by Climate Trends revealed that one out of every four cities failed to set up a real-time pollution monitoring system (CAAQMS). Of the remaining cities, only forty-nine had PM2.5 data for all five years, of which only four cities met the target for PM reduction.[83]

The experience of NCAP shows that no amount of talk or expert committee recommendations are going to save Indian cities without serious money backing it. Given the scale of this pan-India crisis and the overall impact on India's GDP, it is only fair that the biggest chunk of budgetary commitment comes from the Central government. The states must also pitch in. Funding arrangements used for massive infrastructure projects can be emulated to fund ambitious clean air action plans too, such as one used by the Delhi Metro Rail Corporation (DMRC) where the Centre and state contribute a 50:50 equity adding up to 20–30 per cent of the project cost, and the rest being funded through low-cost debt.

The fourth and perhaps the most critical component for a successful roadmap to fix the air pollution crisis is the role of political leadership. It is difficult to imagine the head of any other country whose cities occupy forty-two spots in the top fifty most polluted cities in the world not holding a single meeting in ten years to find a lasting solution or saying anything that suggests this is bothersome. The Union environment minister rarely meets his state-level counterparts to discuss and monitor action plans even during the peak winters. Yet, that is the harsh reality of the missing political leadership when it comes to fixing north India's air pollution crisis.

It is clear that there are no easy solutions to curb pollution. In fact, the most effective solutions will cause some inconvenience and will require considerable effort by the political leadership to convince the voters or stakeholders involved—be it convincing farmers to stop lighting farm fires, or transitioning industries to cleaner fuels, or getting car and bike owners to adopt electric vehicles. That is when the role of political leadership becomes critical to draw up a comprehensive yet realistic action plan, and take accountability to implement it effectively.

The past decade of failed efforts to curb air pollution across north India and particularly the NCR have all been led by non-political actors. For the two decades beginning in the late 1990s, a body of experts under the banner of Environment Pollution Control Authority (EPCA), the precursor to CAQM, was put in charge of coordinating actions against pollution across the NCR. In 2021, this was replaced by CAQM—largely a body of bureaucrats with no direct involvement of the elected leadership within governments. With the real responsibility pawned off to ineffective commissions, the elected leadership in most Indian states as well as the Centre relegated its role to blaming each other for the few days or weeks every winter when air pollution dominates national headlines. Meanwhile, several years have passed by without a single meeting held between the Union environment minister and state environment ministers to discuss air pollution. On one occasion, before the onset of winter in 2019, the Union environment minister, Prakash Javdekar, cancelled three meetings on prevention, control and mitigation of air pollution in NCR with the environment ministers of Delhi, Haryana and Uttar Pradesh because he was busy campaigning for state assembly elections in Maharashtra.[84]

It's time we demand that a problem of such magnitude needs ownership and accountability at the level of the prime minister and of the respective state chief ministers. There must be a public declaration of a 'war against pollution' nationally, much like the national campaign against polio in the 1990s. A suitable governance structure should be created in the form of a national council for war against pollution, chaired by the prime minister and comprising of chief ministers and environment ministers of the concerned states. The GST council is one recent example of political leadership taking charge of decision-making, which can be emulated in fighting air pollution too. Similarly, inter-state councils for war against pollution should be created at a regional 'airshed' level, comprising chief ministers of the concerned states. The role of bodies, such as CAQM, should be restricted to promoting cutting-edge research, rendering scientific advice and monitoring field-level implementation.

All the above four components—acknowledging air pollution as India's biggest public health emergency, announcing a regional action plan that is binding on all concerned states, devoting adequate funds and fixing ownership and accountability of all actions on the political leadership starting with the prime minister—are essential if we are to guarantee our citizens the most precious of all rights—the right to breathe clean air.

Chapter 5

Transport

A New Dawn for Delhi's Transport System

The Delhi Model stands out among other governance models for it prioritizes issues affecting the quality of life of the aam aadmi—the middle and lower classes. Education and health form the foundation for any nation's progress. Air pollution is the leading cause of deaths in India affecting the health of all citizens equally. Efficient and affordable transportation plays an important role in accessing education and job opportunities, thereby furthering social mobility. In particular, robust public transport can go a long way in reducing congestion, pollution and accidents, while contributing to economic growth. In many ways, transportation can be said to be the backbone of urban economies.

The AAP government's vision for Delhi's transport system was first articulated in 2015 by the then deputy chief minister, Manish Sisodia, in his first budget speech. Quoting the former mayor of Bogota, Enrique Peñalosa, Mr Sisodia said, 'A developed country is not a place where the poor have cars. It's where the rich use public transport.' He said the latter will happen only when the comfort of public transport trumps the cost and difficulty of using a private vehicle. He further defined a 'smart city' as one that focuses on moving people rather than vehicles, a city that makes mobility accessible and affordable. 'It is a city where people walk and cycle without fear of being run over . . . a city where public space is distributed equitably rather than it being privileged for the privileged,' said Mr Sisodia.[1]

When the AAP government assumed office in 2015, Delhi's buses formed the mainstay of its public transport system with an all-CNG fleet of 6,118 buses. It had emerged as the world's largest CNG bus fleet after a Supreme Court mandated shift from diesel to CNG in the early 2000s. However, Delhi was still far away from reaching the court mandated fleet size of 11,000 buses. A rapidly ageing bus fleet with no modernization plan or new additions for years resulted in falling ridership year-on-year. Further, Delhi's buses were widely perceived as unsafe for women. In contrast, the Delhi metro emerged as a world-class public transport system that every Indian city aspired to have. However, many parts of Delhi were untouched by the metro and issues with last-mile connectivity persisted.

Meanwhile, Delhi's petrol-and-diesel-fuelled private vehicles grew exponentially—four times in the past two decades—while the number of zero emissions EVs was negligible. This, coupled with poorly designed streets that catered only to motorists, became the main cause for traffic congestion and vehicular pollution in the city. On the administrative side, the Regional Transport Offices (RTO), the front offices of Delhi government's transport department, had a reputation similar to RTOs all over India—as a den of corruption where nothing moved without a bribe. A frustrated Union Transport Minister in 2015 said, 'RTO is the most corrupt organisation in the country; they loot more than the dacoits in the forests of Chambal.'[2]

To curtail rising vehicular pollution caused by private vehicles, the AAP government introduced India's most progressive EV policy in 2020. Launched with a target of ensuring 25 per cent of all newly registered vehicles in Delhi be electric by 2024, Delhi's EV policy provided generous yet targeted subsidies for purchase of electric vehicles and aggressively pushed the creation of a public charging infrastructure. The policy proved to be a turning point in Delhi's and India's transition to zero-emission vehicles. From a mere 3.9 per cent in 2019–20, the share of EVs among newly registered vehicles in Delhi rose to 12 per cent in 2023–24— the highest in India and twice the national average of 6 per cent. Delhi's public charging infrastructure also grew rapidly with over 4,600 EV charging points and battery swapping stations set up by mid-2023—the highest among all states and 30 per cent share of all charging points in India. In 2023, the AAP government created history by becoming the first state government to legally mandate the transition of commercial vehicles to EVs by 2030.

To address the flawed design of existing roads, Mr Kejriwal launched Delhi's first effort to completely redesign its arterial road network, based on international standards, focusing on two key issues. First, functionality issues were addressed by redesigning roads to cater to the needs of pedestrians, cyclists and the specially-abled, while ensuring a smooth traffic flow through uniformly designed lanes. Second, the public character of Delhi's streets was sought to be enhanced to international standards through installation of well-designed street furniture, functional signages and greening of open surfaces to prevent suspension of road dust. After a successful pilot of sixteen road stretches spanning 38 km, the AAP government took a big leap in 2023 by announcing the scale-up of the street redesign project to cover 1,400 km roads in Delhi at a cost of ₹19,500 crore in ten years.

The biggest test for the AAP government was overhauling Delhi's public buses. Over the first nine years of the AAP government, Delhi's ageing public bus fleet transitioned to a largely new, modern fleet of 7,683 buses, 25 per cent of which were electric buses. As a result, Delhi has emerged as the city with the largest fleet of public buses and electric buses in India. By 2025, Delhi's bus fleet is expected to reach 10,480 buses, 80 per cent of which will be electric. This will make Delhi the city with the largest electric bus fleet in the world outside China.

Alongside fleet expansion, Delhi's public bus fleet underwent several major transformations to improve its safety, convenience and reliability. Several reforms were launched, such as the common mobility card, a mobile app to serve all the information needs of public transport users and the Connect Delhi initiative—a route rationalization exercise to connect all corners of Delhi within a 500-metre walk and up to fifteen-minute waiting time of the public bus network. To address the last-mile connectivity problem, the mohalla bus scheme was launched in 2024, deploying small air-conditioned electric buses on short routes connecting residential areas with metro stations and local landmarks.

In 2019, to make public transport inclusive, the AAP government took an unprecedented decision of making bus rides free for women, the first government in the world to do so. The decision was aimed at tackling two major issues— the lack of safety for women in Delhi and the dismal 11 per cent participation of women in Delhi's workforce. Several technological interventions, such as CCTV cameras, panic buttons and live GPS tracking, were also introduced, apart from the deployment of over 13,000 dedicated marshals inside buses to act as first responders. The 'pink ticket' scheme, as the free bus ride initiative is popularly called, had a direct impact on economic empowerment of women by significantly improving their access to education and job opportunities. By May 2024, over 170 crore pink tickets had been issued by Delhi's buses. The scheme has since been adopted by several other states including Tamil Nadu, Kerala, Punjab, Karnataka and Telangana.

The other critical pillar of Delhi's public transport system, the Delhi metro—a 50:50 joint venture between the Centre and the Delhi government—continues to be a success. It is well known that the early phase of the metro was built under successive Congress-led governments in Delhi headed by Chief Minister Shiela Dikshit. Between 1998 and 2015,

Delhi metro added 143 stations and 193 km to its network length i.e. 11.4 km per year. What is less known is that in the first nine years of the Kejriwal government, the Delhi metro doubled its stations and network length to 288 and 393 km respectively. A total of 200 km of metro lines were added in just nine years i.e. 22.2 km per year—doubling the rate of metro expansion. As a result, the daily ridership of the Delhi metro has risen substantially from 24 lakh in 2014 to 60 lakh in 2024.[3]

The AAP government also undertook a series of bold administrative reforms targeting corruption at RTOs. In 2018, the government launched the 'Doorstep Delivery of Public Services' (DDPS) initiative, providing every Delhi resident with an option to avail 100 government services, including many RTO services, by scheduling a home visit by a mobile sahayak rather than personally visiting the RTO. However, this did not eliminate the corruption at RTOs, since some services still required a physical visit and verification, for instance, the learner's licence test. In 2021, the AAP government became the first in India to transition all RTO services into an online, faceless mode, leveraging AI-based face recognition and biometric authentication. Symbolizing the end of an era, Mr Kejriwal physically locked up RTO offices in August 2021 while launching the faceless services initiative. A year later, the Central government emulated the Delhi government's initiative, allowing citizens to access over 58 transport-related services online without needing to visit an RTO.[4] The final blow to corruption at RTOs was dealt in 2023 when Delhi became the first state in India to transition to fully-automated driving test tracks for issuing driver's licenses, shutting down manual assessment of driving tests.

Over the course of the past decade, these measures have changed the face of Delhi's public transport system and, in the process, created many firsts that continues to inspire states across the country. Some of these reforms are still a work-in-progress and when completed, will propel Delhi to claim its rightful place among the top global cities that stand out for their commitment to sustainable and inclusive mobility.

Creating a World-Class Public Bus System

Since the turn of the century, the Delhi metro came to symbolize what a world-class public transport system should be like for the entire country. In contrast, Delhi's public buses in 2015 resembled a poor cousin of the Delhi metro with a fleet that had stagnated in capacity and worsened in quality over the years.

Yet, this wasn't always the case. Before the metro assumed a sizeable scale, public buses were the lifeline of Delhi's public transport system ferrying 47 lakh passengers a day at its peak in 2012–13.[5] Following the Supreme Court's directions, Delhi became the first city in the world to transition to an all-CNG fleet in the early 2000s cutting down pollution. During the 2010 Commonwealth Games, the fleet size of the Delhi Transport Corporation (DTC)—the state-owned bus corporation—was at its highest ever of 6,204 buses, including over 1,200 modern, low-floor AC buses. In mid-2011, Delhi initiated a unique experiment to privatize half of its bus fleet by getting private operators to run a cluster of public bus routes, popularly called the 'Cluster bus scheme'. But these measures failed to increase the fleet size, which reduced marginally to 6,118 buses by March 2015. With an ageing and an outdated fleet that comprised only 20 per cent AC buses, and a widespread perception of a lack of safety for women, the daily ridership of Delhi's public bus system declined to 42 lakh by 2016–17.[6] Winter pollution episodes further made it clear that the gains from an all-CNG fleet had plateaued.

There has been some debate on the question: how many buses does Delhi need? The Supreme Court, while directing the shift to CNG in 1998, had ordered the Delhi government to procure 10,000 buses by 2001. The Delhi High Court increased this target to 11,000 in 2007.[7] Subsequently, the Central government defined a service level benchmark of sixty buses per lakh population for cities, pegging Delhi's requirement at 9,600 buses as per the 2011 census and 10,800 buses as per Delhi's estimated population in 2015.

The Congress government preceding the AAP had failed to achieve the desired bus fleet size in its fifteen years, term, leaving Delhi with a shortfall of 40 per cent capacity in 2015. Making matters worse, the outgoing government had failed to place any new orders for buses before leaving office. Since Delhi was the only Indian city procuring CNG buses then, manufacturers supplied buses based on custom orders with a lead time of two to three years. Any attempt to increase Delhi's bus fleet, therefore, would bear results only after a few years. In addition, several manufacturers declined participating in AAP government's tenders as it mandated maintenance of the buses for twelve years, leading to repeated procurement failures. It was only towards the end of AAP's first term that these issues were ironed out and an aggressive roll-out plan for Delhi's public buses was put in place.

By mid-2024, Delhi's ageing fleet of CNG buses transitioned to a new, modern fleet of 7,683 buses, 25 per cent (1,970) of which were zero-emissions electric buses (e-buses). Accounting for 2,637 retiring buses scrapped between 2015 and 2024, a total of 4,202 buses were inducted by the AAP government in nine years, i.e. nearly 70 per cent of the capacity in 2015. By 2024, Delhi emerged as the city with the largest fleet of public buses in India, followed by Bengaluru with a fleet of 6,634 buses. With orders to manufacturers already placed, the total public bus fleet of Delhi is all set to reach 10,480 by 2025—nearly 80 per cent of which will be electric.

Along with a sizeable expansion in the fleet, Delhi's public bus system has seen five major transformations under the AAP government in the past decade that has taken it closer to the goal of establishing a world-class public bus system in the capital.

First, Delhi's aggressive focus on transitioning to e-buses within just five years is a feat that has few parallels globally. As of mid-2024, Delhi has 1,970 e-buses, the highest in India and third highest in the world in cities outside China and Chile.[8] Delhi's e-bus fleet will witness a massive four-fold expansion to 8,280 buses by end 2025 catapulting it to become the city with the largest e-bus fleet in the world outside China.

This transition wasn't trivial and came with its fair share of challenges. The first was financial. Electric buses are cheaper to run but twice as expensive as CNG buses in terms of their upfront cost, largely due to expensive batteries. A fleet of 8,280 e-buses meant investing over ₹3,000 crore annually or ₹36,000 crore over the twelve years, lifetime of buses.[9] The next challenge was upgrading the electricity infrastructure to enable overnight charging of buses. Delhi's 8,280 e-buses were estimated to increase Delhi's energy demand by 450 MW. Only careful planning would ensure no power outages or grid failures. A wide network of fifty-seven existing bus depots across Delhi were electrified, thirteen new bus depots built from scratch and the electricity grid upgraded—all at a cost of ₹1,500 crore. The other challenge was human. Thousands of staff in Delhi's public transport system, running only CNG buses, had to be retrained to run a fully e-bus fleet.[10]

Yet, all these challenges were surmounted due to Mr Kejriwal's firm commitment to fighting pollution by investing in a clean and green public transport. This was matched by years of careful planning and execution by Delhi's transport minister, Kailash Gahlot, and his team of officials in the transport department and DTC. While the spadework for this began as early as 2018, it was not until 2021 that Mr Gahlot made a bold public commitment on behalf of the AAP government that all its future bus procurements will only be e-buses.[11] Despite the air pollution crisis facing dozens of Indian cities, Delhi is alone in making such a bold pledge. By doing so, Delhi became the only Indian city to join a select league of cities such as London, Paris and Los Angeles driving the climate change agenda by committing a transition to zero-emissions public transport.

The next major transformation was modernizing the bus fleet to enhance passenger safety and convenience. To match the comfort and experience that a ride in the Delhi metro provided, the AAP government prioritized the purchase of low-floor, air-conditioned buses, which could appeal to people of all classes. The government was keen to shed the perception that DTC buses were meant to ferry only those who had no better option. By mid-2024, at least 50 per cent of Delhi's buses were low-floor and air-conditioned, as compared to only 20 per cent in 2015. This number is set to rise further to 90 per cent by 2026. Moreover, the large-scale induction of e-buses meant noiseless travel, drastically improving commuter experience. To tackle the concerns of women safety, all DTC and cluster buses were, for the first time, equipped with GPS devices, CCTV cameras and panic buttons, monitored real-time through a centralized command and control centre. By 2020, all Delhi buses had also become disabled-friendly, a first for any public bus fleet in India.

The third major transformation was the move to digital ticketing and a common mobility card. Most global cities have contactless smart cards that enable seamless travel across their public transport network—London has the Oyster card, Singapore has the EZ-link card and Boston has the Charlie card. While the Delhi metro had already adopted smart cards, they weren't valid in buses. The AAP government decided to adopt the same smart cards for all digital ticketing devices in Delhi's buses so that commuters could travel in any bus or metro using the same card. After two years of planning, the One Delhi card was launched in December 2018, making Delhi the first Indian city to have a common mobility card, valid across its entire public transport system.[12] Interestingly, the branding and design of the One Delhi card was a voluntary effort by a team of design professionals passionate about public transport.

The fourth key step was the launch of Delhi's first common mobility app, called the One Delhi mobile app in March 2019, catering to all the information needs of Delhi's commuters. The app had features such as journey planning in the bus or metro system, live tracking of buses, e-ticketing and locating the nearest EV charger. The app was developed in collaboration with the Centre for Sustainable Mobility at IIIT Delhi, a Delhi government university, and had been downloaded by over 15 lakh smartphone users by mid-2024. The AAP government took another unprecedented step, leveraging data to improve the public transport experience. Delhi's open transit data platform was launched in November 2018, providing open access to static and real-time transit data, so that developers and researchers can co-create innovative and inclusive public transport solutions for Delhi.[13] Over the years, some of the top institutions globally and in India including MapMyIndia, Google, Uber, IIT Madras, IIT Delhi and Harvard University have used Delhi government's open transit data.

Historically, most of Delhi's bus routes were created in an ad hoc manner without any scientific planning, resulting in poor service across most of the city. The AAP government in 2018 launched the Connect Delhi initiative, which sought to carry out a scientific route rationalization and last mile connectivity study along with public consultations to redesign Delhi's bus routes for better accessibility and reliable service. Conceptualized on successful models in Seoul and London, the Connect Delhi initiative aimed to ensure that 95 per cent of Delhi was connected to the public bus system within a 500-metre walk and a maximum fifteen-minute-waiting time from their homes or workplace. In 2015, only 50 per cent of Delhi met these service benchmarks.[14] The initiative also sought to address the issue of last mile connectivity from Delhi metro stations and major bus stops to residential areas, which for decades had been the Achilles heel of Delhi's public transport system. Based on study results, a pilot of the initiative launched in Najafgarh in January 2019 resulted in a 17 per cent increase in daily ridership in nine months.

An important outcome of the Connect Delhi initiative was a finding that smaller-sized buses were ideally placed to resolve Delhi's last mile connectivity issues. Being able to access narrow interior roads of residential areas, these buses would run in short circular routes under a 10-km length, connecting residential areas with all the nearby metro stations and local landmarks. Based on this finding, the AAP government announced an ambitious initiative called *mohalla* buses (neighbourhood buses) introducing smaller air-conditioned e-buses for the first time in Delhi. The first batch of mohalla buses started running in mid-2024 with the aim to induct over 2,000 mohalla buses by 2025.[15]

The AAP government's efforts to revamp Delhi's public bus system have started yielding results. Unlike the declining trend in public bus ridership across major Indian cities, Delhi has managed to maintain its average daily ridership at 42 lakh in 2023–24. The biggest challenge for Delhi's bus system continues to be its archaic route planning systems and disruptions caused by the rapid transition from CNG buses to e-buses. Once the transition is completed by 2025, and the Connect Delhi initiative implemented all across Delhi, bus ridership is expected to rise significantly.

In November 2023, Mr Kejriwal launched another progressive initiative, called app-based premium bus aggregator scheme, to encourage commuters to switch from using private vehicles for their daily commute to premium luxury buses, thereby cutting down on pollution.[16] Rather than being dogmatic about having the sole right to run intra-city bus services, defining their routes, pricing etc., the AAP government established a liberal regime that allows any number of private players to run premium luxury buses in Delhi-NCR, giving them the liberty to decide how many buses to run, on which routes and at what pricing based solely on market demand. The only restriction was that the bus operators had to book passenger rides in advance through their mobile apps. As the first such initiative by any government in India, the premium bus aggregator scheme has the potential to revolutionize city bus systems with the active participation of the private sector. The first set of buses under this scheme were launched in Delhi in mid-2024.[17]

The above initiatives show how the AAP government has ensured that the national capital makes giant strides towards building a world-class public transport system that is reliable, affordable and convenient to use by all sections of society.

For Women, Mobility Is Freedom

In June 2019, Chief Minister Kejriwal cleared the proposal to make bus and metro rides free for women in the national capital. An unprecedented move for any government around the world, it was also the most significant initiative by the AAP government to empower women in Delhi through free and unlimited access to the city's public transport system. While women who wished to avail free rides would be issued pink tickets, those who opted to pay, could do so.

A national debate immediately erupted on issues affecting safety and mobility of women in Indian cities. Many critics wondered whether such a policy was desirable at all. What motivated the AAP government was the status of women in India in general, and in Delhi in particular. The 2018 Global Gender Gap report by the World Economic Forum ranked India at 108 out of 149 countries. India's position has since only worsened, falling to 129 out of 146 countries in 2023. A survey by Thomson Reuters Foundation in 2017 ranked Delhi as the most unsafe megacity in the world for women. As per official data, crimes against women in Delhi had seen a phenomenal increase of 83 per cent between 2007 and 2016.[18] While there are a plethora of factors that contribute to this— ineffective policing, dark spots, unsafe modes of transport, social norms towards women, among others—there is hardly any talk of transformative solutions in policy circles.

The Delhi government's decision resolved an important element concerning women safety by making public transport the default mode of transport for Delhi's women. Experts across the globe vouch for the fact that public transport is the safest mode of travel—there's safety in numbers. In Delhi, a large fraction of women from poor and lower middle classes, often living at the margins of existence, are constrained to walk long distances or use unsafe modes of transport, since they cannot afford buying a bus ticket. The metro is not even an option for most of them. By providing unrestricted access to public transport, the Delhi government's decision provided women an opportunity to reclaim public spaces.

Besides enhancing safety, the policy also had a direct impact on women's economic empowerment by significantly improving their access to education and job opportunities. A 2019 study by the Sustainable Urban Transport Project (SUTP), and supported by the Government of India, showed that women forgo opportunities to work outside their neighbourhoods if they perceive transport fares and services to be expensive and unreliable. A 2017 study by Girija Borker, a World Bank economist, covering 4,000 students in Delhi colleges showed that female students were willing to choose a lower ranking college, travel longer and spend much more than men, in order to travel safely.

These findings become important since India is among the few countries globally to see decreasing participation of women in the workforce in the first two decades of this century, despite stellar economic growth.[19] In Delhi, women account for a dismal 11 per cent of the workforce—perhaps the lowest among Indian cities. It was clear to the government that sustained growth in Delhi's economy will remain a pipe dream if the constraints faced by 50 per cent of its population were ignored.

The second critique of the decision was that of financial sustainability and whether this money could be better used in strengthening public transport services. For the AAP government though, this was never an either-or question. The fiscal space created by substantially increasing Delhi's budget over its first term from ₹30,900 crore to ₹51,200 crore meant higher investments for targeted initiatives that improve the productive capacity of Delhi's people—be that building world class government schools and mohalla clinics or offering free rides to women. This was yet another example of the AAP government's trickle-up model that believed in building its economy bottom-up.

Before it could be launched, the initiative ran into fierce resistance from the Central government, which shot down the inclusion of the Delhi metro, despite assurances that the AAP government would bear the entire subsidy burden. Delhi's bureaucracy also resisted introducing this scheme for all women with the finance department recommending restricting the scheme only to women from economically weaker sections (EWS). But Mr Kejriwal knew what that meant—condemning the poorest women in Delhi to carrying papers all the time. It would also exclude many other women who faced constraints on their mobility. Eventually, the Centre stood its ground whereas Delhi's bureaucracy relented. India's first gender-specific free bus ride scheme was rolled out in October 2019.

The last 24 hours before the scheme's much publicized launch witnessed tense moments and drama. Delhi has a peculiar governance system where bureaucrats often use their discretion to determine if a new initiative can be launched with the approval of the elected government alone, or if the Delhi Lt. Governor's (L-G) approval is also necessary. Officials in Delhi's transport department had finalized the notification of the scheme the evening before launch day. At the very last minute though, some official took a view that legal opinion was necessary whether the file should be sent for L-G's approval or not—an exercise that would put off the scheme's implementation by a week at least. Without informing their Minister, Kailash Gahlot, they shut their offices and left for home without issuing the notification.

When Mr Gahlot learned about it, he was livid. The Delhi government had already announced the launch date and calling it off the last minute would be a huge embarrassment. He immediately summoned the top officials of the transport department from their homes to his office, while getting the offices of the transport department unlocked to retrieve the file. He then summoned the Delhi government's standing counsel from Gurgaon to his office, who reached by 8 pm. It helped that Gahlot was also the Law Minister of Delhi and before that, a practicing advocate in Delhi's High Court and Supreme Court for 16 years. Over the next three hours, the standing counsel gave his formal legal opinion and, together with Mr Gahlot, convinced the officials that the L-G's approval wasn't necessary. Finally, all the officials signed off and the scheme's notification was released at 11 pm.

The initiative proved to be a huge hit right away. Several media reports suggested that women using buses ending up saving ₹1,500 to ₹3,000 per month and felt safe traveling in buses now.[20] In the few months after its rollout, the bus ridership of women went up by 33 per cent, translating to 5 lakh extra trips by women per day and 1.5 crore extra trips every month. By May 2024, over 170 crore pink tickets had been issued by Delhi's buses. In February 2024, the AAP government extended this initiative to include transgenders as well.

When Mr Kejriwal was asked at an interview in 2020, how he would finance the free rides, he said, 'The chief minister of a state (Gujarat) bought a private jet for himself for ₹191 crore. I didn't buy a plane and instead made travel free for my sisters.'[21] The cost of implementing the scheme was ₹145 crore in 2019–20. Kejriwal's response highlighted a much ignored fact about government budgets in India— there's plenty of room to launch innovative welfare schemes for people if there is commitment to cut back on humongous amounts of wasteful expenditure.

An independent study published in 2023 by researchers from Ashoka University and Shiv Nadar University evaluated Delhi's pink ticket scheme and found that it led to a 24 per cent increase in paid work and employment for women, who were from the marginalized sections of society and therefore most likely to gain from affordable public transport.[22] The study also suggests that a universal policy like the pink bus ticket scheme that does not differentiate among end-beneficiaries, is more efficient even if the marginalized section benefits the most.

Apart from free bus rides, the AAP government also appointed bus marshals in each bus to make the public bus system safer for women. While the government was already investing in CCTV cameras and panic buttons in all buses, posting law enforcement personnel inside buses signalled an immediate response mechanism to ward off unruly elements. In 2015, the AAP government launched a pilot initiative, appointing civil defence volunteers and home guards, all wearing khaki uniforms, as bus marshals. By 2019, over 3,300 bus marshals had been appointed, covering half of the bus fleet in one of the two shifts. Based on a performance evaluation of the programme by the DDC, a decision was taken to appoint another 13,000 bus marshals covering every public bus in every shift.[23] Delhi's bus marshal programme is the largest of its kind initiative in India to secure the safety of women in public transport.

These initiatives show that much can be done to strengthen women's safety and promote their greater participation in the workforce in Indian cities by challenging the status quo approaches, even as we continue to work towards strengthening policing and other levers of women empowerment.

Delhi Emerges as India's EV Capital

While the AAP government was taking rapid strides in strengthening Delhi's public transport system, much of the pollution-related gains were being nullified by the increase in private vehicles. The number of registered vehicles in Delhi have increased four times in the past two decades—from 34 lakh in 2000 to nearly 1.4 crore by 2023. In 2023–24, nearly 4 lakh two-wheelers and 2 lakh cars were registered in Delhi. It's clear that any sustainable strategy to cut back on vehicular pollution will have to focus on upgrading the public transport system while also transitioning the burgeoning fleet of private and commercial vehicles to zero-emission EVs.

The national push towards EVs started with the launch of the National Electric Mobility Mission Plan by the UPA government in 2013 followed by the Faster Adoption and Manufacturing of Hybrid and Electric Vehicles (FAME) India scheme launched by the NDA government in 2015. Yet the share of EVs among new vehicle registrations was a paltry 0.8 per cent nationally in 2019–20.

The AAP government made an early push towards promoting EVs by announcing India's first subsidy programme for e-rickshaws in 2015. Besides promoting clean mobility, the government realized e-rickshaws also solve the last mile connectivity problem while providing livelihoods. A subsidy of ₹15,000 per newly registered e-rickshaw was announced in 2015, which was increased to ₹30,000 in 2016. As a result, in 2019–20, EVs accounted for 3.9 per cent of new vehicle registrations in Delhi, of which e-rickshaws and e-carts (e-rickshaws modified as freight vehicles) accounted for 94 per cent. But the share of other electric vehicles, particularly two-wheelers (0.2%) and cars (0.5%) that jointly accounted for 92 per cent of all new vehicles registered, remained miniscule.

All this changed when the AAP government rolled out the most ambitious EV policy by any Indian state in 2020. The Delhi EV policy was framed with the singular goal of reducing air pollution in the national capital; everything else in the policy was made subservient to this goal.[24] The policy was the outcome of a year-long consultation led by the DDC with citizens, experts and industry stakeholders across India.

The Delhi EV policy 2020 was unique in three distinct ways. It was the first policy nationally to declare an upfront target of ensuring 25 per cent of all newly registered vehicles in Delhi be electric by 2024. Starting from a base of 3.9 per cent in 2019–20, many considered Delhi's aspiration to achieve a 25 per cent share of EVs as 'too ambitious'; yet the government committed itself to the target.

Second, national and state-level EV policies in India typically pursued a supply-side approach with an excessive focus on attracting investments for EV manufacturing by giving generous incentives to industry. Even the Central government's FAME India scheme shows this bias, as it is implemented by the Union Ministry of Heavy Industries rather than the transport or environment ministry. Delhi's EV policy, implemented by its transport department, was the first state policy to pursue a demand-side approach, focusing entirely on generating demand for EVs among the masses. This was yet another instance of AAP's trickle-up economic model in action, where it chose to put money into the pockets of EV buyers rather than give tax incentives or waivers to industry to manufacture more EVs.

Third, Delhi's EV policy leveraged local source apportionment data for air pollution to scientifically target financial and non-financial incentives at vehicle segments that contributed the most towards Delhi's pollution—two and three-wheelers constituting nearly 70 per cent of vehicles on Delhi's streets.

Such was the effectiveness of Delhi's EV policy that within three years of implementation, Delhi emerged as the undisputed EV capital of India. In 2023–24, the share of EVs among newly registered vehicles in Delhi reached 12 per cent—the highest for any Indian state and twice that of the national average of 6 per cent in 2023.[25] In December 2023, Delhi's EV penetration reached 20 per cent—a national milestone.[26] Anyone living or visiting Delhi can attest to the fact that rarely do a few minutes go by without a vehicle with a green vehicle registration plate going by.

The scale of Delhi's EV revolution becomes clearer when you look at the absolute number of electric vehicles sold. In 2019–20, 954 electric two-wheelers were sold in Delhi. In 2023–24, that number crossed 38,000—a staggering jump of 40 times! In 2019–20, 780 electric cars (private and commercial) were sold in Delhi. In 2023–24, that number crossed 8,800—a jump by 11 times. In 2023–24, EVs constituted over 70 per cent of all three-wheeler freight vehicles sold in Delhi and 38 per cent of all taxis sold in Delhi (See Table 4).[27] Just Delhi accounted for more than 50 per cent of all electric taxis sold in India in 2023. In the first three years of Delhi's EV policy, over 1,35,000 EVs were sold in Delhi; 89 per cent of these sales happened in the two targeted segments—two and three wheelers, a clear indicator of the policy's success.

So, what did Delhi do differently as compared to other states? Delhi managed to turn the tide on EVs by demonstrating a firm political will to address the three key barriers that have plagued the adoption of EVs across India.

First is the high upfront cost of EVs. Even after factoring in the subsidies given to EV manufacturers by the Central government, there is a wide gap between the upfront cost of petrol/diesel vehicles and comparable models of EVs. This is why the AAP government decided to give generous subsidies to consumers for EVs as compared to other states. Delhi also became the first state to fully exempt road tax and registration fees for all EVs. Further, the eligibility criteria to determine which vehicle models could receive subsidy were broadened. For example, in 2020, the Centre gave subsidy only to EVs with fixed batteries even as new models with swappable batteries were being introduced by manufacturers to reduce upfront costs. Recognizing this as a technological innovation, Delhi became the first state in 2020 to offer the same subsidy to battery swapping models of EVs, a practice that was adopted by the Centre and several states many years later.

Table 4: Segment wise sales of electric and non-electric vehicles in Delhi: 2019–20 vs 2023–24

	All Vehicles		Only Electric		EV Penetration	
	2019-20	2023-24	2019-20	2023-24	2019-20	2023-24
Two Wheeler	4,03,841	4,07,748	954	38,120	0.2%	9%
Three–Wheeler Passenger	5,150	3,556	0	433	0%	12%
Three-wheeler Goods	2,456	11,672	2,456	8,547	0%	73%
E-rickshaw	19,710	18,891	19,710	18,887	100%	100%
E-cart	2,229	2,153	2,229	2,153	100%	100%
Four–Wheeler Private	1,45,923	1,96,509	208	5,923	0.1%	3%
Four–Wheeler Commercial Cab	7,041	7,663	572	2,921	8%	38%
Four-Wheeler Goods	19,373	18,713	0	464	0%	2%
Bus	1,565	2,292	1	1,327	0%	58%

Source: Transport Department, Government of NCT of Delhi.

Announcing generous subsidies is one thing, but making sure citizens can avail it in a time-bound, hassle-free manner is more consequential. To ensure this, the AAP government put in place a cloud-based IT application for transfer of subsidies directly to the buyer's Aadhaar-linked bank account within seven days of an EV purchase. The entire process was managed by the dealer with no hassles or paperwork required from the buyer. A real-time dashboard was created to monitor subsidy payment pendency and avoid delays. In the first three years of the policy, the AAP government disbursed ₹180 crore in incentives to EV buyers, while incurring an additional cost of ₹246 crore as foregone road tax and registration fees.

The second barrier is the unavailability of charging infrastructure. Under the Delhi EV policy, the AAP government had promised to create public charging infrastructure within a 3-km distance from anywhere in Delhi. By mid-2023, over 4,600 EV charging points and battery swapping stations were set up, which is not only the highest for any state in India but also constitutes 30 per cent of all charging points nationally. As per the Central Electricity Authority, Delhi accounted for 55 per cent of the power consumed at EV charging points across the country in 2023.[28]

Delhi's success in rapidly setting up charging infrastructure was built on the back of several innovations, some of which deserve special mention. In November 2021, the AAP government launched India's first single-window facility to enable citizens to install EV chargers faster (within seven days) and cheaper (under ₹2,500 for a slow charger) than anywhere else in India. Under this facility, any consumer could call their local Discom helpline or visit its website for installing an EV charger after selecting from a range of chargers across a list of approved vendors at pre-negotiated prices. By March 2024, over 1,900 chargers were installed in Delhi through the single window facility. Delhi also introduced several regulatory changes, such as the provision of a highly subsidised EV charging tariff that was among the lowest in India.

In early 2022, Delhi became the first Indian state to implement a unique public-private partnership (PPP) model for creating a citywide network of public charging stations. Under the model, the government provided the land at prime locations (metro stations, bus terminals etc.,) at subsidized lease rates and bore the cost for upgrading the upstream electrical infrastructure, while private players took the lead in setting up the EV charging stations and running them for seven years. The bidding criteria was kept as the service fee to be charged to the end consumer over and above the EV tariff charged by the Discom—a unique procurement innovation in India. The model was hugely successful with the government receiving negative bids for service fees, i.e. bidders were ready to subsidize EV charging for consumers to get a share of Delhi's EV market. Delhi citizens can today charge their EVs at these public charging stations at just ₹3 per unit, perhaps the *cheapest in the world*.[29] This translates to mind-boggling last mile travel economics. An electric two-wheeler in Delhi will incur only 7 paise to travel a kilometre as compared to around ₹3 per kilometre for a petrol two-wheeler—a saving of 97 per cent! A 100 such charging stations, with around 900 charging points and 103 battery-swapping stations are being setup across Delhi through this PPP model.

The third barrier that was overcome in Delhi's EV transition was pre-empting resistance from stakeholders—be it ordinary residents or business owners or those in the transport industry—by adopting a collaborative approach to policy design and implementation. From the very initial stages of policy formulation, dialogue and discussion formed the bedrock of Delhi's EV policy. After policy launch, the Delhi EV Forum was set up under the aegis of the DDC that brought together over 200 stakeholders in Delhi's EV ecosystem every six months to assess and provide feedback for effective policy implementation. This approach ensured that the successful transition to EVs was not just the government's vision, but a common mission. Many of the innovations that came about in Delhi, such as the single-window facility for installing private EV chargers or the PPP model for setting up public chargers at the lowest tariffs in the world, were a result of discussions in the Delhi EV Forum.

While Delhi's journey to transition to EVs has gotten off to a good start, the bigger challenge would be to sustain this momentum and ensure an ever-increasing share of EVs in coming years. This is where the role of mandates comes in. Delhi's big shift to CNG-powered commercial vehicles happened in the late 1990s because of a Supreme Court mandate.

However, the AAP government did not wait for court strictures to mandate a shift to EVs. In November 2023, after almost two years of public consultations, the Delhi Motor Vehicle Aggregator and Delivery Service Provider scheme was notified under the Motor Vehicles Act, 1988, making Delhi the first and the only state/UT in India date to legally mandate the transition of commercial vehicles to EVs.[30] Delhi's policy specifically mandated the entire fleet of vehicles with cab aggregators (e.g. Ola, Uber), delivery service platforms (e.g. Zomato, Swiggy) and e-commerce aggregator platforms (e.g. Amazon, Flipkart) to transition to EVs laying out yearly targets for transition and imposing harsh penalties for deviations. The policy set out a deadline of four to five years for different categories of new passenger and commercial vehicles to be only EVs, and an outer deadline of 1 April 2030 by which the entire fleet of commercial vehicles—old and new—would be only EVs. The policy also legalized the operation of bike taxis in Delhi provided they were EVs. In what was a testament to the government's consultative approach in rolling out this progressive reform, over a lakh vehicles of twenty-one different cab aggregators, delivery service providers and e-commerce companies registered under the scheme by mid-2024.[31]

The remarkable success of Delhi's EV policy has not only kick-started Delhi's and India's EV revolution but also made the dream of an all-electric future seem real—something that was inconceivable just four years back.

Building Delhi's Roads on International Standards

Roads in Indian cities are a reflection of our governance. The perennially worn-out, pothole- ridden roads reflect the indifference and endemic corruption in our governments where construction projects are often given to favoured contractors who build poor quality roads that wear out quickly so that a new project can be initiated again. Just like our governments that are beholden to vested interests, our roads too are designed primarily for cars with little thought spared for other users, especially pedestrians, cyclists and the specially-abled. Finally, the state of our traffic and lack of road safety reflects severely deficient planning and design standards.

While the well-planned streets of Lutyens Delhi are often hailed as the symbol of Delhi's road infrastructure, only a small fraction of Delhi's residents use these streets, with the majority depending on the arterial road network of 1,400 km (streets with a width of 60 meters or above) managed by the Delhi government's Public Works Department (PWD). Like the main or arterial roads in most Indian cities, the PWD roads suffered from a host of issues. Construction quality was poor since projects were typically broken into small contracts to be given out to local contractors. Lane markings and footpaths were either absent or present with no uniformity. Needs of all road users apart from cars and bigger vehicles were largely ignored. There was little attention given to design and planning of street furniture (e.g. garbage bins, benches, signages, street lights etc.,) or to cover road edges that contributed heavily to dust pollution. Further, the number as well as the width of lanes on a single road stretch often varied based on available space, creating traffic bottlenecks.

Within a year of coming to office, Mr Kejriwal decided to initiate a complete redesign of PWD roads based on European standards. In his second budget speech in March 2016, the former deputy chief minister Manish Sisodia announced the AAP government's plans to redesign eleven road stretches as a pilot project 'to promote public transport, cycling and making streets friendly for pedestrians and physically challenged people.'[32] Mr Sisodia also announced the government's intention to extend this to all PWD roads based on the results of the pilot.

The primary objective here was to address the multitude of functionality issues arising from the flawed design of existing roads that focused on moving vehicles, not people. By stressing on walkable and cyclable streets for citizens of all ages including the specially-abled, the government embraced principles of sustainable mobility. The second objective was to enhance the public character of Delhi's streets by beautifying them to international standards, which entailed installing creatively designed street furniture, functional signages and greening of all open surfaces to prevent road dust. Delhi is viewed by international visitors as a window into India, and the AAP government was determined to ensure that the national capital passes muster. Achieving both the above goals would have a substantial impact on Delhi's pollution too.

In effect, the AAP government was attempting to build what urban planners call 'complete streets'—a street which is safe, comfortable and convenient for all users and activities. Few cities in India had attempted designing complete streets in the past decade —Bengaluru (Tender SURE project), Pune (Complete streets project) and Chennai (Street redesign project) being the exceptions completing around 70 km each with a focus on city centres. This was going to be Delhi's first attempt at building complete streets, and the largest such initiative taken up in India if scaled to all PWD streets.

Turning this dream to reality turned out to be far more challenging than anticipated because of the mindset of PWD engineers and the lack of adequately trained professionals who could be hired to deliver upon the vision. After a few

short trials, the first set of nine pilot projects were awarded in
October 2019, followed by another seven road stretches soon
after, taking the total to sixteen pilot road stretches spanning
38 kilometres that would provide a glimpse of Delhi's streets
in the future. Announcing the launch of the pilot, Mr Kejriwal
spoke of his vision for redesigning and beautifying Delhi's
roads as per European standards emphasizing especially on
road safety, meeting the needs of all road users and ensuring
smooth traffic flow through uniformly designed lanes.[33]

Delayed due to the Covid-19 pandemic, the sixteen pilot
stretches were completed only by early 2023. These newly
transformed streets received tremendous public response—
with hordes showing up on these streets for fun and leisure
along with their families. The AAP government laid a
special emphasis on placemaking, installing varied modern
sculptures, steel structures, sandstone benches, fountains and
innovative street furniture along the streets that were in tune
with the cultural ethos of Delhi. With the pilot successful, the
AAP government took its next big leap in March 2023 by
announcing the scale-up of the street redesign project to cover
1,400 km of PWD roads in Delhi.

Designed on an unprecedented scale, the project was
conceptualized with three main components.[34] Under the first
component, the roads would be redesigned to fix lane width
inconsistencies, black topped to fix potholes and broken
roads, while lane markings were applied as per prevailing
national standards. The government made the construction
agency doing the initial upgradation in-charge of maintaining
the road for ten years to ensure accountability and quality
work. Under the second component, footpaths alongside the
1,400 km roads and the central verge would be completely
redesigned, obstructions to pedestrians and encroachments
removed and all open surfaces covered by plantations. The
third component emphasized regular upkeep of the roads by
mandating regular washing and mechanized sweeping of the
entire network of 1,400 km of roads.

The AAP government budgeted a whopping ₹19,500 crore over a ten-year duration for this mega project, showing its commitment to investing in large infrastructure projects that directly impact the quality of life and daily commute of Delhi residents.[35] As of mid-2024, the project was yet to hit the ground, stalled by the crisis that enveloped the Delhi government after the L-G wrested control of Delhi's bureaucracy away from the elected government. We will visit this further in the final chapter.

A Vision for Sustainable and Inclusive Mobility

The divide between India and Bharat is apparent in the manner in which our governments treat citizens when delivering essential public services. Often this divide is portrayed as an urban–rural divide, but the truth is that the divide shows up as starkly as to how different socio-economic groups experience governance within urban areas. There is no better example than urban transport systems.

Most governments in India love to extol the virtues of a robust public transport system. But scratch the surface and you see their love limited to shiny, expensive metro rail systems while the public buses that carry the masses continue to deteriorate. Mention transport infrastructure and politicians rattle off the length of roads or national highways or flyovers built for motorists, but they are mum on complete streets or obstruction-free footpaths or cycling tracks that the masses use to commute.

The AAP government's approach over the past decade has been to develop Delhi's transportation system in a manner 'where public space is distributed equitably rather than it being privileged for the privileged.'[36] As the national capital, Delhi has been fortunate to see massive investments in its road and public transport networks over several decades, yet the AAP government can be credited to have a charted a unique path towards the vision of sustainable and inclusive mobility that holds important lessons for Indian cities.

First, our city governments need to prioritize investments for public transport systems that can serve the commuting needs of its people. For far too long, roads and flyovers have dominated any spending on transport infrastructure with the result that personal vehicles have grown exponentially while underfunded pubic transport systems have witnessed steady erosion in ridership. This has been the primary cause behind increasing congestion and pollution in our cities. India invests only 1.7 per cent of its GDP in public transportation, significantly lower than China at 5.5 per cent.[37] Even when our cities do invest in public transport, the default spending is on metro rail systems. Metro systems are now operating in thirteen cities and twenty-nine more are either under construction or at the planning stage. A study by researchers at IIT Delhi shows that most of the metro systems are running at less than 15 per cent of the projected ridership, some even less than 10 per cent. Neither do enough people benefit, nor are operations financially sustainable. Delhi had the highest ridership among all metro systems.[38]

On the other hand, public buses that have for decades formed the backbone of public transport systems in Indian cities have seen either static or falling fleet sizes in major Indian cities. A 2019 report by the Ministry of Housing and Urban Affairs found that there were around 66,000 public buses in India, as against the required number of 1,88,500 (based on 2011 census figures).[39] Based on the same 2011 census figures, only Bengaluru meets the norm of at least sixty buses per lakh population followed by Delhi, with several major cities (Mumbai, Pune, Kolkata) falling short by more than half (Figure 12).[40] A 2022 study found that only twenty Indian cities had state-run bus services.[41] Globally, public bus systems are valued for their flexibility—they can go to any nook and corner—and affordability since they cost a fraction of metro systems. As a result, the majority of the public transport ridership happens in buses, even in cities like London. In contrast, most Indian cities that have bus systems have seen a falling ridership pattern due to lack of adequate investments leading to unreliable services.

Over the past decade, the AAP government in Delhi has prioritized the expansion of both the metro and the bus systems to meet the needs of all commuters. In addition, it initiated a massive modernization plan to ensure Delhi's public buses offer a safe, reliable and convenient experience to all commuters at par with the Delhi metro. Driven by the vision for sustainable zero-emissions public transport, it also initiated a transition plan from CNG to e-buses that will see Delhi's e-bus fleet go from zero to over 8,000 within four years—a feat that has few parallels globally. This has happened only because the Kejriwal government displayed the political will to make unprecedented investments in public transport, treating it as an essential public service, akin to education or health that can connect the most vulnerable populations to jobs and opportunities.

Figure 12: Buses per lakh population

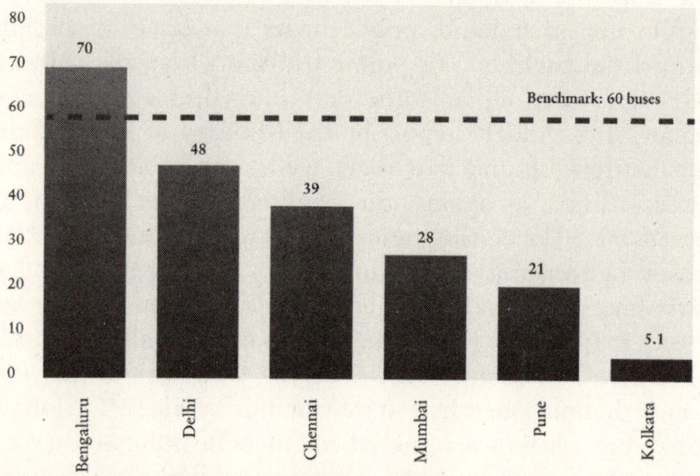

Source: Analysis by Omkar Khandekar for The Morning Context

For instance, the AAP government has spent ₹1,500 crore just to electrify Delhi's seventy bus depots, and committed to spending ₹36,000 crore over the twelve years lifetime of the 8,000 e-buses that will be onboarded by 2025. In contrast, the Central government's most ambitious imitative for promotion of electric vehicles, the FAME scheme, spent approximately ₹2,300 crore over five years (2019–24) to partially subsidize 4,600 e-buses all over India. The contrast in ambition couldn't be more glaring.

The second lesson from Delhi's journey is that transport systems do not become inclusive unless governments design policies for it and actively promote it. Delhi's pink ticket scheme ignited a massive national debate and criticism when it was launched in 2019. Yet, the scheme has been transformational for Delhi's women, with studies finding that women from the most marginalized sections of society experienced significant increases in employment. The scheme is now widely accepted and has been replicated by several states. Globally too, a huge movement has begun with over 100 cities, especially in Europe, making public transport entirely free for its citizens.[42] To keep Delhi's public transport system inclusive and accessible to the most vulnerable populations, the AAP government retained highly subsidized bus fares for the past fifteen years and strongly resisted the doubling of Delhi metro fares in 2018.

Most governments in India, including the BJP-ruled Centre that blocked the AAP government's proposal to subsidize metro rides for women, hesitate in subsidizing public transport. This is due to the flawed economic belief that public transport systems need to be financially sustainable. The proponents of this theory often ignore the contribution that the masses traveling in public transport make to the urban economy as well as its effects on reducing congestion and air pollution. In a paper published in the *American Economic Review* in 2009, researchers developed a mass transit pricing model for twenty US cities factoring in the welfare effects of congestion, pollution and lower accidents. Their results support the efficiency of large fare subsidies starting at 50 per cent of operating costs.[43] In yet another study, researchers examined transit subsidies in London and Santiago. Their advice to policymakers: if you care for equity, then you should put into place subsidies as this will do the most to help the poor and redistribute incomes, compared to the alternatives.[44]

The third lesson that Indian cities need to heed is that a commitment to sustainable mobility means building infrastructure that gives equal priority to the needs of non-motorized vehicles, particularly cyclists and pedestrians. The 2011 Census, though old, shows that 36 per cent Indians either walk or cycle to work while only 16 per cent use private vehicles.[45] Yet, much of our road infrastructure is designed keeping the needs of motorists in mind. As a result, people who prefer to walk or cycle are forced to commute by private vehicles. The AAP government's experiences with road redesign projects, though at early stages, shows that this transition won't be easy and will be met with stiff internal resistance. Yet, each city will need to start its journey towards democratizing public spaces and learn its own lessons along the way, just as Bengaluru, Chennai, Pune and now, Delhi, have.

The fourth lesson is that it is possible to make a permanent dent on vehicular pollution by initiating a mass shift towards EVs. Back in 2020, before the launch of the Delhi EV policy, EVs were viewed as too futuristic a technology for India barring exceptions, such as e-rickshaws. Many cities were in the same bracket as Delhi in terms of EV adoption. Delhi's emergence as India's EV capital over a span of just three years shows that state-level EV policies that offer carefully targeted financial and non-financial incentives, coupled with innovative models to rapidly set up public charging infrastructure, will play a crucial role in catalysing EV adoption in Indian cities. Here too, the AAP government's willingness to allocate substantial budgets (over ₹400 crore) towards this vision and backing it with diligent implementation over the years was crucial in achieving success. In contrast, as of mid-2024, most Indian states, barring a couple, either hadn't notified their EV policies or had lapsed policies showing either the lack of intent or resources to aggressively pursue EV transition plans.

The AAP government's efforts in reimagining Delhi's transport system have shown the extent of change that is possible within a decade if governments are willing to prioritize investments in building efficient transport systems based on the vision of sustainable and inclusive mobility.

Chapter 6

Electricity

From Crisis to Win-Win

In the early nineties as the Indian economy opened up, there were demands for private sector participation in the delivery of essential public services, such as electricity and water. Five decades after Independence, state-run public utilities were ridden with endemic corruption, incurring heavy losses year-on-year while providing poor service. Privatization was expected to deliver better customer service, operational efficiency and financial sustainability. But it came with a new set of challenges. Privatization of utilities in India has typically followed one of two trajectories.

One, where privatization led to improved efficiencies in running of state utilities but led to exorbitant tariffs. For example, Mumbai's private electricity distribution companies (called Discoms) have brought down transmission losses to under 5 per cent, among the lowest in India. At the same time, domestic electricity bills in Mumbai have risen by 127 per cent in the decade after 2014 and are among the highest in India. Second, where state governments prevented tariff increases. This meant a financial crisis for private Discoms, decay in infrastructure and poor service to consumers. Odisha, the first state to privatize its Discoms in the late 1990s, went on this journey; the privatization experiment failed and by 2015 distribution licenses were cancelled.

Over the past decade, the AAP government in Delhi rejected both these beaten paths and created a unique model in the power sector nationally that is both people and business friendly. Today, Delhi enjoys the lowest tariffs in India and its private Discoms have turned a profit while providing 24/7 power supply with among the lowest transmission losses, also referred to as aggregate technical and commercial (AT&C) losses, in the country.

But all wasn't well when the AAP government came to power in 2015. Delhi had already privatized electricity distribution in 2002 as its state utility, Delhi Vidyut Board (DVB), suffered from huge financial losses, long power outages and over 50 per cent AT&C losses. Delhi's distribution system was carved out into distinct territories and licensed to three private distribution companies for a period of twenty-five years—Tata Power Delhi Distribution Limited (TPDDL), BSES Rajdhani Power Limited (BRPL) and BSES Yamuna Power Ltd (BYPL). The government owned a 49 per cent stake in these Discoms, while the majority stake was held by private companies. An independent electricity regulator—Delhi Electricity Regulatory Commission (DERC)—was created to set tariffs without any political pressure as required under the Electricity Act 2003. By 2014 Delhi's private Discoms managed to bring down the AT&C losses substantially to 16 per cent.

Yet, several crises loomed over Delhi's power sector in the years leading up to 2015. Delhi had witnessed runaway hikes in power tariffs for several years in a row, creating widespread discontent amongst the lower and middle classes. Between 2011 and 2014, Delhi's power tariffs were hiked by over 100 per cent, making it unaffordable for many to pay their bills. For instance, Bana Ram, a labourer living in a modest two-room house with six family members in a slum-like area in south Delhi received an electricity bill of ₹15,116 for two months in October 2012, which was his salary for two months.[1] Unable to pay, his power supply was promptly disconnected.

Despite runaway tariff hikes, Delhi's Discoms had amassed huge losses and were on the verge of bankruptcy. In December 2011, the then Congress government was forced to announce a ₹500-crore bailout package for BSES discoms.[2] In February 2014, the Discoms once again threatened to push half the city into darkness, citing their inability to pay for power purchase even for a single day. The situation was averted after the Supreme Court's intervention.[3] Due to their precarious financial condition, the Discoms had stopped making additional investments into the distribution system for many years. With Delhi's energy demand rising every year, instances of old transformers blowing out, and power outages, shot up. The summer of 2014 saw most of Delhi reeling from intense heat with four to five hours of power cuts for several months.[4] Almost every household and business in Delhi that could afford it, invested in inverters or diesel generators, to make up for the inefficiency of the distribution system.

Reforming the power sector was a litmus test for the Kejriwal government. In fact, it was the issue of unaffordable power tariffs that had propelled AAP to the centre stage of Delhi politics. Within months of the party's establishment, Mr Kejriwal decided this was an issue that affected every household in Delhi. Based on documents he had accessed, he alleged that Delhi's high power tariffs were due to a nexus between the Discoms and the Congress government, which failed to scrutinize the false claims of piling financial losses made by Discoms to demand higher revenues.[5] With AT&C losses in Delhi having reduced substantially since 2002, Mr Kejriwal argued that the Discoms were making substantial profits but under-reporting it. In October 2012, he launched a citywide protest against inflated power bills by climbing up the electricity pole and restoring the connection of the labourer, Bana Ram. In March 2013, Mr Kejriwal sat on a fifteen-day fast demanding a tariff reduction, which caught the imagination of Delhi's aam aadmi. Having been elected with a resounding mandate in 2015, it was time to walk the talk.

Over the past decade, not only has the AAP government managed to avert Delhi's power sector crisis, but has also created a unique model unprecedented across India. Delhi is today the only state in India to see zero tariff hikes since 2015. Even better, it has actually seen a reduction in tariffs over this period for all categories of consumers—residential, commercial and industrial. In 2024, Delhi's residential consumers had to pay a 25 per cent lower tariff at the two lowest consumption slabs (0–200 units and 200–400 units) as compared to 2014. Small commercial establishments such as *kirana* stores were billed at a 32 per cent lower slab in 2024 as compared to 2014.

The AAP government reined-in power tariffs and also rolled out India's largest electricity subsidy scheme for domestic consumers, providing free power of up to 200 units every month targeting the poorest households, apart from a 50 per cent subsidy to those consuming between 200 and 400 units. As a result of both these steps, Delhi today offers the cheapest electricity across all Indian cities. As of mid-2024, a family consuming 400 units per month would pay ₹985 in Delhi, a quarter of what it would pay in Mumbai (₹4,463), or a third of what it would pay in Bengaluru (₹3,096) or less than half of what it would pay in Chennai (₹2,385).

The financial health of the Discoms improved significantly over the first term of the AAP government itself. Since electricity distribution is a regulated business, the main concern for any private Discom is whether the revenues collected from consumers as per tariff structure are enough to cover their expenses, including a reasonable return on investment. Revenue gap, if any, would accumulate as regulatory assets (RAs) i.e. dues owed by the consumers to Discoms to be recovered in future. As Mr Kejriwal said, when the AAP government came to power in 2015, it 'inherited a system plagued by years of corruption, incentivised inefficiency and large-scale over-reporting of losses. Delhi's Discoms reported RAs of ₹11,406 crore in 2014–15, which served as the basis of steep tariff hikes year after year'.[6] The combined RAs of

Discoms were only ₹937 crore in 2007–08. From 2009–10 to 2014–15, Delhi's Discoms registered a revenue gap every single year. However, for each year during the first term of the AAP government, Delhi Discoms registered a revenue surplus. For the first time, the Discoms were no longer short on cash. By 2020, the combined RAs of Discoms had reduced to ₹9,063 crore, a drop of nearly ₹2,400 crore in five years.[7]

The operational performance of the Discoms improved considerably too. To rid the national capital from power outages, a massive infrastructure overhaul was initiated resulting in a 43 per cent increase in distribution transformer capacity. This led to a steep reduction in AT&C losses from 16 per cent in 2014 to 6 per cent in 2024—among the lowest in India. To make the Discoms accountable for providing uninterrupted power supply, the government imposed a penalty to be paid by the Discoms to every consumer for every unscheduled power cut—a first for any state in India. However, this policy was struck down by the courts. Nevertheless, the government's efforts resulted in a drastic 92 per cent reduction in load shedding between 2014–15 and 2022–23. Within five years, the capital started experiencing 24/7 power supply even at peak summer. The largest pan-India survey on the state of power supply in 2020 found Delhi to be the leading state providing 24/7 power supply, followed by Kerala and Gujarat. The 2022–23 Consumer Service Ratings released by the Power Ministry gave all three Delhi's Discoms the top A+ rating—the top three among sixty-two Discoms in India.[8]

A significant feature of the Delhi model in the power sector has been the big transition from fossil-fuel based power to clean, renewable power. From virtually nil installations in 2015, over 2,000 MW of wind and solar power was added by mid-2024, making the share of renewable power one-third of the total installed capacity—the highest in Delhi's history. The AAP government has promoted rooftop solar installations among all consumers too by ushering in progressive solar polices. Delhi's first ever solar policy was notified in 2016 that laid the foundation for rooftop solar installations leading to 250 MW installations. In March 2024, the Delhi Solar Policy 2024 was launched with an ambitious goal of tripling the total installed solar capacity of Delhi in just three years. Announcing a generous set of incentives, Chief Minister Kejriwal promised that this policy had the potential of reducing power bills of all residential consumers in Delhi to zero, and of industrial and commercial users to 50 per cent, while helping fight air pollution.

The dramatic turnaround in Delhi's power sector under the AAP government has led to the creation of a unique model that is both pro-people and pro-industry—a rare win-win in India's journey of privatization of state utilities. As of 2024, Delhi has the lowest power tariffs across India, supplies uninterrupted and reliable electricity and the Discoms are profitable. This was as much an outcome of smart policy thinking as diligent implementation spanning a decade. But most importantly, it was the result of an honest government displaying the political will to do what was necessary to provide an essential service impacting the quality of life of its citizens.

Delhi, a City with 24/7 Electricity

A crude, but simple test of whether a country or state has a competent government is whether it is able to provide high quality essential services to its people, such as uninterrupted power. In much of the developed world, power cuts are a once-in-a-decade event that usually happens due to natural calamities and goes on to make front-page news. Not in India. India took seventy-four years after Independence to provide every household—rural or urban—access to electricity. But even those Indian states or cities that achieved 100 per cent electrification decades ago have failed to provide 24/7 power supply. As a result, most Indian homes and businesses run with a backup—an inverter or diesel generator.

The condition of the national capital in 2014 exemplified the mess in India's power supply situation. In the summer of 2014, when Delhi's peak power demand hit 5,925 MW, the city saw four to five hours of daily power cuts for months together.[9] Officials claimed the culprit was a weak transmission and distribution network that tripped the moment demand increased in summers. 'The entire distribution system needs to be overhauled', they said.[10] Poor finances of Discoms, was another factor. A few months earlier, in February 2014, the BSES Discoms had threatened to carry out load-shedding, i.e. forced power cuts due to inadequate supply, for eight to ten hours for almost 50 per cent of Delhi's consumers if the government didn't bail them out.[11]

The situation wasn't any better in the first year of the AAP government in Delhi. The summer of 2015 saw a spate of power cuts lasting for hours every day. Delhi's new power minister, Satyendar Jain, assured people that there was adequate power but years of underinvestment in the distribution infrastructure led to frequent grid failures. The Discoms blamed the densely populated unauthorized colonies of Delhi where augmentation of distribution network posed to be a constant challenge.[12]

Four years later, Delhi had turned a new leaf. In June 2019, Mr Kejriwal proudly proclaimed, 'Delhi is the only city in country to get 24-hour power supply.' The India Residential Energy Survey 2020, conducted by the Delhi-based think tank Council on Energy, Environment and Water (CEEW), assessed the state of power supply by carrying out household sample surveys across twenty-two large Indian states and found Delhi to be the leading state providing 24/7 power supply.[13] UP was rated worst with a daily average of eight hours of power cuts in rural areas and four hours in urban areas. Even Haryana, a much richer state with the fourth highest per capita income, had a daily average of seven hours of power cuts in rural areas and three hours in urban areas. The all-India daily average for power cuts was four hours in rural and two hours in urban areas (Figure 13).

Figure 13: Daily power cuts across India (in hours)

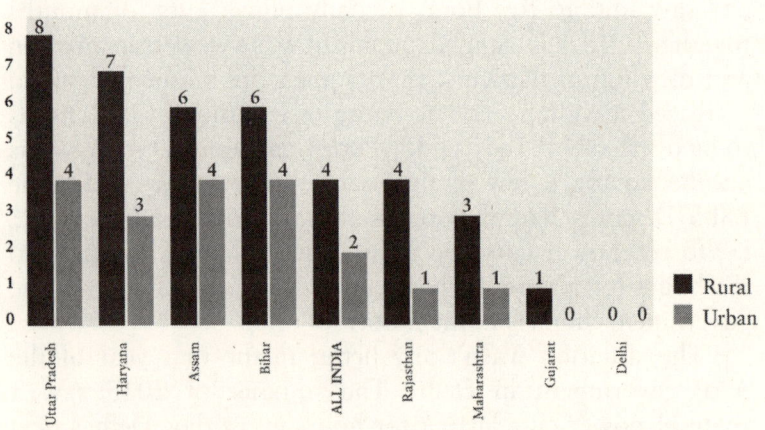

Source: India Residential Energy Survey 2020 by CEEW

Delhi's economic survey data further validates the rapid strides taken by the AAP government to provide uninterrupted power; load-shedding in Delhi has fallen sharply from 117 million units (MU) in 2014–15 to 10 MU in 2022–23—a decline by 92 per cent.[14] By 2020, media reports suggest that inverter sales across several wholesale inverter markets in Delhi had declined sharply by 70 per cent for homes and 60 per cent for offices and societies. Hotel owners reportedly stated, 'Gensets and inverters have become just a showpiece now.'[15]

The AAP government managed to turn around the capital's power supply situation by first addressing the elephant in the room—Delhi's creaking, old transmission and distribution network. A massive overhaul of Delhi's electricity distribution infrastructure was undertaken, making Discoms upgrade old lines and transformers across the city. Apart from relying on Discom officials, the government involved its MLAs to identify areas with persistent power cuts. In many congested areas of Delhi, such as Burari and Okhla, the MLAs became the bridge between the Discoms, government agencies and the local residents to identify suitable land parcels and physically supervise the upgradation of substations. The Discoms too came up with innovations such as 'double decker substations' that occupied 50 per cent less space than conventional substations to provide uninterrupted power in congested areas. The first of these was inaugurated in Sangam Vihar in south Delhi in May 2017.[16]

Over the past decade, Delhi's transmission and distribution infrastructure witnessed the greatest expansion in Delhi's history. The total transmission capacity under Delhi Transco Limited, the state transmission utility that manages the high-voltage power grid, increased by 35 per cent in the past eight years—from 15,570 MVA in March 2015 to 21,090 MVA in March 2023.[17] On the distribution side, the total transformer capacity of Delhi's three Discoms increased by 43 per cent—from 12,311 MVA in March 2015 to 17,545 MVA in March 2024 (Table 5).[18]

Upgrading Delhi's power infrastructure led to a steep reduction in the AT&C losses too, which meant that most of the power supplied to Delhi reached its consumers without being lost in transit. In 2013–14, the AT&C losses of Delhi's three Discoms—BYPL, BRPL and TPDDL—were 22.2 per cent, 17 per cent and 10.6 per cent respectively.[19] A decade later, in 2023–24, the AT&C losses of the three Discoms had reduced to 6.8 per cent, 6.6 per cent and 5.8 per cent respectively—among the lowest in India.[20]

Table 5: Change in distribution transformer capacity in Delhi in 2015 vs 2024

	March 2015 (MVA)	March 2024 (MVA)	% change from 2015
BRPL	4,800	7,107	48%
BYPL	2,620	3,714	42%
TPDDL	4,891	6,724	37%
	12,311	17,545	43%

Source: Economic Survey of Delhi 2014–15 and 2023–24

While overhauling the infrastructure was the necessary first step, it wasn't sufficient to guarantee 24/7 power supply to Delhi's residents. Given the tendency of Discoms to shift the blame on external factors every time there was a power cut, the AAP government decided to impose a framework of accountability on the most essential function of the Discoms—providing uninterrupted power supply. In June 2015, Power Minster Satyendar Jain wrote to Delhi's electricity regulator, Delhi Electricity Regulatory Commission (DERC), directing it to frame a policy through which the Discoms would pay a penalty to every consumer of ₹50 per hour for up to two hours of unscheduled power cuts, and ₹100 per hour thereafter.[21] Scheduled power cuts for repair and maintenance were exempted.

This was an unprecedented step by any state government in India with the potential to upend the relationship between the Indian consumer and Discoms. In May 2016, the DERC issued an order directing compensation to consumers for unscheduled power cuts, making Delhi the first state in India to do so.[22] Predictably, the move met with fierce resistance from Delhi's private Discoms. The order was challenged in courts and struck down by the Delhi High Court as it did not have the lieutenant governor's (LG) approval.[23] It was only in April 2018 that the then Delhi L-G, Anil Baijal, finally approved the AAP government's proposal clearing the stage for implementation of this landmark pro-consumer policy.[24] Based on the approval, the DERC notified this policy in December 2018, but the Discoms promptly challenged the order again in the courts. Four years later in October 2022, the Delhi High Court ruled in the favour of the Discoms holding that the process by which DERC has issued the policy violated the Electricity Act 2023. Though this policy did not see the light of the day, it sent out an important message. It conveyed that while this government was willing to support all plans of the Discoms for strengthening and modernizing the distribution network, power cuts in the national capital would not be tolerated.

Another measure that conveyed the government's no-nonsense approach was close monitoring of the power situation during summers. Discoms were mandated to prepare a 'Summer Action Plan' to ensure zero power cuts, which were reviewed and approved by the power minister well before the onset of summers. The Discoms were also ordered to increase the capacity of the call centres in summers to handle consumer complaints promptly, and position adequate emergency response teams on field to resolve outages. Unhappy with the efforts of the Discoms to prevent summer outages in 2016, the government gave them a week's ultimatum to take corrective actions else it would go to the extent of cancelling their licenses. In 2017, Mr Kejriwal ordered all call centre complaints to be recorded, transcribed and a daily report submitted to him by 11 am with a resolution status.[25] Such persistent monitoring by the government ensured that Discoms were kept on their toes and innovations that effectively reduced power cuts in any part of Delhi were quickly scaled up across all Discoms.

Over the past decade, Delhi Discoms have implemented several innovations to establish smart distribution infrastructure and strengthen grid reliability, many of which were piloted for the first time in India. In 2018, TPDDL launched the advanced distribution management system (ADMS) to remotely monitor and operate each distribution transformer in real-time allowing for enhanced network reliability. In 2019, TPDDL became the first Discom in India to launch a 10 MWh grid-scale battery energy storage system (BESS) at Rohini in Delhi that stores energy during off-peak hours and discharges it during peak hours or when there is a grid failure—working like a mega inverter catering to 2,500 consumers. The project has since been replicated at ten locations across Delhi, the latest being the approval of a 40 MWh BESS system in June 2024—the largest in South Asia. In another innovation, BRPL launched Delhi's first microgrid (solar + battery) in 2019 providing two hours of backup through green power in case of grid failure.

All these efforts significantly improved the health of Delhi's distribution infrastructure and ensured that residents receive 24/7 power supply even though Delhi's peak demand crossed 8,600 MW in June 2024, the harshest summer for over a decade, when much of north India reeled under long power cuts.

The Cheapest Electricity in India

Rising power tariffs year-on-year is accepted as a fact of life in most parts of India. The justification often given by governments is that inflation spares none. The fact that the process for determining power tariffs is so opaque and complex acts as an effective shield against any serious public scrutiny.

Continuously rising power tariffs was among the key issues that defined the last five years of the Congress government in Delhi under Chief Minister Sheila Dikshit (2008–13). In its last three years, Delhi's power tariffs shot up by 22 per cent in 2011, 32 per cent in 2012 and 22 per cent again in 2013.[26] When faced with widespread criticism, Sheila Dikshit had famously responded, 'People will have to pay if they want round-the-clock electricity supply. If people are finding it difficult to pay the hiked charges they should cut down consumption. Use a fan instead of a cooler.'[27]

Delhi's hiked power tariffs also became the most emotive issue that propelled Mr Kejriwal's and AAP's rise in Delhi politics. In the assembly elections in late 2013, reduction in electricity bills was one of AAP's core promises. True to its word, among the first decisions the minority AAP government made after assuming power in December 2013 was announcing a 50 per cent subsidy on electricity bills of up to 400 units of consumption per month. Simultaneously, it launched a direct attack on the transparency of the Discoms' finances. The AAP government initiated a CAG audit of the Discoms' accounts, from their inception in 2002, to determine the true extent of their profits or losses. It also publicly declared its intent to oppose any demand for higher tariffs, unlike the previous Congress government, until the CAG audit had concluded. In return, the Discoms challenged the government's decision in the Delhi High Court and threatened to carry out load shedding for eight to ten hours in large parts of Delhi if tariffs were not allowed to rise![28] Just as the stage was set for a showdown, the AAP government fell.

When the AAP was re-elected in 2015, it picked up the agenda of containing Delhi's power tariffs just where it had left it. Unfortunately, the Delhi High Court ruled in the favour of Discoms in October 2015 deeming that since the majority stake in Discoms of 51 per cent was held by private companies, they are not covered under the ambit of CAG audits. Despite losing the legal battle, the Discoms received the message that this government will battle any unjustified demands to hike power tariffs. The message was reinforced in multiple internal meetings and public statements by the Power Minister Satyendar Jain over the years.[29]

The government cornered the Discoms on two questions— why are power supply costs so high and what can be done to reduce them. It offered Discoms all the support for reforms aimed at containing Delhi's power supply costs, reducing their losses and ensuring efficient operations.

In August 2019, after five years of ensuring no power tariff hikes, Power Minister Satyendar Jain predicted that Delhi will not see a power tariff hike for another five years. Did he get it right? He absolutely did.

In 2024, Delhi earned the distinction of becoming the only Indian state to see no tariff hikes for the past decade. In fact, it did better; Delhi managed to actually reduce its tariffs over this period. Without exception, all categories of consumers were better off. For example, a domestic consumer in Delhi paid ₹4 per unit for the first 200 units and ₹5.95 per unit between 201 and 400 units of consumption in 2014. In 2024, Delhi's domestic consumers were billed at ₹3 per unit for up to 200 units and ₹4.5 per unit between 201 to 400 units—a 25 per cent reduction over ten years.[30] In 2014, all commercial consumers were billed at ₹8.8 per unit whereas in 2024, small commercial establishments (such as *kirana* stores, barber shops, small traders etc.) under the 3kW sanctioned load were billed at ₹6 per unit—a 32 per cent reduction. Even industrial consumers benefitted. In 2014, they paid ₹8.45 per unit whereas in 2024, they paid ₹7.75 per unit.[31]

While doubling down on Delhi's power tariffs, the AAP government also rolled out India's largest subsidy scheme, announcing a 50 per cent subsidy for monthly domestic consumption under 400 units. Those consuming over 400 units had to pay the full bill as per the tariff structure. As the Delhi government's revenues soared under the first term of the AAP government creating sufficient fiscal room, Chief Minister Kejriwal announced the first free electricity scheme in India in 2019. Coining it as a 'lifeline electricity' scheme to ensure that even the poorest could live a life of dignity, the government decided to provide free electricity to those consuming under 200 units per month. Those consuming between 201 to 400 units per month received a fixed subsidy of ₹800 or around 50 per cent of their bills. The full tariff was applicable above 400 units.

As a result of the above two measures—reducing power tariffs and subsidizing electricity for domestic consumers—Delhi emerged as the indisputable leader in providing the cheapest electricity across India. In 2024, a domestic consumer in Delhi consuming 200 units, 400 units and 600 units of electricity in Delhi would have paid zero, ₹985 and ₹3,150 respectively. The same consumer in Mumbai would have paid ₹1,762, ₹4,463 and ₹7,998 respectively, and in Chennai it would be ₹675, ₹2,275 and ₹4,375 respectively (Table 6).[32]

Table 6: Comparison of domestic power bills
in key Indian states in 2024

State	Monthly bill (₹) for consumption at		
	200 units	400 units	600 units
Delhi	0	985	3150
Mumbai, Maharashtra (Tata Power)	1762	4463	7998
Chennai, Tamil Nadu	705	2385	4590
Bengaluru, Karnataka	0	3096	4382
Kochi, Kerala	1284	3564	6028
Ahmedabad, Gujarat	894	2044	3194

*4 kW sanctioned load

Source: Author's analysis of the latest tariff orders of respective states

So how did the AAP government achieve the seemingly impossible task of moving Delhi from being the city with the fastest rising tariffs in 2014 to one offering the cheapest electricity a decade later?

It did so by unravelling the opaque regulatory process responsible for annual tariff hikes and going after every major component that led to higher costs for Delhi consumers, particularly the power purchase costs and AT&C losses. First was the power purchase costs, which contributed to nearly 70 per cent of the cost for Delhi's consumer. Reducing tariffs would not succeed without fundamentally addressing this factor. The government figured that the different long-term power purchase agreements (PPAs) signed by the previous Congress government were among the most expensive in India at ₹5 to ₹8 per unit, most of which was being procured from Central government PSUs like the National Thermal Power Corporation (NTPC). In July 2015, Delhi's Power Minister Satyendar Jain proposed a plan to the Union power minister to surrender 2,225 MW of expensive power from Central PSUs and replace it with cheaper short-term power to reduce overall power costs.[33] But the Centre did not accept the proposal.

It wasn't until 2021 that Delhi was able to rid itself of a costly 750 MW Dadri-I thermal plant in Uttar Pradesh despite opposition from the NTPC and after seeking legal intervention from the Central Electricity Regulatory Commission (CERC). Studies have estimated that Delhi Discoms were incurring an annual burden of over ₹650 crore by procuring costly power from Dadri as compared to cheaper alternatives.[34] The AAP government also realized that Delhi's state-owned gas-based generation plants with nearly 1,800 MW installed capacity produced among the most expensive power due to the high cost of natural gas as compared to more economical options. As a result, it decided to ramp down the production in its own state plants to 24 per cent of the capacity using them largely as a backup in case of exigencies.[35]

While optimizing the allocation from existing power sources, the AAP government took a conscious call to stop signing any new power purchase agreement for expensive and polluting thermal power and instead pursued a large-scale expansion in cheap renewable power. Since 2015, Delhi has added nearly 1,800 MW of utility-scale wind and solar power to its energy mix at an average cost of ₹2.6 per unit.[36] A rapid increase in the share of cheap renewable power has been one of the biggest factors in bringing down power purchase costs in Delhi and reducing the pressure on power tariffs.

Yet another cost factor that contributed to the rising tariffs in Delhi were the high AT&C losses, which—as discussed earlier—were brought down significantly by overhauling the distribution infrastructure. But that didn't take care of power thefts, which were a recurring source of revenue loss for the Discoms. This is where the AAP government's electricity subsidy scheme turned out to be a boon.

Since the scheme required a metered connection for any domestic consumer to avail benefits, it incentivized many households in low-income neighbourhoods to get a metered electricity connection. Consequently, there was a drastic decline in electricity theft, a spurt in metered connections and a widening of the base of billed consumers leading to increased revenues for Discoms. Domestic metered connections in Delhi rose from 41 lakh in March 2015 to 60 lakh in March 2024—a 46 per cent increase in just nine years. In 2023–24, around 65 per cent of Delhi's domestic consumers (38 lakh consumers) received zero electricity bills every month. The fact that Delhi government directly pays this subsidy to Discoms significantly improved their operational efficiencies by cutting down collection costs for these 38 lakh consumers, a massive number, and improving cash flows as the subsidy is paid in advance every quarter. In many ways therefore, AAP's electricity subsidy scheme has proven to be a win-win for the Discoms and the people of Delhi.

When 'free lifeline electricity' was first announced in August 2019, Mr Kejriwal said:

'Every government must provide basic services like education, health care, water, power and transport to every citizen regardless of their ability to pay for them. Every household needs lights, fans, one fridge, cooler in the summer, geyser in the winter to survive. By ensuring free supply of electricity for this level of usage, the government is guaranteeing access to a bare minimum quality of life.'[37]

Mr Kejriwal credited the people of Delhi for having voted an honest government, which had managed to double government revenues and was in a position to invest back in them. Just like with its other schemes, the AAP government used a self-targeting approach to target the bottom 65 per cent of Delhi's population for full subsidy and another 25 per cent for partial subsidy based on their monthly consumption. While Delhi's free electricity scheme for the poor was initially derided by the entire political opposition as a prime example of freebie politics, it has slowly come to be accepted as an essential element of a welfare state over the years. By 2024, Karnataka, Rajasthan, Telangana, Punjab and Tamil Nadu were offering free electricity to domestic consumers up to a monthly consumption limit.

While questions of dignity and equity were the primary drivers behind the launch of the free electricity scheme in Delhi, research shows that increased access to cheap and affordable electricity is a necessary condition for socio-economic development. A systematic review of the socio-economic impacts of rural electrification by the United Nations carried out in fifty-one countries in 2021 found that better access to electricity increased income, consumption, working time and employment status. The review also found positive impacts on gender empowerment and children's education, including an increase in time spent studying and total years of schooling.[38]

The progress made by the AAP government over the past decade to provide the cheapest electricity in India to every resident in Delhi and to provide free or subsidized electricity to nearly 90 per cent of its population has directly served its long-term goal of building Delhi's human capital—a key tenet of the Delhi Model.

Delhi's Big Push for Renewable Energy

In India, a commitment to sustainability is often perceived as obstruction to the idea of development itself. Want cheap energy? Clear out a few million acres of dense forests. Want connectivity? Tear down fragile mountains. If you want to make an omelette, you need to break some eggs, they say. But what if this isn't necessarily true?

The AAP government's big push for renewable energy (RE) over the past decade, which contributed to providing the cheapest electricity in India to Delhi's consumers, is a case in point. This was achieved by pursuing a two-pronged strategy—ensuring all new power generation projects commissioned across India by Delhi's Discoms are only RE projects and by promoting rooftop solar installations within Delhi.

Soon after assuming power in 2015, the AAP government decided that it made little sense to procure more conventional, fossil-fuel based power. With Delhi's pollution levels worsening year-on-year, the government dialled down on thermal power—the main source for Delhi's energy needs till 2015—and initiated a large-scale transition to clean renewable power. It also made economic sense to switch to renewable power, which was available at under ₹3 per unit as compared to Delhi's average power purchase cost of ₹5.5 per unit. But a large-scale shift to RE comes with its own challenges as the sun shines and the wind blows only for a few hours every day. Discoms had to therefore upgrade their systems to manage the variability of RE supply while ensuring grid stability and 24/7 supply to consumers.

Within its first year in office, the AAP government brought the Discoms on board with its energy transition plan. As a result, starting from virtually nil capacity in 2015, nearly 1,800 MW of utility-scale wind and solar power was installed by March 2024 bringing the total share of RE to one-third—the highest in Delhi's history. With another 250 MW of rooftop solar installations in Delhi added during this period, the total RE capacity added to Delhi's energy mix in the past decade crossed 2,000 MW. With several green projects in the pipeline and a commitment to source only green power in the future, the share of RE in Delhi's installed capacity is expected to cross a historic 50 per cent by 2027.[39]

While pushing the Discoms to increase their share of utility-scale RE, the AAP government also decided to promote rooftop solar installations within Delhi's borders. In September 2016, Delhi's first ever solar policy was notified that was widely perceived as among the most progressive solar policies by any Indian state. Prepared by the DDC after wide stakeholder consultations, the policy made it mandatory for large government buildings to install rooftop solar plants and introduced a slew of incentives and tax exemptions to encourage domestic and commercial consumers to go solar. The policy enabled them to set up rooftop solar panels that generate enough solar power to adequately offset the electricity they consume from the grid—a concept known as net metering. Excess solar units generated every month could be rolled over to the next month's bill.

For the first time in India, the policy introduced a generation-based incentive (GBI) of ₹2 per unit of solar power generated by domestic consumers for three years. Until then, the Central government offered a subsidy on the capital cost of installing rooftop plants, which was widely perceived to be encouraging vendors to install sub-standard products to corner the subsidy, leaving the consumers saddled with poorly performing plants. In contrast, Delhi's GBI rewarded effective usage of rooftop solar plants, thereby rewarding high quality installations maintained well over time—a critical gap in India's rooftop solar market. For commercial consumers, the Delhi solar policy 2016 introduced two specific policy innovations for the first time in India—group net metering and virtual net metering—that allowed them to aggregate limited rooftop space across multiple properties to avail policy benefits. The policy successfully kickstarted rooftop solar adoption in Delhi with 250 MW of installations by early 2024.

In March 2024, Mr Kejriwal upped the ante in Delhi's fight against pollution and climate change by launching a new Delhi solar policy 2024 with an ambitious goal of tripling Delhi's solar capacity in just three years. Calling it the most consumer-friendly solar policy in India, Mr Kejriwal promised that this policy had the potential of reducing electricity bills of all domestic consumers in Delhi to zero, and that of industrial and commercial users by 50 per cent.

The AAP government could achieve this by combining the benefits of GBI and net metering with Delhi's electricity subsidy scheme. With nearly two-thirds of Delhi's households covered under the free electricity scheme, Delhi's new solar policy targeted the partially-subsidized (between 200 and 400 units of monthly consumption) and unsubsidized domestic consumers (over 400 units per month monthly consumption) with a generous set of incentives. The government expanded the coverage of GBI by removing eligibility restrictions from the older policy, increased the incentive from ₹2 per unit to ₹3 per unit for small domestic consumers, and the duration of the incentive from three to five years. The new GBI turned into a potent policy tool when combined with net metering benefits and Delhi's electricity subsidy scheme. It enabled every domestic consumer in Delhi to get a return on their investment on a rooftop solar plant in four years while availing zero electricity bill for twenty-five years, the typical life of a solar plant.[40]

The new solar policy also took a path-breaking step by extending the GBI to commercial and industrial consumers for the first time, giving them an incentive of ₹1 per unit of solar power generated for five years. Combined with net metering, this move enabled an average commercial consumer in Delhi to save nearly 50 per cent on their electricity bill and achieve a return on investment for their rooftop plant within four years as well.[41]

The shortage of sufficient rooftop space had traditionally posed a significant challenge to solar installations in Delhi.

To address this obstacle, the AAP government pioneered the 'Community Solar' model for the first time in India under the new solar policy. This approach allowed consumers without suitable rooftops to participate in a community-owned solar system located at a third-party site, ensuring they enjoy all associated benefits, such as net-metering and GBI. The government's Delhi solar portal would act as an aggregator between developers willing to setup community solar plants and households wanting to own a share.

The new policy also laid out the roadmap for aggressively increasing the procurement of solar power from utility-scale solar plants outside Delhi to reach an installed capacity target of 4,500 MW by 2027. To pursue this goal, Delhi became among the first few states in India to participate in a tender for renewable energy round the clock (RE-RTC) power—an innovative model that combines solar, wind and battery installations at multiple sites to provide round the clock power at lower prices than fossil fuel based power. If successful, RE-RTC power has the potential to replace costly and polluting thermal power with renewable power at a fixed tariff for twenty-five years.

The AAP government's concerted push for renewable energy in the past decade demonstrates a progressive approach towards sustainability that doesn't inflict a cost or make people suffer; instead it makes their lives more prosperous.

Vision for Affordable and 24/7 Power for Every Indian

No country or its people can prosper without access to affordable and reliable power. For the poor, it holds an even higher stake as it can make all the difference between maintaining a minimum quality of life and accessing opportunities. Yet, as a country that sees vociferous protests and public debate on every hike in prices of petrol, diesel and LPG cylinders, we see very little of this fury on the issue of rapidly rising electricity bills that claim an even bigger share of the aam aadmi's wallet.

The last decade has seen a rapid rise in the electricity bills for domestic consumers across the country. Most people accept these ritualistic year-on-year tariff hikes as a fact of life, with governments and Discoms conveniently pinning it on inflation. This is nothing but a flawed and a lazy excuse that hides inefficiencies and often even corruption. A big conundrum in India's power sector is that consumers are forced to pay more every year even as the share of cheap renewable power keeps rising. The AT&C losses across the distribution sector also keep reducing and new and more efficient technologies are available across the value chain. True, the price of coal—the fuel that powers most of the electricity in Indian homes—has risen since 2021 due to greater reliance on costly imported coal. As we will see shortly, this too was an avoidable burden on the people and a failure of the Central government to ramp up domestic coal production in time.

Delhi's reforms in the power sector under AAP have shown that a government determined to provide affordable power to all consumers can take several steps to not just rein in tariffs but actually reduce them. A comparison of monthly domestic electricity bills for 400 units of consumption across eight states between 2014 and 2024 shows the starkly different trajectory that Delhi has traversed compared to the others (Table 7).[42] In 2014, three of the eight states offered cheaper electricity to domestic consumers than Delhi. However, over the past decade, Delhi emerged as the state offering cheapest electricity in India. Delhi is also the only state where electricity bills reduced, with or without subsidy, while bills have risen by an average of 50 per cent in other states, with Maharashtra (Mumbai) registering the highest increase by 127 per cent.

Delhi's success in providing affordable power to its residents holds many lessons for other states. To begin with, there is no reason to accept the homily of 'cost-reflective tariff' that is often peddled by advocates of constantly rising tariffs without asking the question that the AAP government asked in 2015—why are power supply costs so high in the first place and what can be done to reduce them? It was only after asking this question relentlessly over the years that a strategy to reduce costs by rejigging the allocation from existing power sources, and launching a plan for massive expansion in cheap renewable power, was arrived at. Over the past decade, India has fared well by ramping up renewable power generation by adding 107 GW capacity and bringing the share of renewable power to over 40 per cent in 2023. Yet, most consumers have been deprived from seeing the benefit of this transition in their electricity bills.

It is time for the central and state governments to consider providing free electricity to the country's lower and middle classes to the extent their budget allows. Delhi too started by providing only a 50 per cent subsidy initially and moved to the free electricity scheme four years later when there was enough fiscal room to sustain it. Delhi's free electricity scheme costs 4 per cent of its budget but has had a transformational impact on the bottom two-thirds of Delhi's population—the backbone of Delhi's economy—assuring them of a basic quality of life while providing an essential cover against inflation.

Table 7: Change in monthly electricity bills for domestic consumers
across eight states in 2014 and 2024

State	Electricity bill for 400 units consumption in 2014 (in ₹)*	Electricity bill for 400 units consumption in 2024 (in ₹)*	% change
Delhi-Private Discom	2,196	985 (with subsidy)/ 1,785 (without subsidy)	-61%/ -19%
Assam	2,228	3,543	59%
Karnataka (Bengaluru)	2,400	3,096	29%
Kerala	2,764	3,564	29%
Madhya Pradesh	2,620	3,854	47%
Maharashtra (Mumbai) –Private Discom	1,964	4,463	127%
Tamil Nadu (Chennai)	2,056	2,340 (with subsidy)	14%
Uttar Pradesh	2,100	2,956	41%

Source: 2014 tariff data: Report of Central Electricity Authority, March 2015;
2024 tariff data: Author's analysis of the latest tariff orders of the respective states.

During the 2024 Lok Sabha election campaign, Mr Kejriwal announced a plan to provide 200 units of electricity free to every household in India at an annual cost of ₹1.5 lakh crore. This is similar to the average value of loans that Indian banks, most of which are public sector banks, have written-off for rich corporates every year for the past ten years under the Narendra Modi government.[43] The only difference is that the former is quickly latched upon as an example of 'freebie' politics, while the latter isn't. The truth is: money that could have been used to provide free lifeline electricity to every Indian was used to provide a free lunch to the rich corporates.

Of course, cheap power means little if it is unreliable or interrupted. The fact that an overwhelming majority of India is yet to experience 24/7 power from the grid, without relying on any power backup, is a stark reminder of the failure of our governments in reforming the power sector even seventy-five years after Independence. When the summer of 2024 brought with it a now familiar heat wave across northern India, Delhi was the only state that continued providing uninterrupted power. During this period, Lucknow, Indore and Gurugram—the top cities of their respective states—faced multiple outages each day lasting up to eight hours.[44] One can only imagine the state of the power supply in rural parts of these states. The stated goal of the chief minister of Uttar Pradesh is to provide eighteen hours of power supply in rural areas, making it anybody's guess how many more decades will the 185 million people living in UP's villages have to wait to get 24/7 power supply.[45]

The most perplexing aspect about India's power supply crisis is that India is a power-surplus nation with a total installed generation capacity of 418 GW in mid-2024; almost double the peak demand of 221 GW.[46] The crisis is a result of two underlying failures in governance: failure in ramping up domestic coal production, and failure to upgrade grid infrastructure. First, there has been a gross mismanagement in supplying adequate domestic coal to power India's thermal power plants. India is among the top five countries globally in terms of coal reserves. India's coal reserves are estimated at 344 billion tonnes, which can last India 400 years as per a 2022 report of the Standing Committee on Energy.[47] Yet, the Central government has failed to ramp up production, leading to a shortage of domestic coal at power plants across India, many of which run at 50 per cent capacity—a double whammy as it increases the cost per unit of power produced.

In 2022, faced with an almost depleted domestic coal stock, the Central government took the unprecedented step of mandating the use of minimum 10 per cent imported coal, which is ten times costlier. Several expert bodies like the All India Power Engineers Federation (AIPEF) pointed out that this will push up power prices in India by 30 per cent and the Central government should focus on ramping up domestic coal production. While the Central government is yet to heed this advice, some state governments with captive coal mines such as Punjab, have. In 2023, the AAP government in Punjab pushed back on the Centre's coal import mandate and ran all its state-run thermal power plants at full capacity using domestic coal only, thereby saving ₹500 crore annually.[48]

The second underlying cause has been the continued failure of state-run Discoms to augment their transmission and distribution infrastructure to meet the increasing electricity demand. State-run Discoms, which still supply over 90 per cent of power across India, continue to accumulate huge financial losses every year with over ₹3 lakh crore of losses accumulated in the five years ending 2022–23.[49] This failure to ensure timely upgradation of the distribution infrastructure—transmission lines, sub-stations, transformers etc.,—has meant that even when there is enough capacity to produce power in India, it is of no use since that power is unable to reach homes. Until late 2023, it was the official policy of the Haryana government to not build new substations for hundreds of new housing societies developing in Gurugram and instead directing the builders to do so. Most of them failed to make these investments relegating the societies to run on 24/7 power backup through diesel generators.[50]

Over the past decade though, government figures suggest considerable progress in reducing pan-India AT&C losses from 25 per cent in 2015 to 16.5 per cent in 2022. Yet, these figures hide substantial disparities with many large states such as Uttar Pradesh, Bihar, Odisha and Jharkhand still experiencing losses above 30 per cent in 2022.[51] The Centre's new Revamped Distribution Sector Scheme (RDSS) introduced in 2021–22, makes all the right noises about overhauling and modernizing distribution infrastructure across India with an outlay of ₹3 lakh crore over five years. With much of this money yet to be spent, the jury is still out whether the scheme will make a substantial impact in heralding India towards 24/7 power supply.

In spite of knowing the problems that stand in the way of providing affordable and 24/7 power supply, governments in India—states and the centre—have failed to meet this goal even seventy-five years after independence. The Delhi Model shows that it is indeed possible to realize the vision within five years, not decades, if the government has the political will to do so. Delhi's experience also shows that privatization can be an enabler in bringing this change, but it is a double-edged sword. If wielded without checks and balances, it can lead to disasters like that of Odisha or the looming power outages in Delhi till 2015. Regardless of whether states choose to go down the privatization route or not, it is clear that India needs to set a time-bound goal for providing affordable and uninterrupted power supply to all its people much before it can even dream of becoming a developed nation.

Chapter 7

Water

Striving for Equity and Self-Reliance in Water Supply

'City's tanker mafia makes a killing'[1]
'Water Shortages Lead to "Tanker Mafia" in New Delhi'[2]

Between 2013 and 2014, several headlines like these dominated the national and international news, detailing Delhi's desperate water woes. The national capital had, in 2010, emerged fresh from hosting the celebrated Commonwealth Games with infrastructure that most Indian cities could only dream of— including tree-lined boulevards, dozens of flyovers, a world-class metro rail system and modern sports complexes. Yet, on one count it resembled the worst of any other Indian city. A dysfunctional and overwhelmed water supply system had made the daily lives of most people, particularly the poor, miserable. When the government failed to meet demand, tanker mafias swooped in and made headlines.

The chief cause behind the water scarcity was that the Delhi Jal Board (DJB), the public water and sewerage utility, had failed to create adequate water supply infrastructures to respond to population growth. For several decades after independence, lack of affordable housing impelled hordes of migrants to settle in Delhi's informal settlements. By 2015, over a third of Delhi's population lived in 1,799 unauthorized colonies spread mostly around the city's borders. The DJB laid down piped water supply in half of the unauthorized colonies by 2015, but the actual supply was ridden with deep inequities. A better-off neighbourhood of South Delhi was supplied 225 litres per person per day, whereas poorer villages a few kilometres away got a meagre 3 litres per person per day, according to a Comptroller and Auditor General (CAG) report.[3]

Here, management failures and arbitrary distribution of resources created rampant water shortages. People were forced to rely on private water tankers to meet daily needs. Water tanker mafias swooped down on the fertile ground; a close nexus was nurtured between the tanker mafia and local politicians who ensured water supply to these areas remained disrupted to preserve business interests.[4] Reports estimate the mafia business to be worth ₹400 crore annually.

More than time and money, this experience meant sacrificing human dignity every day at the altar of survival. A 2014 news report recounts this indignity: 'Tankers usually stop for just 15 minutes, while dozens of people crowd around waving buckets and plastic tubes. Tempers flare in the fierce heat; fights are frequent. In some areas, people get just three liters.'[5]

Rising water bills added to people's woes. When Arvind Kejriwal sat down for an indefinite fast in March 2013, it was to protest the twin issues of inflated electricity and water bills. He alleged there had been an 18-times jump in water bills over the last nine years. The responsibility, Mr Kejriwal said, lay with the Congress government: its policies mandated a 10 per cent hike in water tariff every year, and the party was colluding with private contractors at the expense of the common man.[6]

When AAP formed the 49-day government in December 2013, the promise that resonated the most with people was

'Bijli haaf, paani maaf'. In public rallies, Mr Kejriwal asked: 'If a poor family cannot afford to pay water bills, should they stop drinking water?', and proclaimed water as a basic human right. In the landmark 2000 case of *Narmada Bachao Andolan vs. Union of India*, the Supreme Court held that access to water is intrinsic to the right to life, and thus a fundamental right. The top court also emphasised that the 'state is responsible for providing clean drinking water to the citizens'.[7]

Delhi's water sector was ridden with deep inefficiencies when AAP came to power. Such was the scale of the crisis that Mr Kejriwal directly steered the water department as the Minister-in-charge for more than a year. He held no other department throughout the two terms of the AAP government in Delhi.

Over the years, the AAP government's approach towards the water sector has aimed at putting two key principles in action—equity and self-reliance.

Ensuring Equity in Water Supply

The principle of equity has a perspicuous demand: a government should do everything possible to ensure an adequate supply of clean, drinking water as a basic right to every resident, especially those from the most marginalized sections. Mr Kejriwal, immediately after assuming office in 2015, made 20 kilolitres of water per month (around 700 litres per day) of 'lifeline water' free to every household. The lifeline would ensure adequate supply for an average family to maintain a healthy and hygienic lifestyle. The scheme was conceptualized with the dual goals of promoting water conservation and promoting water metering to check water theft. To encourage water metering, the scheme made the installation of a functional water meter as a pre-condition for receiving subsidies.

The results were immediately evident. Until 2015, only 82 per cent of Delhi's domestic consumers had metered connections; unmetered connections were on the rise, increasing from 3.1 lakhs to 4.1 lakhs in four years. These trends reversed within the first five months of the free lifeline water scheme as metered connections in Delhi rose by 75,000. By March 2023, the unmetered connections have reduced by nearly 75 per cent.[8]

Data and anecdotal evidence both suggested positive trends in household water conservation as well. The per day per person consumption in Delhi has reduced from an average of 190 litres between 2009 and 2014, to 180 litres over the first three years of the AAP government.[9] The number of households availing lifeline free water subsidy too has increased by 70 per cent in less than a decade. As of 2024, beneficiaries of the free water scheme constituted 63 per cent of all domestic consumers of water.[10]

But implementing the free water scheme was not the challenging part. AAP's promise of water as a fundamental right would remain an empty rhetoric unless every household of Delhi had a piped water connection, particularly those living in informal settlements who were under the clutches of the tanker mafia. Shocking as it may sound, even in the national capital of India, only 81 per cent of households had piped water supply per the 2011 census.[11] AAP's manifesto for the 2015 Delhi elections acknowledged this gap and promised to make a time-bound plan for covering all residents irrespective of their legal status. It read: 'There will be no discrimination between planned/non-planned; authorized/nonauthorized; regularized/non-regularized; city or village. Within five years piped water connections will be made available to as many as 14 lakh households (50 lakh people) in Delhi that do not have a piped water connection at present.'

Under the AAP government, Delhi has seen a historic expansion in its piped water supply network primarily targeting the informal settlements. The government has installed over 5,200 km of water pipelines in unauthorized colonies. This has almost doubled the share of colonies connected to the water supply network, from 54 per cent in

2015 to 99.6 per cent in March 2024.[12] This figure excludes the 113 colonies built on forest/archaeological survey of India (ASI) land where it wasn't permissible or technically feasible to lay water pipelines. Another 2,100 km of water pipelines were laid to service rural areas, urban villages and resettlement colonies of Delhi, ensuring 100 per cent water supply to these areas by 2023.[13]

As the mega expansion in Delhi's water supply network started gathering pace, the government soon faced an unforeseen challenge: those who finally received a piped water supply in their colonies hesitated to apply for individual water connections. A high one-time connection fee charged by the DJB bogged them down. The AAP government in 2019 waived off the development charges, reducing it to a flat fee of ₹2,310 for both water and sewer connections. The decision enabled people with a land of 200 square meters and above to amass savings of over ₹1 lakh.[14]

The above three initiatives—free lifeline water for those with metered connections, expansion of the water supply network and waiving off development charges for new connections—have heralded a massive change. For the first time in decades, almost 9,34,000 people in the national capital have access to free drinking water in their households. Consequently, the usage of water tankers has also substantially reduced and remains restricted largely to the few informal settlements, such as Delhi's slums or jhuggi-jhopri clusters, where it wasn't feasible to lay water pipelines. Here, the AAP government in 2023 decided to roll out 'water ATMs'. These decentralized water supply systems would take water from borewells and treat it through reverse osmosis (RO) plants to provide clean, drinking water to the local community. To access these machines, all residents in the area were provided with a smart card, entitling them to 20 litres of free RO water per day. Any consumption beyond that, or for those without cards, was charged at ₹1.60 per 20 litres. Seven such water ATMs have been installed as of September 2023, with plans underway to deploy 500 such units in unserved communities across Delhi.[15]

As of 2024, the water supplied by DJB and private tankers combined constituted less than 1 per cent of the city's total water supply.

Making Delhi Self-reliant for Its Drinking Water Needs

A pursuit of self-reliance was embedded into AAP's reforms for the water sector.

Only 10 per cent of the state's drinking water needs were met through groundwater usage. For the remaining 90 per cent, Delhi leaned on surface water from neighbouring states. River Yamuna passing through Haryana provided the largest share of Delhi's water at around 60 per cent. This share was frozen for a thirty-year period, pursuant to a 1994 water sharing agreement between five north Indian states whose chief ministers formed the Upper River Yamuna Board.[16] Another 30 per cent share of water coming via River Ganga through Uttar Pradesh was also fixed. These unyielding ratios did not account for a population boom: between 1994 and 2015, Delhi's population doubled to two crore. In 2015, DJB was supplying 840 million gallons per day of water against a demand of 1,140 MGD—a deficit of almost 30 per cent. It was clear that Delhi was heading towards a precipice.

The AAP government came up with an unorthodox solution, which was conceived in response to another crisis. In 2016, agitators protesting job quotas sabotaged Haryana's Munak canal that supplied almost 60 per cent of water coming into Delhi, affecting the water supply for several days.[17] The brainstorming that unfolded in the Delhi Secretariat led to the development of a bold and innovative blueprint to make Delhi self-reliant for its drinking water needs.

With the strong backing of the Chief Minister, the government decided to value treated wastewater as precious a commodity as fresh water. Until 2015, only a small fraction of the treated wastewater was being reused, primarily for gardening and irrigation purposes, while the rest was discharged back to the Yamuna. The AAP government now decided to use treated wastewater to revive and rejuvenate hundreds of Delhi's neglected lakes and waterbodies, and through them, recharge the aquifers. With unchecked urbanization, these natural water reservoirs had either become dumping grounds of solid waste or were encroached upon and forgotten. Breathing life into these water bodies was not impossible: a government survey revealed that 600 of these could be revived. This water could then be extracted through tubewells and treated and supplied to meet the city's water needs. Thus the 'city of lakes' project was born—an innovative, decentralized approach to using treated wastewater so that Delhi could achieve self-reliance in its water infrastructure.

A pilot project was conducted at Rajokri village, located on the outskirts of south Delhi. Until 2017, the dying water body at Rajokri was swollen with untreated sewage and cattle dung waste.[18] The AAP government opted for natural treatment methods over chemical treatment and installed a decentralized sewage treatment plant that used scientifically designed wetlands to treat sewage and recharge the 2,000-square metre lake. At the same time, the adjacent space of nearly 10,000-square metre was transformed into an aesthetic, vibrant public site that the local communities could use for recreation and leisure. The environmental impact was evident. The Rajokri lake restoration reduced the pollution load of wastewater by 90 per cent and increased water tables.[19] Diverse species of migratory birds were spotted in the surrounding locality. Community engagement and ownership means local families commit to keeping it clean, besides seeing it as a safe space for families and children. This first-of-a-kind initiative won a Ministry of Jal Shakti excellence award in 2020, and a commendation from the National Green Tribunal in 2019.[20]

Buoyed by Rajokri lake's turnaround, Mr Kejriwal, as Delhi's water minister in December 2018, announced the plan to revive 159 dying lakes and waterbodies at a budget of ₹376 crore. 'Delhi will become a city of lakes after the completion of the projects. It will reduce pollution, recharge groundwater and make our city beautiful,' he said. [21] The plan was expanded to cover all 600 water bodies, starting with 265 waterbodies in the first phase.

Till mid-2024, over 50 water bodies had been revived across Delhi under the 'city of lakes' project including 16 large lakes and 34 natural water bodies. The areas around these water bodies have registered a rise in groundwater levels by 3–6 metres within a couple of years, per a Centre for Science and Environment study.[22] A notable success story is of the Pappankalan lake near Dwarka spread over 11 acres. The lake has resulted in a staggering rise in groundwater levels by 13 metres in just two years and left an ecological impact too.[23] 'In the last two years, we have seen a constant rise in the number of waterbirds like spot-billed ducks, red-naped ibis, white-breasted waterhens, cormorants, medium egrets, cattle egrets, little egrets, etc. We have noticed their breeding population here,' said Sumit Dookia, assistant professor at the school of environment management, Guru Gobind Singh Indraprastha University.[24] The areas surrounding the revived lakes recorded 5 to 7 degrees lower temperatures than the rest of the city's average temperature, providing relief from the urban heat island effect, according to a DJB study.[25]

The government also piloted an innovative floodwater harvesting technique to move towards self-reliance. Under this initiative, excess floodwater coming through river Yamuna during peak monsoons would be captured and used to recharge the aquifers for future use in lean summer months. The initiative was piloted in 2019 at the floodplains near Palla village in northwest Delhi. The government leased land from resident farmers to build a 26-acre desilted pond that could recharge 50 million gallons of water daily. The project successfully led to an average of 2 metres increase in groundwater levels, recharging around 1,000 million gallons of water every year.[26] The government, encouraged by the success of the Palla floodwater harvesting project, plans to cover 1,000 acres of recharge ponds in the Yamuna floodplains in the future.

Besides harvesting treated wastewater and Yamuna floodwaters, the AAP government has also taken steps to promote rainwater harvesting (RWH) to recharge Delhi's aquifers. In 2021, the government announced financial assistance up to ₹50,000 and a 10 per cent rebate on water bills on installation of rooftop RWH systems.[27] The scheme is yet to see a wider take-up though. The government had also made it mandatory for owners of existing and new properties measuring over 100-square metre to install RWH structures. Over 85 per cent of Delhi government buildings had complied with this mandate by mid-2024.

In the next phase, the Delhi government has planned to address the water deficit by installing 200 MGD capacity of decentralized mega reverse osmosis (RO) plants around lakes and high-water table areas. Groundwater will be extracted through tube wells and treated through RO plants of 5 MGD and 10 MGD capacity to get high-grade drinking water, which would be blended in the local underground reservoirs (UGRs). This will allow drinking water to be directly augmented in the target area to ensure minimal distribution losses.

The government's comprehensive efforts to augment water supply have yielded results: Delhi's water availability has increased by 20 per cent from 840 MGD in 2015 to 1,009 MGD in early 2024.[28] However, the government still finds itself in a deficit as Delhi's water needs have also risen to 1,290 MGD due to the rising population. As the 'city of lakes' initiative gains momentum, the government hopes to reuse at least 70 per cent of the treated wastewater (600 MGD in 2024) to entirely eliminate the water deficit.

The AAP government has simultaneously undertaken initiatives to ensure minimal wastage and leakage of water through the city's vast water supply network. Over 3,500 km of old water pipelines in Delhi's main water supply network were replaced between 2017 and 2024. For this, the government established a supervisory control and data acquisition-based (SCADA) system, the first of its kind, at DJB headquarters to monitor water consumption in real time. A large number of bulk flow metres were also installed throughout the water supply network—from the water treatment plants to the underground reservoirs located in neighbourhoods across Delhi . Linked to the SCADA system, these digital bulk flow meters would relay the real-time water flow through the system, allowing immediate identification of any line disruptions. The bulk flow meters in Delhi's water supply network have increased over 10 times—from just 350 in 2015 to over 3,600 by early 2024.[29]

Delhi's water supply network is often criticized for the high proportion of non-revenue water (NRW)—52 per cent as per DJB's records in March 2024. An equivalent of the AT&C losses in the electricity distribution sector, NRW is commonly understood as a measure of water lost or stolen in transit and therefore not billed to the consumer. However, this isn't the case in Delhi, where the real figure for water leakages or theft is bound to be much lower. This reason is that although a large number of pipelines have been placed connecting unauthorized colonies, rural areas, urban villages etc. in the past decade, the process of providing legal water connections is relatively slow. So, though the water has reached the colonies and is being used by the people, it is reflected as unbilled or non-revenue water.

Over its two terms, the AAP government has succeeded in providing water as a basic right to all. While deep system-level reforms undertaken in this period have comprehensively overhauled Delhi's water supply system, significant challenges still remain. Delhi is still as dependent on the share of water incoming from surrounding states. The share of water coming from Haryana in the summer of 2024 suddenly dropped by 100 MGD for weeks together at the peak of a searing heatwave, affecting the supply of nearly 28 lakh residents.[30] The only path for the AAP government to provide a 24/7 reliable water supply is to hasten the pursuit towards self-reliance.

Another challenge is Delhi's antiquated stormwater drainage system that allows frequent waterlogging of Delhi's roads every monsoon within a few hours of rain.

The government attempted, in 2018, to draw a drainage masterplan in collaboration with IIT Delhi. However, the execution of the ideas proposed in the masterplan into field-level projects is still pending—chiefly due to the multiplicity of agencies responsible for managing the city's drainage network including PWD, municipal corporations, Delhi Jal Board, DDA and the flood and irrigation department.[31]

Cleaning River Yamuna

Yamuna is said to be Delhi's lifeline. Its historical, cultural and ecological significance aside, the river has historically been a steady source for addressing Delhi's domestic, industrial and agricultural needs. This source, however, is quickly being drained of its vitality. Rapid urbanization, industrial waste, agricultural run-off and domestic sewage discharge have turned Yamuna into one of the most polluted rivers in the world. Such is the scale of fouling that the 22 km stretch of the Yamuna that passes through Delhi, comprising 2 per cent of its length, contributes to more than 76 per cent of the total pollutants. The Yamuna Action Plan (YAP) in 1993 ambitiously set out to cleanse the river in three phases but has remained limited in success. Reviving the Yamuna thus figured prominently in AAP's 70-point manifesto for the 2015 Delhi elections.

The YAP, jointly funded by the Centre and the Delhi government, was one of the largest river restoration projects in the country. The third phase is still underway in 2024, but its notable achievement so far has been the expansion and development of Delhi's sewage treatment plants (STPs). In addition, there is now a network of interceptor sewer lines that traps most of the polluted water passing through eighteen major drains of Delhi and diverts it to the STPs for treatment, rather than letting them discharge straight into the Yamuna.[32] The biggest failing of YAP, however, was that it did little to trap the domestic sewage generated at source. Delhi in 2015 had an STP capacity of 592 million gallons per day against the daily estimated sewage discharge of 672 MGD. However, only 55 per cent of this discharge was being trapped and treated in the STPs. The rest found its way into the Yamuna.[33]

Reviving Yamuna's health was one of the prominent reforms AAP envisioned for Delhi in its manifesto. After assuming office, one of the first decisions was to extend Delhi's sewer network to cover 100 per cent of Delhi's households. Similar to the crisis of water shortage, the DJB had left most informal settlements of Delhi, especially the 1,799 unauthorized colonies and 675 slums or *jhuggi-jhopri* clusters, out of its network. AAP's wasn't an easy decision. There are huge budgetary implications attached to expanding sewer networks, explaining why no large Indian city has managed to provide sewer connections to all its residents. Yet, the AAP government decided to pursue this goal—not just to achieve its vision for a clean Yamuna, but to correct historical inequities and ensure that every resident of Delhi, especially the poor, can live a life with dignity and without disease.

The government has over the years invested in installing over 4,400 km of sewer lines. This has increased the share of unauthorized colonies connected to the main sewer network from a meagre 13 per cent in 2015 to 57 per cent in March 2024.[34] The work to connect the remaining colonies with the main network or with decentralized sewage treatment plants is expected to be completed by 2027. Progress was also made in connecting the waste from community toilet complexes in slums to the main sewer network; by mid-2023, 85 per cent of the slums had been covered. This massive expansion in the coverage of sewer network has alone cost the AAP government ₹4,400 crore—more than the combined cost of the three phases of the Yamuna action plan.

New solutions breed new problems, however. The government found that the take-up of individual household sewer connections was very poor despite a reduction in the connection charges in 2016. In November 2019, Mr Kejriwal launched the 'Mukhyamantri Muft Sewer Connection Yojna' to provide free household sewer connections in every colony connected to the sewer network. This decision was taken despite the additional budgetary outlays that it required. In the last decade, thanks to the above initiatives, the AAP government has provided over 4,10,000 new household sewer connections.[35]

By mid-2023, Delhi also recorded substantial progress in the interceptor sewer project, completely trapping thirteen of the eighteen major drains falling into Yamuna and diverting the polluted water to STPs for treatment. The work on trapping the remaining five drains is at an advanced stage.

Both these efforts—trapping domestic sewage at the source and diverting it to STPs—have significantly reduced the discharge of untreated wastewater into the Yamuna. The wastewater treated by Delhi's STPs has increased by 60 per cent to around 600 MGD in just nine years. As a result, even though Delhi's daily estimated sewage discharge rose due to its population boom, 75 per cent of this wastewater was trapped and treated by early 2024, as against 55 per cent in 2015.

The government has also invested in initiatives to ensure 100 per cent treatment of wastewater to meet the current and future demand. A three-pronged strategy was put in place. First, four new centralized STPs were constructed and the capacity of two existing ones were enhanced. Second, a novel initiative was undertaken to construct 40 decentralized STPs, which occupy a smaller space and could be created in unauthorized colonies that were being connected to the sewer network for the first time. These plants proved to be far more cost-effective than centralized STPs. Third, the government upgraded the technology across existing STPs to increase their capacity, and to ensure their discharge meets the enhanced effluent norms notified by the Central government in 2017. All these initiatives are expected to be completed by 2025, increasing Delhi's total sewage treatment capacity from 592 MGD in 2015 to 935 MGD in 2025—enough to meet the capital's needs.

Towards the end of its second term, the AAP government adopted an ambitious plan to translate its vision of a clean Yamuna into reality. In April 2023, it decided to carry out in-situ treatment of the three largest drains in Delhi—Najafgarh, Shahdara and Supplementary drains—so that nearly 80 per cent of the pollutants in these drains get treated while in transit. This would reduce the load on the STPs while turning these foul-smelling drains into clean water channels. In-situ treatment methods include innovative techniques, such as installation of floating booms, aeration devices and chemical dosing at strategic locations for wastewater treatment.[36] Scaling up this cost-effective approach would also take care of over 150 MGD of polluted, untreated water—around 20 per cent of Delhi's wastewater load—entering from neighbouring Haryana and Uttar Pradesh before it falls into the Yamuna.

The AAP government has thus made a series of concerted efforts, backed by adequate investments, to achieve its vision of a clean Yamuna. In 2024, this dream looks closer than ever before.

Chapter 8

Democracy Under Attack

Who Gets to Govern the National Capital?

The Elected or Selected

The lowest point in AAP's history came in 2014, in the months following its complete rout in the Lok Sabha elections in much of India including Delhi. Political commentators wrote mawkish obituaries: Arvind Kejriwal's decision to resign as Delhi Chief Minister after 49 days, to chase national ambitions, was political suicide, they decreed. Internally too, the chips were down and out, and Mr Kejriwal was close to quitting politics. AAP's fortune reversed just eight months later. It mounted a stunning electoral comeback, winning sixty-seven out of the seventy seats in the 2015 Delhi assembly elections, and managed to halt BJP's national winning spree by sweeping all state assembly elections after the 2014 Lok Sabha results.

Much was written about AAP's wildly successful 2015 electoral campaign. [1] But few truly understood that a more daunting challenge awaited Arvind Kejriwal: the task of governing the national capital with his biggest political adversary at the Centre. It's one thing for a small party like the AAP to win an electoral battle against the might of the BJP. It's another thing altogether to fight the all-powerful Central government to preserve the institution of democracy itself in the national capital. How the Kejriwal government fought the battle for democracy while delivering upon the promise of the Delhi Model over the past decade is a story few know.

Mr Kejriwal always knew that Delhi wasn't a full state, and as such, his sphere of power would be restricted. While the rest of India was reorganized into states in the 1950s, the Indian parliament deemed it fit to make Delhi a union territory and placing all decision-making powers firmly under the Centre's control. The 1970s and 1980s saw sustained demand for statehood from the Jana Sangh and its descendent BJP, with leaders including Atal Bihari Vajpayee, Lal Krishna Advani and Madan Lal Khurana leading popular protests. The Congress government under Prime Minister Narsimha Rao eventually caved in, in 1991. The 69th Constitutional Amendment was enacted, granting Delhi partial statehood and a special status, with a legislative assembly and an elected chief minister with subdued powers

The Constitutional Amendment Act outlined the shared power arrangement. The newly incorporated Article 239AA allowed the Central government to retain full executive control over Delhi's land, police and public order (the 'reserved subjects') through a Lieutenant Governor, an official nominated by the Centre. For the remaining subjects under the State and Concurrent list (the 'transferred subjects'), Article 239AA transferred the executive powers to the elected National Capital Territory (NCT) of Delhi government. The L-G's role would be similar to a Governor in states on these transferred subjects, bound by the aid and advice of the elected government. Further, all legislative bills cleared by the Delhi assembly were required to be approved by the Centre before being enacted as laws.

Madan Lal Khurana, the first chief minister of the NCT of Delhi in 1993, lamented that the House appeared like a body without a soul. BJP's Sahib Singh Verma, who took on the mantle next, said he felt like a powerless chief minister. Sheila Dikshit, the longest-serving Congress chief minister in

Delhi from 1998 to 2013, too rued the lack of powers, and demanded full statehood throughout her rule.

Still, during these twenty-one years, the status quo remained unchallenged: the Central government never encroached upon the limited powers of Delhi's chief minister, including during the 49-day AAP government.

But 2015 was different. Mr Kejriwal, uplifted and eager after a historic mandate, hadn't accounted for the fact that the Constitutional segregation of powers between Delhi's elected government and the L-G could be treated as pliable. Reality swept in soon enough. Over AAP's two terms, the BJP-ruled Centre spared no effort in bending all rules and breaking all conventions, taking away the limited powers from the chief minister and vesting them with the L-G, to cripple the functioning of the AAP government. These actions betrayed a political ideology that viewed electoral defeat as unacceptable, and only a starting point to destabilize opposition governments or block them from carrying out their democratic mandate.

The first salvo was fired on 21 May 2015, within three months of the AAP government assuming office. The Ministry of Home Affairs issued a notification to take away the Delhi government's control over 'Services', a transferred subject, and gave it to the L-G.[2] A state government's services department controls the transfers, postings and disciplinary proceedings over all the officers of the government. As the de facto 'HR department' of the government, it also looks after the recruitment of staff that do not fall under the ambit of the Union Public Services Commission (UPSC), such as teachers, doctors, mid-level and junior administrative staff, etc. Article 239AA of the Constitution envisaged for Delhi's chief minister to exercise control over this body for the simple fact that accountability forms the bedrock of any democratic form of governance. The elected government is held accountable every five years through the ballot box; the officials in turn hold bureaucracy accountable too by rewarding those who perform efficiently and reprimanding those who don't.

The Centre's calculated move reversed the principle of accountability in the Delhi government. The Centre started rewarding Delhi officers who were seen as obstructing the work of the elected government. For example, the Centre extended the term of a particular chief secretary of Delhi not once but twice in 2023 and 2024, even though the AAP government contended in the Supreme Court that there was an 'absolute breach of communication, trust and faith of any kind between the incumbent chief secretary and the Delhi government.'[3] To think of a corporate analogy, imagine running a giant multinational with a ₹75,000 crore (about $10 billion) annual turnover where the HR department works under the directions of the main business competitor with no guardrails.

With the control over its officers forcibly taken away, the day-to-day functioning of the AAP government has been impacted in many ways over the years:

Officers shuffled like playing cards in a deck

Ever since the L-G assumed control of the services department, senior bureaucrats and IAS officers started receiving transfers far more frequently than the average posting of one-and-half years. The elected government was rarely consulted; this often caused major disruptions in the flow and functioning of the departments. Between mid-2016 and early-2019 i.e. in two-and-a-half-years, the chief secretary of Delhi was changed four times and principal secretaries were constantly shuffled across major departments: eight in urban, seven in environment, five in public works and four in transport. In education, the epicentre of AAP's reform, secretaries were replaced four times between 2019 and 2022. What could be more telling than the fact that Delhi might be the only state to have seen eight health secretaries in the first two years of the Covid-19 pandemic?[4] Mr Sisodia in the Delhi assembly alleged these transfers were intended to cripple the development works in the city: 'There is a circus going on in the services department and the L-G is behaving like the ringmaster.'[5]

Flagship initiatives stalled by bureaucracy

In India's parliamentary form of governance, the ministers or the cabinet hold responsibility for the government's decisions, with the bureaucracy assisting them in recommending sound policy options and implementing their decisions. Severing the accountability between the elected government and bureaucracy has led to continuous insubordination and non-cooperation in implementation of policy. For example, in 2023, health department officers refused to clear the bills of many private hospitals providing cashless payment to road accident victims under the Farishtey scheme.[6] The AAP government had to move against its own officers in the SC for the funds to be released. Similarly, payments for salaries and tests in all mohalla clinics were stopped for three months preceding the 2022 Delhi municipal elections, affecting their services. Mr Sisodia, in a letter to the L-G, demanded an FIR against conspiring officers who willingly delayed payments to tarnish the image of the AAP government ahead of elections.[7] In 2023, the bus marshal scheme was shut down, based on frivolous objections by the same officers who smoothly ran the scheme for eight years.[8] In April 2024, the AAP government knocked on the Supreme Court's doors again, seeking action against its own finance department officers, who defied their Minister and blocked the release of nearly ₹2,000 crore for the DJB.[9]

These are a few among the hundreds of instances when routine work was disrupted due to open defiance by officers—an act that would lead to direct suspension or dismissal anywhere else in India. On several occasions, the chief minister or the concerned minister would directly appeal to the L-G to intervene and penalize erring officers to disprove that the officers were under pressure to defy the elected government at the behest of the BJP-ruled Centre. The L-G typically responded with a vehement refusal of any malfeasance, yet in each instance, the L-G did not accept the government's request to take disciplinary action against the defying officials.

Officers stopped attending meetings and ceased responding to ministers:

It has become a routine practice for heads of departments or senior bureaucrats to skip meetings convened by their ministers and to send junior officers instead. For instance, in 2022, out of the twenty meetings called by Delhi's environment minister to prepare a winter pollution action plan, only one meeting was attended by the environment secretary. The PWD secretary attended only one of the four meetings convened in October 2022 to finalize an ambitious plan for redesigning Delhi's roads to European standards. 'Apart from skipping meetings, senior officers also routinely do not attend to phone calls of Ministers or respond to their verbal requests to meet them in their offices to discuss official matters,', stated Mr Sisodia in an affidavit filed in the Supreme Court in 2022.[10]

Spiralling vacancies across departments:

Staff shortages have plagued several departments after the elected government lost control over the recruitment process of government staff. The epidemic of vacancies stretches from the transport department to schools to hospitals. As of mid-2024, over 30 per cent positions for specialists and doctors lay vacant at Delhi government hospitals, severely hitting expansion plans for hospitals as well as polyclinics.[11] Almost 50 per cent positions of principals and vice-principals in Delhi's government schools were vacant as of March 2024.[12] The recruitment of permanent teaching staff has also lagged, making government schools reliant on guest or contractual teachers. The vacancies in the transport department stood at 55 per cent.[13]

The above instances show how nearly impossible it is to run a government that does not have control over its officials. Mr Kejriwal has often joked he might be the first chief minister in India who can neither appoint nor sack even a peon from his office. The AAP government will go down in history as the only state government in Independent India to face such a situation that is no less than a constitutional coup by the BJP-ruled Centre to render an opposition-ruled government powerless even after securing a historic mandate from the people. So how did the AAP government still manage to deliver the unprecedented outcomes across sectors and give birth to the Delhi Model?

It was largely due to the sheer political will, perseverance and moral authority of the Kejriwal government that helped it deliver most of its promises and return to power in 2020 with yet another historic mandate. It helped that many government officers, though not obligated to listen to the elected government, did so because they knew that constitutionally it was the right thing to do. A small but important factor was also that the first two L-Gs of Delhi during AAP's term, Najeeb Jung (until December 2016) and Anil Baijal (December 2016 to May 2022), were former IAS officers who, while doing the Centre's bidding on important policy matters, didn't go out of the way to obstruct the plans of the AAP government.[14] The situation changed in May 2022 with the appointment of Vinai Kumar Saxena as Delhi L-G. He was the first private individual to be appointed as Delhi L-G; all previous L-Gs came either from bureaucratic or defence backgrounds.

On one hand, as the AAP government pushed Delhi's bureaucracy against all odds to deliver upon its flagship initiatives, on the other hand, a fierce legal battle ensued in the Delhi High Court with the AAP government challenging the May 2015 order issued by MHA. Eventually, it took a long and arduous legal fight, spanning eight years and multiple benches in the High Court and the Supreme Court that culminated in a landmark 5-0 verdict of a Chief Justice of India (CJI)-led constitutional bench in May 2023 that gave the elected government in Delhi complete control over the bureaucracy.[15] The CJI observed reading out the verdict: "If a democratically elected government is not given the power to control the officers, the principle of accountability will be redundant. If the officers stop reporting to the ministers or do not abide by their directions, the principle of collective responsibility is affected."

Under normal circumstances, this would have been the end of the matter, but not in this case. Setting aside all constitutional norms, the Central government passed an ordinance within days and subsequently enacted a law that nullified the unanimous decision of the constitutional bench—a perversity that has few precedents in our country's history.[16] As per this new law, the Delhi Services Act 2023, the final authority on all service matters was to be the Delhi L-G. The AAP government promptly challenged the constitutionality of the new law in the SC, which was yet to constitute a bench to hear the matter as of mid-2024.[17]

While the AAP government was already battling the Centre usurping control over Delhi's bureaucracy, a new front opened up in August 2016 when the Delhi high court ruled that the L-G is the administrative head of the National Capital Territory on all matters, and is not bound by the aid and advice of the elected government.[18] This was a body blow to democracy, turning Delhi back to a full-fledged union territory where the elected government was no more than an advisor to the L-G, even on transferred subjects. The AAP government appealed this order in the SC, which gave a historic verdict in July 2018, ruling the L-G had no independent decision-making powers and was bound to follow the 'aid and advice' of the elected government on transferred subjects. It also explicitly said that the elected government is under no obligation to wait for the L-G's concurrence on subjects that fall within its domain but should nonetheless keep him informed. For the next two-and-half years, the AAP government got its powers back although the matter of the services was still undecided.

In March 2021, the Central government launched another assault on the powers of the elected government in Delhi by passing the Government of NCT of Delhi Amendment Act 2021 that made it mandatory for the L-G's opinion to be obtained before the government took any executive action.[19]

In effect, this overturned the July 2018 SC judgment that held that the L-G had no independent decision-making powers on transferred subjects and his concurrence or opinion on such matters held no significance. The AAP government appealed the constitutionality of this act too in the SC in early 2022, but two years later, a bench was yet to be constituted.

Meanwhile, post the 2021 Act, the L-G has routinely used his powers to summon files on transferred subjects and pass directions, often masked as opinions or queries, stalling the decisions taken by the elected government. This constant attack and encroachment by the BJP-ruled Centre, acting through the L-G, on the AAP government's executive domain over the past decade has meant that for the first time anywhere in India, an elected government had to resort to *dharnas* to get their programmes—such as mohalla clinics, CCTVs on streets for women's safety, doorstep delivery of ration or sending teachers abroad for training—back on track. While there are countless instances of such interference, sharing two will suffice.

The L-G objected to the AAP government's plan to send a batch of teachers to Finland for training in October 2022, although the government had been sending teachers and principals abroad for training for the previous six years. The L-G marked 'queries' on the file seeking a cost-benefit analysis for the training, asking why this couldn't be done in India. After the L-G did not give a go-ahead after three months of files going back and forth, Mr Kejriwal lashed out at the L-G saying, 'It seems like *"Begani Shaadi Mein Abdullah Deewana"* (A person who takes far too much interest in the affairs of others). Why is the L-G sitting on our head? If an elected CM cannot send his schoolteachers abroad for teachers' training, then what is the purpose of such election and democracy?'[20] This was followed by a street protest led by the chief minister, his cabinet ministers and MLAs. Eventually, after a delay of six months, the L-G gave his approval in March 2023, but only after the scheduled departure date for the teachers visit had elapsed. Their programme had to be cancelled.[21]

Since this incident, no teacher or principal in a Delhi government school has travelled abroad for training.

In another incident, the Delhi L-G took a suo motu decision in June 2024 to dissolve the DDC, the policy think-tank of the Delhi government. Mr Kejriwal's brainchild, the DDC was established in 2015 with a mandate to study innovations globally and advise the government in finding sustainable, people-centric solutions to the critical developmental challenges facing Delhi. Over the next nine years, the DDC served as a fountainhead for some of the flagship and innovative initiatives implemented by the AAP government. For instance, the DDC led the process of formulation of the Delhi EV policy 2020, Delhi solar energy policy 2024, tree transplantation policy 2020, among several other reforms. From its inception, the DDC functioned under the sole jurisdiction of the Delhi chief minister, who acted as its chairman. Official notifications giving the chief minister the sole jurisdiction over the DDC were approved by the Delhi cabinet and the previous L-Gs of Delhi. But in June 2024, L-G Vinai Saxena abruptly ordered the bureaucracy to dissolve the DDC, completely bypassing the elected government.[22]

Sanjay Singh, the AAP Rajya Sabha MP from Delhi, eloquently expressed Delhi government's situation in parliament as: 'tying down someone's hands and legs, pushing them in a swimming pool and asking them to win the race'.[23] The framers of the Indian Constitution may have dreamt of an independent India ruled by the elected, but governance in its national capital has steadily turned into a rule of the selected. On one end is a political ideology that sees the Constitution and Supreme Court orders as transactional documents to be upheld when it suits their ends, and bypassed, when it does not. On the other end is a democratically elected government that has to fight every single day to translate the will of the people, expressed through the ballot box, to reality. How long will this struggle, or rather, the siege of the elected government in the national capital continue, will be determined only by the parliament or by the Supreme Court.

Investigative Agencies, Unleashed

India has a long history of governments in power abusing federal investigative agencies to target political opponents and shield political allies. It was in 2013, under the Congress-led UPA government at the Centre that the Supreme Court denounced the Central Bureau of Investigation (CBI) as a 'caged parrot' and 'its master's voice'. However, things changed for the worse after the BJP formed a government at the Centre in 2014 under Prime Minister Narendra Modi. Over the past decade, India's top investigative agencies have seen an unprecedented scale of politicization and abuse of authority to target, harass and arrest opposition leaders.

An investigation by the *Indian Express* revealed that between 2014 and 2022, 95 per cent of the 124 CBI cases were against prominent opposition parties, whereas this figure was 60 per cent in the ten years of UPA rule. Similarly, 95 per cent of the 121 prominent politicians probed by the Enforcement Directorate (ED) in this period were Opposition leaders, whereas this figure was 54 per cent under UPA rule.[24] Another investigation by the same newspaper in 2024 revealed that of the twenty-five opposition leaders who faced a corruption probe and crossed over to the BJP since 2014, twenty-three got a reprieve.[25] Many have labelled this phenomenon in Indian politics as 'washing machine'.

Since law and order in Delhi falls under the jurisdiction of the Central government, the Delhi police reports to the Centre. The two other branches of a state government that typically investigate corruption cases—the Anti-Corruption Branch (ACB) and the Vigilance directorate—were both reporting to the Delhi chief minister until 2015. By June 2015, the Centre snatched control of both these institutions, making the AAP government powerless to implement one of its key promises of the election campaign—rooting out government graft. This move has had a perverse impact as well. Just as the ED and CBI were unleashed on opposition parties across India, the Centre also unleashed the full fury of every investigative agency in Delhi upon the AAP government, its ministers and MLAs over the past decade.

Till 2024, over 200 cases had been filed against AAP leaders, including over fifty-five MLAs in Delhi. Mr Kejriwal himself was the target of over fifty civil and criminal cases, and Mr Sisodia of twelve. On multiple occasions, Mr Kejriwal asserted that AAP is the most persecuted political party in India's history and the cases were a conspiracy to finish off the party.[26] After AAP's spectacular victory in the Punjab assembly elections and its rise as India's youngest-ever national party in 2022, the persecution campaign worsened. A spate of corruption investigations were initiated in Delhi targeting the AAP government and its flagship initiatives.

Between 2022–24, two CBI probes and an ACB probe were launched targeting government hospitals and mohalla clinics; one probe was launched by the Vigilance directorate targeting government schools, one ACB probe targeted the installation of CCTV cameras on Delhi's streets by the public works department, one CBI and ACB probe each targeted procurement of government buses, and five separate probes were launched targeting the DJB involving the ED, CBI and the ACB. Till mid-2024, none of these probes found any evidence of corruption or recovery against any minister of the AAP government. In fact, the investigation was yet to conclude and trial yet to begin in all cases. Nevertheless, they have served the purpose of instilling fear in the entire bureaucracy, and to some extent, stalling important government initiatives.

The probe that attracted the most attention, occupying national headlines throughout 2023 and 2024 after the Centre unleashed the full fury of the ED and the CBI to investigate trumped-up corruption charges, was the AAP government's new excise policy. It was the first instance in Indian history where a sitting chief minister, a deputy chief minister (also the excise minister) and a Rajya Sabha MP were arrested on corruption allegations, charged under the stringent provisions of the Prevention of Money Laundering Act (PMLA) and jailed without trial for up to 17 months. It is important to note here that it was the Modi government itself that had passed eight amendments to the PMLA in 2019 that gave the ED virtually unlimited powers of arrest and incarceration, and made it extremely difficult for any accused person to get bail.[27] Post these amendments, PMLA, a law enacted to curb heinous crimes such as terrorism and drug financing, has been increasingly used to target political opponents across the country.

Let's first understand the genesis of Delhi's new excise policy and the twin problems it was trying to solve—stamping out Delhi's liquor mafia and increasing state revenue.[28] Illicit sale of liquor flourishes when there is either partial or complete prohibition on its sale, such as in Gujarat. The pre-2021 excise regime in Delhi was synonymous with partial prohibition with half of the capital's municipal wards having either none or one liquor shop.[29] Illicit sale of liquor also flourishes under a regressive tax regime. Delhi's old excise policy collected a meagre annual licence fee of ₹8 lakh per liquor shop, but imposed heavy excise fees on the sale of liquor, sometimes up to 300 per cent. This created a big incentive to bypass official sales channels, leading to the increased risk of sale of spurious liquor besides causing revenue loss. An additional issue in Delhi prior to 2021 was a policy regime dominated by sales through government-run shops that offered few brands and an undignified store experience. As a result, consumers preferred buying from shops outside Delhi or through illegal channels.

Delhi's new excise policy ushered in a progressive regime that addressed all these flaws. First, it brought about an equitable distribution of liquor shops across all wards of the city without increasing the total number of shops. Second, it rolled out a progressive tax regime by subsuming excise fees into licence fees and ensuring retail players bid for licences through auctions and paid their taxes upfront based on anticipated sales. This one step completely eliminated the incentive to indulge in illegal sales. Finally, it marked an exit of government-run liquor shops, letting the private sector operate shops and offer a modern retail experience. A transparent auction-based process for licenses for retail shops was introduced for the first time in Delhi. The success of Delhi's new policy could be gauged from the fact that the annual license fees for shops jumped from ₹8 lakh to ₹8 crore. Officials anticipated the total collections from the new policy, based on competitive bidding for licences, to double from an average of ₹5,500 crore per annum in the previous three years, to over ₹10,000 crore in the first year itself.[30] The policy was welcomed by all stakeholders and even held up as a model excise policy. That is, before the politics took over.

Delhi's new excise policy was drafted after public consultation, cleared by the Cabinet, vetted twice and approved by the then Delhi L-G, Anil Baijal, before being notified in July 2021. However, just 48 hours before the rollout of the new policy regime in mid-November 2021, the L-G intervened to unilaterally introduce a new condition in the policy. The change prohibited retail shops from opening in unauthorized colonies of Delhi, which house a third of Delhi's population, without the approval of the municipal corporation and the DDA, both of which weren't under the control of the AAP government.[31]

This last-minute change in the Delhi excise policy reimposed partial prohibition in many parts of the city, limiting the number of shops that could be legally opened, and the licence fees that was due to the government. To make matters worse, the policy rollout, starting mid-November 2021, was met with stiff political opposition from local BJP leaders, who did not allow many private retail shops to open even in conforming areas. As a result, just over 50 per cent of retail shops could open in Delhi by July 2022. The ones that did open also faced continuous threats from local authorities, forcing many private owners to exit. Simultaneously, the Delhi L-G announced a CBI inquiry and suspended eleven excise department officials. Faced with plummeting excise revenues and a Gujarat-like prohibition scenario in Delhi, the AAP government was forced to revert to the old excise regime.

Over the next two years, both the ED and the CBI doubled down upon the entire AAP leadership, turning their and their associates' homes and offices upside down in search for evidence and 'kickback' money that they alleged had exchanged hands between them and the owners of Delhi's liquor businesses. After two years of investigation and carrying out over 500 raids, not a single rupee of the money trail was recovered from any AAP leader or any of the other accused persons—a fact accepted by the investigative agencies in the courts. In the normal course of events, this would be the end of an investigation. But the CBI and ED still went on to arrest AAP leaders, based on the statements given by the co-accused, who turned government approvers after long periods of incarceration, despite giving several contradictory statements earlier. It turned out later that two key approvers who gave incriminating statements against AAP leaders had BJP connections—one had donated ₹50 crore to the BJP through electoral bonds after his arrest by the ED in the same case, and the other received a Lok Sabha ticket from an alliance partner of the BJP from Andhra Pradesh.[32]

It is ironical that the ED and the CBI were alleging corruption and loss to the state exchequer from an excise policy that was all set to double the tax revenues within a year and rein in the liquor mafia, before its implementation was derailed by competitive politics. Incidentally, a similar excise policy, when implemented by the AAP government in Punjab in 2022–23, led to increase in annual state revenues by 41 per cent.[33]

As of October 2024, all three key architects of the Delhi Model had been granted bail by the courts after long periods of incarceration. Mr Kejriwal and Mr Sisodia spent six months and seventeen months respectively in jail in the excise policy case before the SC granted them bail in both the ED and CBI cases. Mr Jain, who was arrested by the ED in May 2022 in an entirely different case under PMLA, was granted bail by the trial court after two years of incarceration. In each of their cases, the courts made similar remarks: there was no money recovered and even after two years, the investigation was yet to conclude and trial yet to begin. The courts invoked Article 21 (right to life and personal liberty) of the Constitution, holding the right to speedy trial as superior to the stringent bail conditions under PMLA. When granting bail to Mr Kejriwal, the SC repeated its reference to CBI as a 'caged parrot' after 11 years and for the first time under Prime Minister Modi's tenure, indicating that not much had changed as far as the politicization of India's top investigative agencies was concerned.

The Delhi Model took shape over the past decade, delivering unprecedented outcomes and setting new benchmarks in governance across multiple sectors, despite the AAP government facing multiple handicaps. First, Delhi was only a partial state with the state government exercising no control over functions such as land, urban planning, law and order, etc., which can substantially aid the delivery of various initiatives. Second, the AAP government under Mr Kejriwal never got the opportunity to exercise even the powers of a partial state as envisaged under the Constitution ever since the BJP-ruled Centre usurped control over Delhi's bureaucracy and empowered the L-G to such an extent that he could scuttle any initiative of the government. Third, much of this progress took place in the face of an unprecedented attack on AAP leaders and ministers, including the chief minister, through federal investigative agencies that has few parallels in Indian democracy. Despite these handicaps, the fact that the Delhi Model bore results in a short span of time and continues to impact the everyday lives of the millions residing in the national capital should make citizens all over the country demand much, much more of their governments, than what they have been used to.

Resolving Delhi's Governance Crisis

When India hosted its first G20 summit in September 2023, the Modi government launched a massive PR blitz all over India with the slogan—'mother of democracy'. For the people of Delhi, which played host to the summit, the slogan rang hollow. In the seven decades since Independence, the national capital had grown to be one of India's key economic engines and the fastest growing city in Asia. As the seat of all embassies, Delhi is a window into India for many foreign dignitaries and tourists. Yet, on the one measure that India prides itself the most globally—world's largest democracy—its national capital has a regrettable track record.

It bears repetition that all the chief ministers of Delhi preceding Mr Kejriwal had full authority over all subjects of the state and concurrent lists barring the three 'reserved subjects' of land, police and public order. Yet, they felt powerless to deliver upon the expectations of the people. In contrast, the AAP government that came to power in 2015 faced a reality far worse. Faced with a hostile Centre, Mr Kejriwal was asked to deliver on the biggest electoral mandate received by any government in India's history without any control over his bureaucracy, the anti-corruption branch taken away and with the Centre's nominee—the L-G—exercising unbridled powers to routinely interfere and cripple the day-to-day functioning of his government.[34] Delhi's brush with three decades of partial statehood has taken a heavy toll on the lives of its people.

Take law and order for instance. It is a travesty of a representative democracy that the home minister of a country with 1.4 billion people, who is battling the crisis in Manipur and terrorism in Jammu and Kashmir, has to simultaneously look after every law-and-order issue of the 22 million residents of Delhi—be it a chain snatching incident in Burari, a car theft in Vasant Kunj or the gruesome rapes and murders happening all over Delhi every day. The Delhi police's complete lack of accountability towards the elected state government is one of the reasons behind Delhi's rise as

India's crime capital. As per the 2022 national crime records bureau (NCRB) data, Delhi registered over 1,800 crimes per 1 lakh residents, the highest in the country. Delhi was also ranked as the 'most unsafe metropolitan for women in the country' accounting for 30 per cent of all crimes against women reported in nineteen major cities across India.[35] After the horrific Nirbhaya rape in 2012, rape cases in Delhi have doubled over the last decade, while the conviction rates in crimes against women stood at a dismally low figure of 3 per cent in 2022.[36] Any home minister or police chief with this track record deserves to be fired, but not in Delhi.

The Delhi chief minister's lack of control over land, and associated functions such as urban planning and affordable housing, has had dire consequences too. The DDA, a Central government agency in charge of this function, was unresponsive to the needs of a massive migrant population coming to Delhi post-Independence resulting in a failure to create an adequate stock of affordable housing. This is the chief reason why over 50 per cent of Delhi residents today stay in informal settlements—slums and unauthorized colonies. DDA's failure to create adequate commercial space for malls and businesses in Delhi was a key factor behind the growth of Gurugram and Noida as business hubs. Every two decades, the DDA indulges in a fanciful urban planning exercise of creating Delhi's masterplan, typically after much delay and with minimal participation from the elected state government that holds the authority to implement it. The DDA's masterplan 2041 that was scheduled to be notified in January 2022 was still pending as of mid-2024, forcing the Supreme Court to note that, 'an utter mess has been made in the city'.[37] Meanwhile, all Delhi chief ministers have struggled to get land allocated for the core needs of the city's residents—schools, colleges, hospitals, clinics, bus depots etc.

The lack of a sufficiently empowered state government is also a key factor behind the multiplicity of agencies that has been a perpetual fault-line in Delhi's governance. For example, Delhi has nine agencies that manage roads and drains; three at the local level; four in the Delhi government and two in the Central government. Besides being a source of constant confusion amongst the public and the media, this makes it very convenient for any one agency to avoid accountability and pass the buck to others in case of any crisis, like after every incidence of waterlogging in the national capital. Similar overlaps in responsibility exist in multiple other areas. The MCD, the Delhi government and the Central government all simultaneously run schools, hospitals and dispensaries in the capital. To run streetlights, as many as fifteen agencies are involved—probably a record in itself.[38]

Delhi urgently needs to fix this corrosion in its basic governance architecture that represents a 'web spun by a drunken spider'—a phrase originally used to describe the overlapping agencies in New York State in 1915. This was at the dawn of the era of Progressivism in American cities and states that radically transformed its administrative set-up. Only an empowered chief minister and a Centre willing to let go of interference in the day-to-day administration of the national capital can ensure this.

So where do we start to fix Delhi's governance crisis? First, the immediate solution. The Central government must withdraw both the regressive amendments made to the Government of NCT of Delhi act in 2021 and 2023, with the perverse motive to overturn the landmark judgments by the SC Constitution benches in 2018 and 2023 respectively. Through these judgments, the SC has unambiguously clarified that the intent of Article 239AA of the Constitution was to strengthen democracy and create a fully-empowered elected government in Delhi that had independent decision-making powers on all subjects in the state and concurrent list including services, except for the three reserved subjects. If the Centre is unable to rise above political point-scoring, it falls upon the SC to uphold the sanctity of its own judgments within weeks or months, and not years, which seems to be the case now. Unless this is done, Delhi will continue to experience confrontation and gridlock in its daily administration irrespective of who is in power.

As for a long-term solution to Delhi's problems—there's really only one—full statehood. After three decades of experimenting with partial statehood, we now know the shortcomings of the current dysfunctional governance structure in the national capital that holds everyone responsible for every fault, but nobody accountable. Democracy works optimally only when you unleash its full power or else it reduces itself to a tyranny of the bureaucracy or unelected individuals like the Delhi L-G. The Constitution's vision of a federal structure has stood the test of time, enfranchising people through state governments that are closer to them, represent their needs, and are responsible to the electorate. Over decades, several erstwhile union territories have been converted into full-fledged states. This is testimony to the value of a representative form of government as well as the wisdom of our parliamentarians.[39]

Critics of granting full statehood to Delhi often point to the need to place national interests above local, and that many capital cities around the world follow a similar governance pattern. Such arguments aren't just flawed, they also betray the ignorance of a comparative perspective. An analysis of governance structures of large national capitals in modern democracies shows that India has by far the most regressive form of governance for its national capital. For example, it is the local city government in London (UK), Berlin (Germany), Mexico City (Mexico) and Ottawa (Canada) that exercises control over police, land and city planning, housing, traffic and transport planning, and appointment and transfer of officials—all missing in Delhi.[40] Comparisons with Washington DC (USA) and Canberra (Australia), tiny capital cities with the population equivalent to a suburb of Delhi, are inappropriate, although their local governments too have more powers than Delhi including that of police.

The BJP and the Congress have both supported the idea of full statehood for Delhi since the 1970s. BJP even went to the extent of introducing a full statehood bill in Parliament in 2003 through the then Union Home Minister, LK Advani.

Every single BJP manifesto for Delhi till the 2015 elections has prominently included this demand. However, after AAP's victory in the 2015 Delhi assembly polls, the BJP has made a U-turn on this demand, acting instead to diminish the powers of Delhi's elected government. Though the Congress was credited with granting partial statehood to Delhi in 1991, it did nothing towards granting full statehood during the two terms of the UPA rule. However, its former Delhi chief minister Sheila Dikshit voiced this demand as early as 2002 and several times during her three terms in office. The Congress also included this demand in its 2015 manifesto for Delhi elections.

This suggests that both the traditional political parties of India know this is the only practicable, long-term solution. Over the past decade, the AAP has been the biggest champion of this demand, going to the extent of officially releasing their draft bill on full statehood for Delhi in May 2016, seeking to build a political consensus. [41] Unfortunately, it received no support from the ruling BJP at the Centre.

The AAP government's draft statehood bill offers the most realistic contours of an enduring solution to Delhi's governance crisis. It proposes to divide Delhi into two parts— the core New Delhi area that houses all the institutions of the Central government as well as the foreign embassies that would become a full-fledged union territory to be controlled only by the Central government. Popularly called Lutyens Delhi, this accounts for 3 per cent of Delhi's geographical area and 2 per cent of its population. The rest of Delhi, where the 98 per cent of the population live over a vast expanse of over 1,400 sq km should be declared a full-fledged state with its own police, administrative machinery and all the powers of any state government. Over the years, several independent experts have endorsed a similar proposal as the only alternative that works for all.[42]

The history of democracy around the world tells us that cities thrive when their people find a voice through an elected legislature and a popular government, and when both of them are adequately empowered. Giving full statehood to Delhi will need abiding faith in the power of democracy and federalism among our parliamentarians, far removed from the pressures of competitive politics that plague modern Indian politics. Only then will Delhi achieve its true potential and rightful place among the greatest cities in the world, and the deserving capital of the world's greatest, not just biggest, democracy.

Afterword

Much of this book has been devoted to giving a detailed account of *what* the Delhi Model is and the impact it has had in the lives of the people of Delhi. But *how* the AAP government went about implementing this reform agenda deserves a special mention too.

It is no secret that the bureaucracy leads policy design and implementation in most of the governments in India. In my decade-long stint in the development sector until 2016, I worked closely with governments, advocating for reforms in education, health and urban governance issues. I met dozens of ministers in central and state governments across India, and every single one of them, without exception, would leave the room within ten minutes after sharing their 10,000 feet vision, asking the bureaucrats to 'sort out' how to get it done. This disconnect of the political leadership from the nuts-and-bolts process of administering reforms is a big reason why our governments are riddled with policies that look excellent on paper, but make little impact on the ground. A defining aspect of the AAP government's style of functioning in Delhi has been elevating the role of the minister's office to the captain of their departmental ships, steering every major or minor policy reform from start to finish.

Chief Minister Arvind Kejriwal led the way by driving clarity into the reform agenda, and working meticulously with each of his ministers and senior officers to ensure policies were implemented in a manner that truly benefitted the aam aadmi. I distinctly remember the multiple hour-long sessions with Mr Kejriwal on Delhi's draft EV policy where he engaged in a threadbare discussion on every single policy intervention and its implementation strategy to ensure they make a meaningful dent on vehicular pollution. An engineer from IIT Kharagpur and a former IRS officer, Mr Kejriwal's remarkable administrative acumen set him apart in being able to shape many blue-sky policy ideas into realistic plans.

Mr Kejriwal's entire team of ministers, notably Manish Sisodia (a seasoned journalist), Satyendar Jain (a professional architect), Gopal Rai (a post-graduate in sociology), Kailash Gahlot (a supreme court lawyer), Imran Hussain (graduate in business management) and later on Atishi (a Rhodes scholar with degrees from Oxford and Cambridge) and Saurabh Bharadwaj (a software engineer and lawyer), who became ministers in 2023, exemplified this hands-on approach to governance as well. An educated group of ministers directly leading a well-thought out reform agenda with empathy and persistence, rather than letting the bureaucracy run the entire show, has been crucial to the success of the Delhi Model.

Assisting the ministers in taking full ownership of the reform process was a group of full-time advisors who brought the necessary technical depth and professional competence. Working collaboratively with the bureaucracy and external experts, they led the delivery of the many reforms that make the Delhi Model. Atishi served as an advisor to the education minister until 2018, followed by Shailendra Sharma from the senior leadership team of India's largest education NGO, Pratham. Gopal Mohan (IIT Delhi), the advisor to chief minister and a DDC member, was the force behind doorstep delivery of services and many tech-led reforms of the government. Shaleen Mitra (MBA, currently pursuing a PhD in psychology) worked on mohalla clinics and several health reforms. Ankit Srivastava (IIT Mumbai) guided reforms in water and Yamuna cleaning, and was the brain behind the city of lakes initiative. Reena Gupta (lawyer and environmentalist, formerly at the World Bank) assisted the environment minister on initiatives to combat air pollution. Aswathi Muralidharan (mass communication expert) and Vijay Vupputuri (ex-tech head of a R&D company), both DDC members, supported the implementation of several flagship reforms.

Supporting the ministers and advisors were a host of young professionals, recruited through fellowship schemes, such as the chief minister's urban leaders fellowship programme, who provided crucial research and on-ground support to ensure that implementation of reforms stayed on course. Over the years, the AAP government has attracted dozens of extremely well qualified young professionals from top universities in India and globally, such as the London School of Economics (LSE), University of Cambridge, IIM Ahmedabad, IIT Kharagpur, Delhi School of Economics, TISS, etc.—many of them leaving far more remunerative options to experience the unique experiment that was the Delhi Model.

Yet another layer of support has been the contribution of countless AAP volunteers, many of them working professionals, in the last mile delivery of the reforms. For instance, the SMCs leveraged volunteers embedded in local communities to strengthen accountability in the delivery of a flagship government initiative. Volunteers also played important roles in monitoring the performance of mohalla clinics, coordinating the government's Covid-19 response including distribution of cooked meals and rations, ensuring smooth implementation of the odd-even scheme, among several other efforts that required strong community participation.

None of this diminishes the role of the government staff, especially the frontline workers who are the real stars of the Delhi Model. Countless teachers, principals, engineers, doctors, nurses, bus drivers, bus marshals and others—many of whom felt respected and empowered for the first time in their jobs—stepped up to serve with passion and dedication, eventually touching the lives of the people of Delhi.

Personally, it has been immensely satisfying to see that AAP's politics not only created space for honest, well-educated Indians to enter the muddy waters of Indian politics, but also fostered an ecosystem of talented professionals passionate about public service. Together, they helped establish a new model of governance that transformed the lives of millions. For all of them, including myself, being part of the Delhi Model has been an experience of a lifetime.

Acknowledgements

Writing this book seemed like a daunting challenge from the very moment the idea struck me two years ago. For the Delhi Model is the result of collective action by a large number of passionate individuals who dreamt that governments in India can deliver the impossible, and who worked tirelessly for years to achieve it despite all odds. I could think of writing the story of the Delhi Model only because I had the privilege to be a part of this brilliant team led by the former Chief Minister of Delhi, Arvind Kejriwal. I am eternally grateful to Mr Kejriwal and Mr Sisodia for entrusting me with the responsibility of working in a leadership role in the government and for serving the people of Delhi.

If there is one person without whom this book would have never even begun, let alone see the light of day, that is my better half—Padmapriya. She has been a true intellectual companion and my biggest critic throughout my life journey, and this book was no different. She latched on to the idea of this book the moment it was conceived and made sure I never let go of it. As a writer and public policy professional, she took on additional roles of reviewing each of my early drafts, correcting, commenting and editing it. It was only due to her encouragement throughout the journey of writing this book that I could get this far.

This book was a collaborative project in many ways for I had to lean on several friends and colleagues to piece together the true story of the Delhi Model across multiple sectors. Atishi, who started her journey as an adviser to

Delhi's education minister in 2015 and went on to become the chief minister of Delhi in September 2024, provided her valuable inputs in many chapters. I am extremely grateful to Shailendra Sharma, Shaleen Mitra, Ankit Srivastava, Abhishek Ranjan, Dimpy Suneja and Tushar Dhiman for generously sharing their time and wisdom, enabling me to do justice to this book. Shilpi Sharma took on the most difficult role of providing research assistance and verifying the accuracy of the data cited in this book. Priyadarshi Singh supported with research on the transport sector. Arundhati Prasad and Sparsh Raj Singh assisted with the book cover design, and Sunaina Mehrotra with the design of graphs and tables. Pritam Pal Singh, Aishwarya Titus and Lalit Maurya helped shortlist the images that are part of this book.

My editor at Penguin, Radhika Marwah, did the impossible job of turning this book around in an extremely tight schedule while constantly encouraging me at every stage. I am also grateful to the rest of the editorial team including Saumya Kalia, Aninda Das and Swarupa for giving the final manuscript such fantastic shape.

My parents, Arun and Rekha Shah, and my brother, Premal Shah, have been pillars of support throughout my journey in public service. I owe them everything for being able to get to where I am. My in-laws, Vijayalakshmi and Brig V.K. Janakiraman (retd), were a source of constant encouragement at every step of this journey.

Notes

Introduction

1 Pragya Kaushika, Mayura Jaywalker, 'Arvind Kejriwal government: 49 days, 49 steps', *Indian Express*, 6 April 2015, https://indianexpress.com/article/cities/delhi/hardlook-49-days-49-steps/

2 'Analysis of electoral trends in India', *Election Commission of India*, 2024, https://www.eci.gov.in/eci-backend/public/api/download?url=LMAhAK6sOPBp%2FNFF0iRfXbEB1EVSLT 41NNLRjYNJJP1KivrUxbfqkDatmHy12e%2FzVx8fLfn 2ReU7TfrqYobgIuGxFb0TguIZDlYt6lm81avhS2EFlXHdNHu VrXN22hJOkCT4PobZAPuSvSgAQo8vCfqwT0qe5ns34A Gmng5OpZc%3D.

Chapter 1: What Really Is the Delhi Model?

1 ET Bureau, 'Use less power if you cannot afford hiked charges: Sheila Dikshit', *Economic Times*, 25 February 2013, https://economictimes.indiatimes.com/news/politics-and-nation/use-less-power-if-you-cannot-afford-hiked-charges-sheila-dikshit/articleshow/18659933.cms?from=mdr

2 AAP 70-Point Action Plan, Delhi Assembly Election 2015 https://timesofindia.indiatimes.com/AAP-Manifesto/photo/46075319.cms

3 Delhi Government Website, https://finance.delhi.gov.in/sites/default/files/generic_multiple_files/budget_speech_2015-16_2.pdf

4 Special Correspondent, 'Education can eradicate poverty in one generation: Kejriwal', *The Hindu*, 17 September 2022), https://www.thehindu.com/news/cities/Delhi/education-can-eradicate-poverty-in-one-generation-kejriwal/article65899490.ece

5   FP Archives, "Make India First': Arvind Kejriwal attacks PM
     Modi's Make in India project', Firstpost, 27 September 2015,
     https://www.firstpost.com/india/make-india-first-arvind-kejriwal-
     attacks-pm-modis-make-in-india-project-2446786.html
6   United Nations Development Programme Website, https://www.
     undp.org/india/press-releases/india-shows-progress-human-
     development-index-ranks-134-out-193-countries
7   PTI, 'India ranks 129 on Global Gender Gap index; Iceland on top:
     WEF', The Hindu, 12 June 2024,
     https://www.thehindu.com/business/Economy/india-ranks-129-
     on-global-gender-gap-index-iceland-on-top-wef/article68280347.
     ece
8   Ibid
9   'State Finances : A Study of Budgets', Reserve Bank of India website,
     https://rbi.org.in/Scripts/PublicationsView.aspx?id=22297
10   Vishal Kant, 'I pity people who think infrastructures is just flyovers:
     Sisodia', Hindustan Times, 13 February 2016, https://www.
     hindustantimes.com/delhi/i-pity-people-who-think-infrastructure-
     is-just-flyovers-sisodia/story-798KCWwf9J7Yo6WOfdQSKJ.html
11   '1,414 Delhi govt. school children passed NEET, says Atishi',
     The Hindu, 8 June 2024, https://www.thehindu.com/news/cities/
     Delhi/1414-delhi-govt-school-children-passed-neet-says-atishi/
     article68263986.ece
12   Karan Deep Singh, 'Clean Toilets, Inspired Teachers: How India's
     Capital Is Fixing Its Schools', New York Times, 16 August 2022,
     https://www.nytimes.com/2022/08/16/world/asia/india-delhi-
     schools.html
13   Outcome Budget 2023–24, Delhi Government, 2023, https://
     delhiplanning.delhi.gov.in/planning/outcome-budget
14   Council on Energy, Environment and Water website, https://
     www.ceew.in/sites/default/files/CEEW-State-of-electricity-access-
     Executive-Summary-1.pdf
15   Centre for Science and Environment website, https://www.cseindia.
     org/Report-Jan3-4-End-of-2023-state-of-air-pollution.pdf
16   Directorate of Information and Publicity, Government of NCT of
     Delhi website, https://publicity.delhi.gov.in/publicity/delhi-creates-
     history-unprecedented-minimum-wages-hike-3rd-march-2017
17   Samreen Wani, 'Over dozen states have higher inflation than
     national average of 4.83% in April', Business Standard, 14 May
     2024,   https://www.business-standard.com/economy/news/over-

dozen-states-have-higher-inflation-than-national-avg-of-4-83-in-april-124051301218_1.html

18 Ibid

19 Press Information Bureau, https://static.pib.gov.in/WriteReadData/specificdocs/documents/2024/may/doc2024513336501.pdf

20 Staff Correspondent, 'Days before relaunch, government gives antigraft helpline more teeth', *The Hindu*, 2 April 2015, https://www.thehindu.com/news/cities/Delhi/days-before-relaunch-govt-gives-antigraft-helpline-more-teeth/article7059892.ece

21 FP Archives, 'Will make Delhi one of the 5 least corrupt cities in the world: CM Arvind Kejriwal', Firstpost, 6 April 2015, https://www.firstpost.com/india/will-make-delhi-one-5-least-corrupt-cities-world-cm-arvind-kejriwal-2185609.html

22 IANS, 'Modi not letting ACB work, alleges Kejriwal', *Business Standard*, 9 August 2015, https://www.business-standard.com/article/news-ians/modi-not-letting-acb-work-alleges-kejriwal-115080900535_1.html

23 HT Correspondent, 'Centre took away my most potent weapon against graft: Kejriwal', *Hindustan Times*, 12 February 2016, https://www.hindustantimes.com/delhi/centre-took-away-my-most-potent-weapon-against-graft-kejriwal/story-fytCZpL9McM93CbcQ6SmiP.html

24 Jatin Anand, 'In last 8 years, 104 Delhi government officials held by ACB over graft charges', *Indian Express*, 9 May 2023, https://indianexpress.com/article/cities/delhi/in-last-8-years-104-delhi-govt-officials-held-by-acb-over-graft-charges-8598876/

25 Aneesha Bedi, 'Why 19 Bills passed years ago by AAP-led Delhi assembly remain hanging', ThePrint, 8 January 2020, https://theprint.in/india/governance/why-19-bills-passed-years-ago-by-aap-led-delhi-assembly-remain-hanging/345764/

26 Moushumi Das Gupta, '3 years since launch, Lokpal is a non-starter. Complaints dry up, questions rise over intent', ThePrint, 11 January 2020, https://theprint.in/india/3-years-since-launch-lokpal-is-a-non-starter-complaints-dry-up-questions-rise-over-intent/795110/

27 Saurav Das, 'Corruption allegations felled the UPA, but Modi's bribery-fighting Lokpal has little to do', Article-14, 22 January 2022, https://article-14.com/post/corruption-allegations-felled-the-upa-but-modi-s-bribery-fighting-lokpal-has-little-to-do-61eb797944414

28 Express News Servive, 'In surprise move, Kejriwal sacks Food
    Minister Asim Ahmed over corruption charges', *Indian Express*,
    10 October 2015, https://indianexpress.com/article/cities/delhi/
    aap-govt-sacks-delhi-food-minister-asim-khan-over-corruption-
    charges/
29 Ibid
30 Vijay Pushkarna, 'Delhi Report Card: Doorstep delivery of services
    may prove winner for AAP as UT readies to vote', Firstpost, 8
    February 2020, https://www.firstpost.com/politics/delhi-report-
    card-doorstep-delivery-of-services-may-prove-winner-for-aap-as-
    ut-readies-to-vote-8017201.html
31 Jatin Anand, 'Former touts ask government for a second chance',
    The Hindu, 12 September 2018, https://www.thehindu.com/news/
    cities/Delhi/former-touts-ask-government-for-a-second-chance/
    article24930232.ece
32 Claudia Eyzaguirre, Shaloo Jeswani, Taekyeong Yoo, Vrashabh
    Kapate, 'At your doorstep: Transforming governance in
    Delhi', *Berkeley Public Policy Journal*, 20 April 2022, https://
    bppj.studentorg.berkeley.edu/2022/04/20/at-your-doorstep-
    transforming-governance-in-delhi/
33 7 Years of DDC: 70 Innovations, Redefining Governance,
    Government of NCT of Delhi, https://ddc.delhi.gov.in/sites/
    default/files/reports/7_years_of_ddc_report.pdf
34 Alok K.N. Mishra, 'All government driving test tracks are now
    automated in Delhi', *Hindustan Time*s, 29 April 2023, https://www.
    hindustantimes.com/cities/delhi-news/delhis-13-government-run-
    driving-test-tracks-go-fully-automated-pass-percentage-drops-
    to-50-101682792754219.html
35 India Corruption Survey 2019 report, https://transparencyindia.
    org/wp-content/uploads/2019/11/India-Corruption-Survey-2019.
    pdf
36 Transparency International website, https://www.transparency.
    org/en/cpi/2023
37 PTI, 'Laws hampering retail trade will be done away with: Arvind
    Kejriwal', 27 December 2015, *Financial Express*, https://www.
    financialexpress.com/policy/economy-laws-hampering-retail-
    trade-will-be-done-away-with-arvind-kejriwal-184324/
38 Budget Speech 2016–17, Delhi Government, 2016, https://finance.
    delhi.gov.in/finance/budget-speech
39 Ibid

40 Ibid

41 Ibid

42 Atul Mathur, 'Manish Sisodia disbands entire team of tax inspectors', *Times of India*, 27 October 2018, https://timesofindia.indiatimes. com/city/delhi/sisodia-disbands-entire-team-of-tax-inspectors/ articleshow/66384952.cms

43 Ibid

44 PTI, 'Govt says 448 infrastructure projects hit by cost overrun of ₹5.55 lakh crore in Oct-December', *Economic Times*, 28 April 2024,   https://economictimes.indiatimes.com/news/economy/ infrastructure/govt-says-448-infra-projects-hit-by-cost-overrun-of-rs-5-55-lakh-cr-in-oct-dec/articleshow/109660649.cms?from=mdr

45 BT Desk, 'We saved money on this as well, Arvind Kejriwal opens Sarai Kale Khan flyover, says saved ₹557 crore in 30 projects', *Business Today*, 23 October 2023, https://www.businesstoday. in/latest/story/we-saved-money-on-this-as-well-arvind-kejriwal-opens-sarai-kale-khan-flyover-says-saved-rs-557-cr-in-30-projects-403017-2023-10-23

46 'The Economic Mantra Behind AAP's Health Initiatives - Satyender Jain in Conversation with Arvind Jha', uploaded by Aam Aadmi Party, 14 July 2017, https://youtu.be/VDOjkG1KIHs?si=sM_3WhOuoykZYKaZ

47 Jasmine Shah, 'Outcomes, not slogans', *Indian Express*, 7 April 2017, https://indianexpress.com/article/opinion/columns/ delhi-government-budget-manish-sisodia-outcomes-not-slogans-4602690/

48 Ibid

49 The Comptroller and Auditor General of India website, https://cag. gov.in/en/audit-report/details/116532#:~:text=Chapter%20I%20 is%20an%20overview,to%20meet%20the%20revenue%20 expenditure.

50 Sweta Goswami, 'Biggest proof of honesty: Kejriwal, Sisodia hail CAG report on surplus revenue', *Hindustan Times*, 6 July 2022, https://www.hindustantimes.com/cities/delhi-news/biggest-proof-of-honesty-kejriwal-sisodia-hail-cag-report-on-surplus-revenue-101657088242388.html

51 Reserve Bank of India website https://rbidocs.rbi.org.in/ rdocs/Publications/PDFs/19_STATEMENT11122023D 187AD89FC48486EB104402B1FDC219E.PDF

52 Ibid

53 Business Today Desk, "Should everybody be poor': PM Modi
    counters income inequality charge with an aviation example',
    Business Today, 17 May 2024, https://www.businesstoday.in/
    india/story/should-everybody-be-poor-pm-modi-counters-income-
    inequality-charge-with-an-aviation-example-429861-2024-05-16
54 Joseph E. Stiglitz, *The Great Divide: Unequal Societies and What
    We Can Do About Them* (2015).
55 *Joseph Stiglitz: Trickle-down economics is 'absolutely wrong'*,
    Uploaded by Intelligence Squared,https://www.youtube.com/
    watch?v=Auuk2oXK8tE
56 'The Economic Consequences of Major Tax Cuts for the Rich',
    eprints.lse.ac.uk/107919/1/Hope_economic_consequences_of_
    major_tax_cuts_published.pdf. Accessed 22 August 2024.
57 Robert Reich, 'Why is trickle-down economics still with us?',
    Guardian, 9 October 2022, https://www.theguardian.com/
    commentisfree/2022/oct/09/why-is-trickle-down-economics-still-
    with-us
58 Press Information Bureau website, https://pib.gov.in/
    Pressreleaseshare.aspx?PRID=1779403
59 PTI, 'NPA: Banks write off ₹1456 lakh crore NPAs in last nine
    financial years', *Economic Times*, 7 August 2023, https://
    economictimes.indiatimes.com/industry/banking/finance/banking/
    banks-write-off-rs-14-56-lakh-crore-npas-in-last-nine-financial-
    years/articleshow/102503282.cms?from=mdr
60 '₹10.4 lakh crore NPAs, 9 years: Which banks wrote off, recovered
    how much?', Newslaundry, 1 March 2024, https://www.
    newslaundry.com/2024/03/01/rs-104-lakh-crore-npas-9-years-
    which-banks-wrote-off-recovered-how-much
61 Devidas Tuljapurkar, 'A Decade of Write-Offs: How the
    government and banks failed NPAs and helped big corporations',
    The Wire, 30 October 2023, https://thewire.in/banking/a-decade-
    of-write-offs-how-the-govt-and-banks-failed-to-tackle-npas-and-
    helped-big-corporations
62 Nitin Kumar Bharti , Lucas Chancel , Thomas Piketty, and Anmol
    Somanchi, 'Income and Wealth Inequality in India, 1922–2023:
    The Rise of the Billionaire Raj', World Inequality Lab, https://
    wid.world/wp-content/uploads/2024/03/WorldInequalityLab_
    WP2024_09_Income-and-Wealth-Inequality-in-India-1922-2023_
    Final.pdf
63 Ibid

64 'India Employment Report 2024: Youth employment, education and skills', International Labour Organization, 29 March 2024, https://www.ilo.org/publications/india-employment-report-2024-youth-employment-education-and-skills

65 ET Bureau, '12.5 million new jobs created since 2014: Labour minister Bhupender Yadav', *Economic Times*, 23 June 2023, https://economictimes.indiatimes.com/news/india/massive-job-creation-in-nine-years-1-25-crore-got-employment-since-2014-bhupender-yadav/articleshow/101188570.cms?from=mdr

66 Maitreesh Ghatak, 'The rise of the affluent is the real India growth story', *Hindustan Times*, 29 February 2024, https://www.hindustantimes.com/opinion/the-rise-of-the-affluent-is-the-real-india-growth-story-101709211988507.html

67 Ibid

68 Joseph E. Stiglitz, 'A Progressive Agenda for the Twenty-First Century', Progressivism in America: Past, Present and Future, David B. Woolner and John M. Thompson (eds.), New York: Oxford University Press, 2015, pp. 215–232.

69 Joseph E. Stiglitz, 'Inequality and Economic Growth', *Political Quarterly*, 22 July 2016, https://onlinelibrary.wiley.com/doi/10.1111/1467-923X.12237

70 Abhijit V. Banerjee, Esther Duflo, *Good Economics for Hard Times* (Hachette Book Group, 2019)

71 'Budget Speech 2018–19', Finance Department, Government of Delhi, 2018, https://finance.delhi.gov.in/sites/default/files/generic_multiple_files/budget_speech_2018-19_2.pdf.

72 Ibid

73 Planning Department, Government of National Capital Territory of Delhi website, https://delhiplanning.delhi.gov.in/sites/default/files/Planning/generic_multiple_files/study_on_impact_of_subsidies_of_the_delhi_government_on_the_socio-economic_status_of_citizens_and_the_local_communityi.pdf

74 Press Information Bureau website, https://pib.gov.in/PressReleaseIframePage.aspx?PRID=2035278

75 Christophe Jaffrelot, 'India's jobs crisis & flaws in Gujarat model of development', *Mint*, 8 January 2019, https://www.livemint.com/Politics/RllLejcmnaOxT5IvfNoeUN/India-jobs-crisis--flaws-in-Gujarat-model-of-development.html

76 Atul Mathur, 'Capital gains: How Delhi turns a startup hub', *Times of India*, 1 February 2022,

https://timesofindia.indiatimes.com/city/delhi/capital-gains-how-delhi-turns-a-startup-hub/articleshow/89257491.cms

77 Aditya Rangroo, 'Economic Survey 2022: Delhi dethrones Bengaluru as startup capital of India', *Economic Times*, 31 January 2022, https://economictimes.indiatimes.com/tech/startups/economic-survey-2022-delhi-dethrones-bengaluru-as-startup-capital-of-india/articleshow/89249066.cms

78 PTI, 'Over 10 lakh got jobs in 2 years through Delhi govt's Rojgar Bazaar portal: Manish Sisodia', The Economic Times, 3 July 2022, https://economictimes.indiatimes.com/news/india/over-10-lakh-got-jobs-in-2-years-through-delhi-govts-rojgar-bazaar-portal-manish-sisodia/articleshow/92636992.cms?from=mdr

79 Delhi Government Website, https://finance.delhi.gov.in/sites/default/files/generic_multiple_files/budget_speech_2022-23_2.pdf

80 Ibid

81 Neil Baron, 'Biden's 'trickle-up economics' is just what America Needs, the *Hill*, 23 April 2021, https://thehill.com/opinion/finance/550007-bidens-trickle-up-economics-is-just-what-america-needs/

82 White House website https://www.whitehouse.gov/briefing-room/statements-releases/2023/06/28/bidenomics-is-working-the-presidents-plan-grows-the-economy-from-the-middle-out-and-bottom-up-not-the-top-down/

83 AAP's X account https://x.com/ArvindKejriwal/status/1203522341143101440

84 'National Election Studies', Lokniti, 2023, https://www.lokniti.org/national-election-studies.

85 Christophe Jaffrelot, 'What 'Gujarat Model'?—Growth without Development—and with Socio-Political Polarisation', *South Asia: Journal of South Asian Studies*, (2015), 38:4, pp. 820–838, DOI: 10.1080/00856401.2015.1087456

86 Ibid.

87 Maitreesh Ghatak, Sanchari Roy, 'Did Gujarat's Growth Rate Accelerate under Modi?', *Economic and Political Weekly of India*, April 12, 2014.

88 'Gujarat model was development on steroids: free land, large loans, nearly zero interest rates', The Print, 1 December 2023, https://theprint.in/pageturner/excerpt/gujarat-model-was-development-on-steroids-free-land-large-loans-nearly-zero-interest-rates/1313695/.

89 'The truth behind the Gujarat growth model', The Wire, 5 October 2023, https://thewire.in/202952/the-truth-behind-the-gujarat-growth-model.

90 Ashok Kotwal and Arka Roy Chaudhuri, 'The Perplexing Case of Gujarat', http://econ.sites.olt.ubc.ca/files/2014/03/pdf_paper_ashok-kotwal-perplexing.pdf.

91 'The truth behind the Gujarat growth model', The Wire, 5 October 2023, https://thewire.in/202952/the-truth-behind-the-gujarat-growth-model.

92 https://www.rbi.org.in/Scripts/PublicationsView.aspx?id=22177

93 'Multidimensional Poverty Index 2022', NITI Aayog, 2024, 'MPI 2022: National Multidimensional Poverty Index Report', NITI Aayog, 2024, https://www.niti.gov.in/sites/default/files/2024-01/MPI-22_NITI-Aayog20254.pdf

94 '1,606 primary schools in Gujarat functioning with just one teacher, govt tells Assembly', Economic Times, 10 October 2023, https://economictimes.indiatimes.com/news/india/1606-primary-schools-in-gujarat-functioning-with-just-one-teacher-govt-tells-assembly/articleshow/107628914.cms?from=mdr.

95 'How Gujarat faces an acute shortage of school teachers', India Today, 10 October 2023, https://www.indiatoday.in/india-today-insight/story/how-gujarat-faces-an-acute-shortage-of-school-teachers-2447097-2023-10-10.

96 'Gujarat's annual school inspection: Will another round change the reality?', Economic Times, 20 October 2023, https://economictimes.indiatimes.com/news/politics-and-nation/gujarats-annual-school-inspection-will-another-round-change-the-reality/articleshow/45153944.cms?from=mdr.

97 'Gujarat's annual school inspection: Will another round change the reality?', Economic Times, 20 October 2023, https://economictimes.indiatimes.com/news/politics-and-nation/gujarats-annual-school-inspection-will-another-round-change-the-reality/articleshow/45153944.cms?from=mdr.

98 '90% of govt schools shut, 500 merged in Gujarat since 2020: Govt data', Indian Express, 12 October 2023, https://indianexpress.com/article/cities/ahmedabad/90-govt-schools-shut-500-merged-in-gujarat-since-2020-govt-data-7835207/.

99 'Table 8.3: Sectoral Growth Rates of GDP', Economic Survey, Ministry of Finance, Government of India, 2023, https://www.indiabudget.gov.in/economicsurvey/doc/stat/tab83.pdf.

100 'ASER 2023: Beyond Basics', ASER Centre, 2023, https:// asercentre.org/aser-2023-beyond-basics/.

101 RBI study of state finances: https://rbi.org.in/Scripts/ PublicationsView.aspx?id=21684

102 'Shining Gujarat has a health problem: Missing MBBS doctors in rural PHCs', The Print, 20 October 2023, https://theprint.in/the-fineprint/shining-gujarat-has-a-health-problem-missing-mbbs-doctors-in-rural-phcs/1921246/.

103 'Annual Report 2022–23', Reserve Bank of India, 2023, https://m.rbi.org.in/scripts/PublicationsView.aspx?id=21401.

104 'The wide disparities in human development', The Hindu, 10 October 2023, https://www.thehindu.com/opinion/op-ed/the-wide-disparities-in-human-development/article66641610.ece.

105 Christophe Jaffrelot, 'India's jobs crisis & flaws in Gujarat Model of development', Mint, 8 January 2019, https://www. livemint.com/Politics/RllLejcmnaOxT5IvfNoeUN/India-jobs-crisis--flaws-in-Gujarat-model-of-development.html

106 'CAG warns Gujarat of falling into debt trap', Indian Express, 12 October 2023, https://indianexpress.com/article/ cities/ahmedabad/cag-warns-gujarat-of-falling-into-debt-trap-7846910/.

107 'Opposition parties mock PM Modi's classroom visit in Gujarat', ETV Bharat, 21 October 2023, https://www.etvbharat. com/english/state/gujarat/opposition-parties-mock-pm-modi-classroom-visit-in-gujarat/na20221021163252586586501.

Chapter 2: Education

1 'Study on School Education Reforms in Delhi 2015–20: An independent report by BCG', Boston Consulting Group, 2020, pp. 7, https://web-assets.bcg.com/1d/3e/9dceac2d4243a4d6a8d 3292e3172/school-education-reforms-in-delhi-2015-2020.pdf.

2 Manish Sisodia, Siksha: My Experiments as an Education Minister, (PRHI Gurgaon, 2019), p. x.

3 https://www.facebook.com/AamAadmiParty/photos/a.300369023 396198/701565799943183/?type=3

4 'CBSE Class XII results: Delhi govt schools' national pass percentage', Indian Express, 29 May 2023, https://indianexpress. com/article/cities/delhi/cbse-class-xii-results-delhi-govt-schools-national-pass-percentage-9326350/

5 'Delhi scores over 94% in CBSE board results', *Hindustan Times*, 29 May 2023, https://www.hindustantimes.com/cities/delhi-news/delhi-scores-over-94-in-cbse-board-results-101715623934891.html

6 '1,414 Delhi govt school children passed NEET, says Atishi', *The Hindu*, 29 June 2023, https://www.thehindu.com/news/cities/ Delhi/1414-delhi-govt-school-children-passed-neet-says-atishi/ article68263986.ece

7 'Study on School Education Reforms in Delhi 2015–20: An independent report by BCG', *Boston Consulting Group*, 2020, pp. 1–40, https://web-assets.bcg.com/1d/3e/9dceac2d4243a4d6a8d 3292e3172/school-education-reforms-in-delhi-2015-2020.pdf.

8 'Economic Survey of Delhi 2018–19', *Delhi Government*, 2019, https://delhiplanning.delhi.gov.in/planning/economic-survey-delhi-2018-19
'Directorate of Education, Delhi Government', *Delhi Government*, 2024,

9 Directorate of Education, Delhi Government.

10 'Reverse swing: 900 students choose this Delhi govt school over private ones', *Hindustan Times*, 1 August 2023, https:// www.hindustantimes.com/delhi-news/reverse-swing-900-students-choose-this-delhi-govt-school-over-private-ones/story-nNMnT6zUsL8O2HSdoE1LgJ.html.

11 'Study on School Education Reforms in Delhi 2015–20: An independent report by BCG', *Boston Consulting Group*, 2020, https://web-assets.bcg.com/1d/3e/9dceac2d4243a4d6a8d3292e3172/ school-education-reforms-in-delhi-2015-2020.pdf.

12 'Study on School Education Reforms in Delhi 2015–20: An independent report by BCG', *Boston Consulting Group*, 2020, p. 7, https://web-assets.bcg.com/1d/3e/9dceac2d4243a4d6a8d3292e3172/ school-education-reforms-in-delhi-2015-2020.pdf.

13 Manish Sisodia, *Siksha: My Experiments as an Education Minister,* (PRHI Gurgaon, 2019), p. xvi.

14 Ibid., p. xiv.

15 Ibid., p. xvi.

16 Budget Speech 2015–16, Delhi government, https://finance. delhi.gov.in/sites/default/files/generic_multiple_files/budget_ speech_2015-16_2.pdf

17 RBI, 'State Finances: A Study of Budgets', https://rbi.org.in/Scripts/ PublicationsView.aspx?id=22291

18 'Study on School Education Reforms in Delhi 2015–20:
    An independent report by BCG', *Boston Consulting Group*, 2020,
    https://web-assets.bcg.com/1d/3e/9dceac2d4243a4d6a8d3292e3172/
    school-education-reforms-in-delhi-2015-2020.pdf.

19 Ibid. p.97.

20 Directorate of Education, Delhi Government.

21 'The Delhi Model of Education', *The Hindu*, 2020, https://
    www.thehindu.com/opinion/op-ed/the-delhi-model-of-education/
    article30796187.ece.

22 'Outcome Budget 2023–24', Delhi Government, 2023, https://
    delhiplanning.delhi.gov.in/planning/outcome-budget-2023-24.

23 'Budget Speech 2024–25', Delhi Government, 2024, https://
    finance.delhi.gov.in/sites/default/files/Finance/generic_multiple_
    files/budget_speech_2024-25_english.pdf.

24 Directorate of Training and Technical Education, Delhi
    Government.

25 'Delhi Teachers University Will Churn Out New Age
    Educators: Manish Sisodia', *Hindustan Times*, 2022, https://
    www.hindustantimes.com/cities/delhi-news/delhi-teachers-
    university-will-churn-out-new-age-educators-manish-
    sisodia-101646425935881.html.

26 'AAP Responds to Firstpost Story on Pass Percentage in Delhi
    Schools, Says Report Doesn't Reflect Data Fully', Firstpost, 2020,
    https://www.firstpost.com/politics/delhi-assembly-election-2020-
    aap-responds-to-firstpost-story-on-pass-percentage-in-delhi-
    schools-says-report-doesnt-reflect-data-fully-7991881.html.

27 Manish Sisodia, *Siksha: My Experiments as an Education Minister,*
    (PRHI Gurgaon, 2019), p. 10.

28 Ibid., p. 21.

29 Ibid., p. 23.

30 Ibid., p. 13.

31 Ibid., pp. 15–16.

32 Budget Speech 2024–25, Delhi Government, https://finance.delhi.
    gov.in/sites/default/files/Finance/generic_multiple_files/budget_
    speech_2024-25_english.pdf

33 Manish Sisodia, *Siksha: My Experiments as an Education Minister,*
    (PRHI Gurgaon, 2019), p. 12.

34 Directorate of Education, Delhi government

35 'DDA gave us only one plot of land in last four years to make
    school', *Indian Express*, 2024, https://indianexpress.com/article/

cities/delhi/dda-gave-us-only-one-plot-of-land-in-last-four-years-to-make-school-education-department-5759505/.

36 Manish Sisodia, *Siksha: My Experiments as an Education Minister,* (PRHI Gurgaon, 2019), p. 49.

37 Directorate of Education, Delhi Government.

38 '2020 BCG Study on School Education Reforms in Delhi 2015–20', *BCG,* 2020, p. 24, https://web-assets.bcg.com/1d/3e/9dceac2d4243a4d6a8d3292e3172/school-education-reforms-in-delhi-2015-2020.pdf.

39 '2020 BCG Study on School Education Reforms in Delhi 2015–20', *BCG,* 2020, p. 24, https://web-assets.bcg.com/1d/3e/9dceac2d4243a4d6a8d3292e3172/school-education-reforms-in-delhi-2015-2020.pdf.

40 '90 Principals of Delhi Government School to Visit Cambridge University', *NDTV,* 2023, https://www.ndtv.com/indians-abroad/90-principals-of-delhi-government-school-to-visit-cambridge-university-1338734.

41 State Council of Education Research and Training (SCERT), Delhi Government.

42 'Clear bill to regularise guest teachers: Manish Sisodia to L-G Baijal', *Hindustan Times,* date not specified, https://www.hindustantimes.com/delhi-news/clear-bill-to-regularise-guest-teachers-manish-sisodia-to-l-g-baijal/story-ukB5izxgvbmVmmGeAX8FuJ.html.

43 '2020 BCG Study on School Education Reforms in Delhi 2015–20', BCG, 2020, p. 38, https://web-assets.bcg.com/1d/3e/9dceac2d4243a4d6a8d3292e3172/school-education-reforms-in-delhi-2015-2020.pdf.

44 Manish Sisodia, *Siksha: My Experiments as an Education Minister,* (PRHI Gurgaon, 2019), p. 52.

45 Manish Sisodia, *Siksha: My Experiments as an Education Minister,* (PRHI Gurgaon, 2019), pp. 42–43.

46 Manish Sisodia, *Siksha: My Experiments as an Education Minister,* (PRHI Gurgaon, 2019), pp. 61–87.

47 State Council of Education Research and Training (SCERT), Delhi Government

48 '60 Delhi govt school principals to go to Cambridge', *Business Standard,* 2018, https://www.business-standard.com/article/news-ians/60-delhi-govt-school-principals-to-go-to-cambridge-118100100862_1.html.

49 'Delhi govt restructures SCERT, DIET for better teacher training opportunities', *Hindustan Times*, 20 January 2021, https://www. hindustantimes.com/cities/others/delhi-govt-restructures-scert-diet-for-better-teacher-training-opportunities-101610647831927. html.

50 Manish Sisodia, *Siksha: My Experiments as an Education Minister,* (PRHI Gurgaon, 2019), p. 96.

51 'AAP to allocate funds to school management committees', *The Hindu*, 29 December 2017, https://www.thehindu.com/news/cities/ Delhi/aap-to-allocate-funds-to-school-management-committees/ article22321382.ece.

52 Manish Sisodia, *Siksha: My Experiments as an Education Minister,* (PRHI Gurgaon, 2019), p. 97.

53 Manish Sisodia, *Siksha: My Experiments as an Education Minister,* (PRHI Gurgaon, 2019), p. 102.

54 Manish Sisodia, *Siksha: My Experiments as an Education Minister,* (PRHI Gurgaon, 2019), pp. 106–108.

55 'Sisodia interacts with members of school management committees', *Hindustan Times*, 27 December 2017, https://www.hindustantimes. com/education/sisodia-interacts-with-members-of-school-management-committees/story-B2h2hZgRAGN01azhtqC6ZN. html.

56 '2020 BCG Study on School Education Reforms in Delhi, 2015–20', *Boston Consulting Group*, 2020, https://web-assets.bcg. com/1d/3e/9dceac2d4243a4d6a8d3292e3172/school-education-reforms-in-delhi-2015-2020.pdf.

57 Ibid. p.58.

58 'Half of Class 6 students in Delhi's govt schools cannot even read', *Hindustan Times*, 3 May 2017, https://www.hindustantimes.com/ delhi/half-of-class-6-students-in-delhi-s-govt-schools-cannot-even-read/story-Rwb4RtqQgkC4NMrYBc93eN.html.

59 'Teaching at the Right Level to improve learning', *Abdul Latif Jameel Poverty Action Lab*, 2018, https://www.povertyactionlab. org/case-study/teaching-right-level-improve-learning.

60 Directorate of Education, Delhi Government

61 Mindset Curricula booklet, Directorate of Education, Delhi Government

62 'The Happiness Curriculum: inculcating mindfulness and social and emotional learning amongst students every day', OECD

Observatory of Public Sector Innovation, 2021, https://oecd-opsi.org/innovations/the-happiness-curriculum-inculcating-mindfulness-and-social-and-emotional-learning-amongst-students-every-day/.

63 Manish Sisodia, *Siksha: My Experiments as an Education Minister,* (PRHI Gurgaon, 2019), p. 138.

64 'Development of student and teacher measures of HC factors', Brookings Institution, 19 August 2020, https://www.brookings.edu/wp-content/uploads/2020/08/Development-of-student-and-teacher-measures-of-HC-factors-FINAL-081920.pdf.

65 Ibid.

66 Manish Sisodia, *Siksha: My Experiments as an Education Minister,* (PRHI Gurgaon, 2019), p. 138.

67 Mindset Curricula booklet, Directorate of Education, Delhi government.

68 'Awards and recognitions: CHVTL', State Council of Educational Research and Training, Delhi, 2023, https://scert.delhi.gov.in/scert/awards-and-recognitions-chvtl.

69 'Melania Trump attends happiness class in govt school, says curriculum inspiring', *The Hindu*, 25 February 2020, https://www.thehindu.com/news/national/melania-trump-attends-happiness-class-in-govt-school-says-curriculum-inspiring/article30912161.ece.

70 'Happiness classes likely in Uttarakhand schools from July', *Hindustan Times*, 11 March 2020, https://www.hindustantimes.com/education/happiness-classes-likely-in-uttarakhand-schools-from-july/story-H8ivDeyWXzdKibkkUsOHOK.html.

71 Manish Sisodia, *Siksha: My Experiments as an Education Minister,* (PRHI Gurgaon, 2019), p. 160.

72 Ibid., p. 163.

73 Directorate of Education, Delhi Government.

74 'Happiness classes likely in Uttarakhand schools from July', *Hindustan Times*, 11 March 2020, https://www.hindustantimes.com/education/happiness-classes-likely-in-uttarakhand-schools-from-july/story-H8ivDeyWXzdKibkkUsOHOK.html.

75 Mindset Curricula booklet, Directorate of Education, Delhi government.

76 Directorate of Education, Delhi Government.

77 '30330 schools to be affiliated to New Delhi state board, says Sisodia', *Hindustan Times*, 14 April 2022, https://www.hindustantimes.com/

cities/others/30-schools-to-be-affiliated-to-new-delhi-state-board-says-sisodia-101627409719914.html.

78 'Assessment Framework Draft version', Delhi Directorate of Education, 28 June 2022, https://www.edudel.nic.in/dbse/resources/pdfs/Assessment%20Framework_Draft%20version_280622_F.pdf.

79 'Delhi Board of School Education (DBSE) sets new benchmark with 99.49% pass rate in Class 10 and 99.25% in Class 12 exams', *Hindustan Times*, 10 July 2023, https://www.hindustantimes.com/cities/delhi-news/delhi-board-of-school-education-dbse-sets-new-benchmark-with-99-49-pass-rate-in-class-10-and-99-25-in-class-12-exams-101684175104772.html.

80 'About SOSE', Delhi Directorate of Education, 2023, https://www.edudel.nic.in/about/sose.

81 'Govt schools perform well in JEE Advanced too', Millennium Post, 17 June 2023, https://www.millenniumpost.in/delhi/govt-schools-perform-well-in-jee-advanced-too-568026.

82 '1,414 Delhi govt school children passed NEET, says Atishi', *The Hindu*, 27 July 2023, https://www.thehindu.com/news/cities/Delhi/1414-delhi-govt-school-children-passed-neet-says-atishi/article68263986.ece.

83 '32 kids from first batch of Delhi Armed Forces School clear NDA written exam', *Indian Express*, 19 April 2023, https://indianexpress.com/article/cities/delhi/32-kids-first-batch-delhi-armed-forces-school-clear-nda-written-exam-8959012/.

84 'Delhi's virtual school model: Arvind Kejriwal', *Indian Express*, 24 August 2023, https://indianexpress.com/article/cities/delhi/delhi-virtual-school-model-arvind-kejriwal-8122434/.

85 'Human Development Report 2023–24', United Nations Development Programme, 2023, https://hdr.undp.org/content/human-development-report-2023-24

86 'ASER 2023: Main Findings', ASER Centre, 2023, https://asercentre.org/wp-content/uploads/2022/12/ASER-2023_Main-findings-1.pdf

87 'India Skills Report 2024', Wheebox, 2024, https://wheebox.com/india-skills-report.htm.

88 'Young Indians more likely to be jobless if they are educated: ILO data', *Business Standard*, 29 March 2024, https://www.business-standard.com/economy/news/young-indians-more-likely-to-be-jobless-if-they-are-educated-ilo-data-124032900038_1.html.

89 World Inequality Report 2022, https://wir2022.wid.world/

90 'Cadre for the Indian Administrative Service', Parliament of India, 19 November 1948, https://eparlib.nic.in/bitstream/123456789/763029/1/cad_19-11-1948.pdf.

91 Analysis of the Union Budget: CBGA, https://www.cbgaindia.org/publications/analysis-of-union-budget/

92 RBI study of state finances 2023, Expenditure on Education - As Ratio to Aggregate Expenditure

93 Economic Survey of India 2023–24, https://www.indiabudget.gov.in/economicsurvey/

94 UDISE+ dashboard, Government of India, https://udiseplus.gov.in/

95 'Education Ministry reports over 8 lakh teaching vacancies in govt schools', News18, 5 February 2024, https://www.news18.com/education-career/education-ministry-reports-over-8-lakh-teaching-vacancies-in-govt-schools-8692309.html.

96 'PM SHRI Schools', Department of School Education and Literacy, 2023, https://dsel.education.gov.in/pm-shri-schools

Chapter 3: Health

1 Karthik Muralidharan, Nazmul Chaudhury, Jeffrey Hammer, Michael Kremer, F. Halsey Rogers, 'Is There a Doctor in the House? Medical Worker Absence in India', 12 April 2011, https://econweb.ucsd.edu/~kamurali/papers/Working%20Papers/Is%20There%20a%20Doctor%20in%20the%20House%20-%2012%20April,%202011.pdf

2 Ishan Anand, Anjana Thampi, 'Less than a third of Indians go to public hospitals for treatment', Livemint, 4 May 2020, https://www.livemint.com/news/india/less-than-a-third-of-indians-go-to-public-hospitals-for-treatment-11588578426388.html

3 'Report on Trend and Progress of Banking in India 2022–23', Reserve Bank of India, 2023, https://rbi.org.in/Scripts/PublicationsView.aspx?id=2229

4 Reserve Bank of India website, https://rbi.org.in/Scripts/PublicationsView.aspx?id=22302

5 Delhi Government website, , https://delhiplanning.delhi.gov.in/sites/default/files/Planning/budget_highlights_2024-25_english_0.pdf

6 State Health Intelligence Report, Delhi government website, https://dgehs.delhi.gov.in/dghs/annual-report

7 Ibid

8 Census of India website, https://censusindia.gov.in/census.website/data/SRSB

9 Ibid

10 'The Economic Mantra Behind Aap's Health Initiatives - Satyender Jain in Conversation with Arvind Jha', Uploaded by Aam Aadmi Party, 14 July 2017, https://www.youtube.com/watch?v=VDOjkG1KIHs

11 Chandrakant Lahariya, 'Access, utilization, perceived quality, and satisfaction with health services at Mohalla (Community) Clinics of Delhi, India'. *J Family Med Prim Care,* 31 December 2020; https://pubmed.ncbi.nlm.nih.gov/33681011/

12 Taniya Sah, Neha Bailwal, Rituparna Kaushik, 'Are Mohalla Clinics Making the Aam Aadmi Party Healthy in Delhi?', the Wire, 20 June 2019, https://thewire.in/health/are-mohalla-clinics-making-the-aam-aadmi-healthy-in-delhi

13 Ibid

14 Charu C. Garg, Roopali Goyanka, 'A comparison of the cost of outpatient care delivered by Aam Aadmi Mohalla Clinics compared to other public and private facilities in Delhi, India', *Health Policy and Planning Journal,* 6 May 2023, https://doi.org/10.1093/heapol/czad033

15 'Supporting the Government of Delhi to Improve Primary Healthcare via the Mohalla Clinic', IDInsight, 16 June 2019, https://www.idinsight.org/article/supporting-the-government-of-delhi-to-improve-primary-healthcare-via-the-mohalla-clinic-programme/

16 Ibid

17 Ibid

18 HT Correspondent, 'AAP MLAs "protest"' inside L-G office, demand approval of mohalla clinic project', *Hindustan Times,* 30 August 2017, https://www.hindustantimes.com/delhi-news/aap-mlas-protest-inside-l-g-office-demand-approval-of-mohalla-clinic-project/story-6hG7tQILWCYzKE5C2m7mjO.html

19 PTI, 'DDA not handing over sites for mohalla clinics, Delhi govt tells HC', *Indian Express,* 1 February 2019, https://indianexpress.com/article/cities/delhi/mohalla-clinics-delhi-aap-dda-high-court-5565050/

20 PTI, 'Makeshift mohalla clinics in north Delhi face "demolition"', *Indian Express,* 3 September 2016, https://indianexpress.com/

article/cities/delhi/makeshift-mohalla-clinics-in-north-delhi-face-demolition-3011870/

21 'Mohalla Clinics Recognised by Fast Company's Innovation by Design Awards', Architecture Discipline, September 2022, https://www.architecturediscipline.com/news-listing/mohalla-clinics-recognised-by-fast-companys-innovation-by-design-awards/

22 'Delhi: Health clinics at 20 government schools to ensure physical, mental well-being', *India Today*, 8 March 2022, https://www.indiatoday.in/cities/delhi/story/delhi-health-clinics-launched-at-20-government-schools-1922027-2022-03-08

23 IANS, 'Kejriwal inaugurates four Mahila Mohalla Clinics exclusively for women', *Business Standard*, 3 November 2022, https://www.business-standard.com/article/current-affairs/kejriwal-inaugurates-four-mahila-mohalla-clinics-exclusively-for-women-122110201743_1.html

24 'Fill vacancies in Govt. hospitals, HC asks Centre', *The Hindu*, 25 November 2021, https://www.thehindu.com/news/cities/Delhi/fill-vacancies-in-govt-hospitals-hc-asks-centre/article37674748.ece

25 Lahariya C. 'Access, utilization, perceived quality, and satisfaction with health services at Mohalla (Community) Clinics of Delhi', India. J Family Med Prim Care 2020; 9:5872-80

26 PTI, 'Delhi government hospitals OPD timings extended by 2 hours', *Business Standard*, 9 October 2017, https://www.business-standard.com/article/pti-stories/delhi-govt-hospitals-opd-timings-extended-by-2-hours-117100901268_1.html

27 Priyanka Sharma, 'To address unavailability of drugs in Delhi govt hospitals, AAP government to strengthen procurement of medicine', *India Today*, 17 June 2017, lhttps://www.indiatoday.in/mail-today/story/arvind-kejriwal-hospital-free-medicines-980121-2017-05-31

28 Astha Saxena, 'Helpline comes to patients' aid at Delhi govt hospitals', *Indian Express*, 25 November 2019, https://indianexpress.com/article/cities/delhi/helpline-comes-to-patients-aid-at-delhi-govt-hospitals-6135120/

29 PTI, 'Arvind Kejriwal pays surprising visit to DDU hospital', *Indian Express*, 2 June 2017, https://indianexpress.com/article/cities/delhi/arvind-kejriwal-pays-surprise-visit-to-ddu-hospital-4686212/

30 PTI, 'Arvind Kejriwal pays Delhi govt hospital a surprise visit, finds violation in prescription', Firstpost, 16 June 2017, https://www.

firstpost.com/india/arvind-kejriwal-pays-delhi-govt-hospital-a-surprise-visit-finds-violation-in-prescription-3705017.html

31 Anonna Dutt, 'Govt gives free medicine, sales down at nearby private pharmacies', *Hindustan Times*, 6 May 2016, https://www.hindustantimes.com/delhi/govt-gives-free-medicine-sales-down-at-nearby-private-pharmacies/story-sXaodMtToJ8EewWymmjtEM.html

32 PTI, 'Delhi health minister Saurabh Bhardwaj gets irked by lapses in cleanliness at govt hospitals, directs strict action', *Deccan Herald*, 14 December 2023, https://www.deccanherald.com/india/delhi/delhi-health-minister-saurabh-bhardwaj-gets-irked-by-lapses-in-cleanliness-at-govt-hospital-directs-strict-action-2811754

33 'The Economic Mantra Behind Aap's Health Initiatives - Satyender Jain in Conversation with Arvind Jha'. Uploaded by the Aam Aadmi Party, 14 July 2017, https://youtu.be/VDOjkG1KIHs?si=pXP_4Ql85xmTDP6O

34 Abhinav Rajput, 'LG ignored several requests by me on vacant health posts: Saurabh Bharadwaj', *Times of India*, 5 August 2024, https://timesofindia.indiatimes.com/city/delhi/delhi-health-minister-accuses-lg-of-inaction-on-vacant-health-posts/articleshow/112272060.cms

35 Sakthivel Selvaraj, Anup K. Kara, Swati Srivastava, Nandita Bhan, Indranil Mukhopadhyay, 'India Health System Review', Health Systems in Transition, https://iris.who.int/bitstream/handle/10665/352685/9789290229049-eng.pdf?sequence=1

36 Geetanjali Kapoor, Aditi Sriram, Jyoti Hoshi, Arindam Nandi, Ramanan Laxminarayan, 'COVID-19 in India: State-wise estimates of current hospital beds, intensive care unit beds and ventilators', An analysis by the Center for Disease Dynamics, Economics & Policy, 20 April 2020, in April 2020: https://onehealthtrust.org/wp-content/uploads/2020/04/State-wise-estimates-of-current-beds-and-ventilators_24Apr2020.pdf

37 Delhi Arogya Kosh, Delhi government website, https://dgehs.delhi.gov.in/dghs/delhi-arogya-kosh

38 Ibid

39 'Delhi L-G Finally Gives Nod to Kejriwal's Quality Healthcare for All Plan', India Today, 17 January 2018, https://www.indiatoday.in/mail-today/story/delhi-l-g-finally-gives-nod-to-kejriwal-s-quality-healthcare-for-all-plan-1147377-2018-01-17

40 State Health Intelligence Report, Delhi government website, https://dgehs.delhi.gov.in/dghs/annual-report

41 The World Bank, 'Traffic Crash Injuries and Disabilities: The Burden on Indian Society', 13 February 2021, https://www.worldbank.org/en/country/india/publication/traffic-crash-injuries-and-disabilities-the-burden-on-indian-society

42 Ministry of Road, Transport and Highways website, https://morth.nic.in/sites/default/files/RA_2022_30_Oct.pdf

43 Government of NCT of Delhi website, https://ddc.delhi.gov.in/sites/default/files/reports/7_years_of_ddc_report.pdf

44 Abhishek Dey, 'In 3 months, 430 more CATS ambulances put on Covid duty, cuts response time', *Hindustan Times*, 22 August 2020, https://www.hindustantimes.com/india-news/in-3-months-430-more-cats-ambulances-put-on-covid-duty-cuts-response-time/story-pS1YbzREX6FwsSGedJpFgL.html

45 Outcome Budget 2021–22 and Department of Health and Family Welfare, GNCTD

46 World Health Organization website, https://www.who.int/news-room/fact-sheets/detail/universal-health-coverage-(uhc)

47 National Health Mission website, https://nhm.gov.in/images/pdf/publication/Planning_Commission/rep_uhc0812.pdf

48 National Health Policy 2017, Ministry of Health and Family Welfare website, https://mohfw.gov.in/sites/default/files/9147562941489753121.pdf

49 Centre for Budget and Government Accountability website, https://www.cbgaindia.org/wp-content/uploads/2024/02/Of-Monies-and-Matters-An-Analysis-of-Interim-Union-Budget-2024-25-2.pdf

50 Reserve Bank of India website, https://rbi.org.in/Scripts/PublicationsView.aspx?id=22292

51 'Budget 2024 debate: FM Nirmala Sitharaman tears into Opposition, says no state being denied any money - Key points', Livemint, https://www.livemint.com/budget/fm-nirmala-sitharaman-responds-to-budget-debate-in-lok-sabha-india-fastest-growing-economy-opposition-sectors-capex-push-11722339077914.html

52 National Health Systems Resource Centre, https://nhsrcindia.org/sites/default/files/2023-04/National%20Health%20Accounts-2019-20.pdf

53 NITI Aayog website, https://www.niti.gov.in/sites/default/
    files/2021-10/HealthInsurance-forIndiasMissingMidd
    le_28-10-2021.pdf

54 Prachi Salve, 'Modi Govt Doubled Spending On Insurance, Not
    Enough On Health Infrastructure', IndiaSpend, 17 April 2024,
    https://www.indiaspend.com/health/modi-govt-doubled-spending-
    on-insurance-not-enough-on-health-infrastructure-904388

55 Rural Health Statistics 2021–22: https://hmis.mohfw.gov.in/
    downloadfile?filepath=publications/Rural-Health-Statistics/
    RHS%202021-22.pdf

56 National Health Accounts 2019–20: https://mohfw.gov.in/sites/
    default/files/5NHA_19-20_dt%2019%20April%202023_web_
    version_1.pdf

57 Tabassum Barnagarwala, 'The Modi government's much-hyped
    health centres are failing', Scroll.in, 29 May 2024, https://scroll.
    in/article/1067868/the-modi-governments-much-hyped-health-
    centres-are-failing

58 Prachi Salve, 'Health Expenses Pushed 55 Million Indians
    Into Poverty In 2011–12', India Spend, 19 July 2018, https://
    www.indiaspend.com/health-expenses-pushed-55-million-
    indians-into-poverty-in-2017-2017/#:~:text=Mumbai%3A%20
    Out%2Dof%2Dpocket,according%20to%20a%20new%20
    study

59 Natasha Agnes D'Criz, 'Risky Insurance: The Pradhan Mantri Jan
    Arogya Yojana in Jharkhand', Economic and Political Weekly,
    7 November 2020, https://www.epw.in/engage/article/risky-
    insurance-pradhan-mantri-jan-arogya-yojana

60 Durgesh Nandan Jha, '80% of public health facilities are
    substandard: govt survey', Times of India, 29 June 2024, https://
    timesofindia.indiatimes.com/india/80-of-public-health-facilities-
    are-substandard-govt-survey/articleshow/111350919.cms

61 Tabassum Barnagarwal, 'The pandemic's hidden cost: much-hyped
    health insurance scheme failed to cover hospital bills', Scroll.in,
    24 March 2022, https://scroll.in/article/1020201/the-pandemics-
    hidden-cost-much-hyped-health-insurance-scheme-failed-to-cover-
    hospital-bills

62 Ibid

63 Tabassum Barnagarwala, 'Modi government's insurance scheme
    pushes hospitals into debt–threatening patient admission', Scroll.

in, 11 March 2024, https://scroll.in/article/1064819/modi-governments-insurance-scheme-pushes-hospitals-into-debt-threatening-patient-admissions

Chapter 4: Air Pollution

1 Interaction Design Foundation website, https://www.interaction-design.org/literature/topics/wicked-problems

2 Central Pollution Control Board website, https://cpcb.nic.in/namp-data/

3 Press Information Bureau website, https://pib.gov.in/newsite/printrelease.aspx?relid=110654

4 IQAir website, https://www.iqair.com/in-en/world-most-polluted-cities

5 *Report on South Asia Air Quality Management – Delhi NCR*, TERI, https://www.teriin.org/sites/default/files/2018-08/Report_SA_AQM-Delhi-NCR_0.pdf.

6 Abhinaya Harigovind, 'This year, new system to pinpoint sources of air pollution in Delhi-NCR', *Indian Express*, 25 September 2021, https://indianexpress.com/article/cities/delhi/new-system-sources-air-pollution-delhi-ncr-7534401/.

7 Kushagra Dixit, 'Over 70% of Delhi's pollution not its creation, from NCR & beyond', 4 November 2022, *Times of India*, http://timesofindia.indiatimes.com/articleshow/95286066.cms?utm_source=contentofinterest&utm_medium=text&utm_campaign=cppst.

8 'Delhi PM2.5 levels rose by 68 per cent within a day in early November: CSE', *Down to Earth*, https://www.downtoearth.org.in/news/air/delhi-pm2-5-levels-rose-by-68-per-cent-within-a-day-in-early-november-cse-92649.

9 'Dear editor, I disagree: On air pollution, the Centre and BJP governments share the blame', *Indian Express*, https://indianexpress.com/article/opinion/dear-editor-disagree-air-pollution-centre-bjp-governments-share-blame-9017024/.

10 'Report on SA AQM in Delhi-NCR', The Energy and Resources Institute, https://www.teriin.org/sites/default/files/2018-08/Report_SA_AQM-Delhi-NCR_0.pdf.

11 'Good green policies make for good politics: Kejriwal in climate summit address', *Hindustan Times*, https://www.hindustantimes.com/cities/good-green-policies-make-for-good-politics-kejriwal-

in-climate-summit-address/story-yr8godnv6KCg8ZSOfS1DmN.
html.

12 Budget Speech 2018–19, https://finance.delhi.gov.in/sites/default/files/
    generic_multiple_files/budget_speech_2018-19_2.pdf.

13 'More than a third of power consumed in Delhi is green', *Times
    of India*, 5 November 2023, https://timesofindia.indiatimes.com/
    city/delhi/more-than-a-third-of-power-consumed-in-delhi-is-green/
    articleshow/105972288.cms.

14 'End of 2023: State of Air Pollution', Centre for Science and
    Environment, 2023, https://www.cseindia.org/Report-Jan3-4-End-
    of-2023-state-of-air-pollution.pdf

15 CPCB real-time air quality data taken for PM2.5 from 2014–23
    and for PM10 from 2018–2023. The PM10 data for 2014–17 was
    taken from Delhi Pollution Control Committee (DPCC), a Delhi
    government agency, due to unavailability of CPCB data for that
    period. Data for 2014–17 is averaged from six monitoring stations
    and from 2018–2023 is averaged from thirty-eight monitoring
    stations in Delhi.

16 *Hindustan Times*, 'Air Quality in Delhi Showing Gradual
    Improvement, Says Economic Survey', 16 February 2023,
    https://www.hindustantimes.com/cities/delhi-news/air-quality
    -in-delhi-showing-gradual-improvement-says-economic-
    survey-101675190018348.html
    Press Information Bureau, 'Press Release on Economic Survey',
    31 January 2023, https://pib.gov.in/PressReleaseIframePage.
    aspx?PRID=1991970

17 'End of 2023: State of Air Pollution', Centre for Science and
    Environment, 2023, https://www.cseindia.org/Report-Jan3-4-End-
    of-2023-state-of-air-pollution.pdf

18 Press Information Bureau, 'Press Release on Period During January-
    October', 3 November 2022, https://pib.gov.in/PressReleaseIframePage.
    aspx?PRID=1973418#:~:text=The%20period%20during%20
    January%2DOctober,barring%20the%20COVID%20affected%20
    2020

19 https://www.teriin.org/sites/default/files/2018-08/Report_SA_
    AQM-Delhi-NCR_0.pdf

20 *Economic Times*, 'Supreme Court Nod to Green Cess on
    Trucks Passing Through Delhi', 2 October 2015, https://
    economictimes.indiatimes.com/news/politics-and-nation/supreme-

court-nod-to-green-cess-on-trucks-passing-through-delhi/
articleshow/49295228.cms?from=mdr

21 Delhi Government, 'Budget Speech 2024–25', 2024, https://
finance.delhi.gov.in/finance/budget-speech

22 https://pib.gov.in/PressReleaseIframePage.aspx?PRID=1987802

23 https://www.teriin.org/sites/default/files/2018-08/Report_SA_
AQM-Delhi-NCR_0.pdf

24 https://pib.gov.in/Pressreleaseshare.aspx?PRID=1694709

25 *Down To Earth*. 'The Undisclosed Air Pollutants,' 2023, https://www.
downtoearth.org.in/blog/air/the-undisclosed-air-pollutants-56786.

26 *Down To Earth*. 'Commission for Air Quality Management Orders
Phase Out of Coal in Delhi-NCR by January 1, 2023,' 2023,
https://www.downtoearth.org.in/news/pollution/commission-for-
air-quality-management-orders-phase-out-of-coal-in-delhi-ncr-by-
january-1-2023-83210.

27 https://pib.gov.in/PressReleaseIframePage.aspx?PRID=1908953

28 Centre for Science and Environment. 'Coal-Based Thermal Power
Plants Ignoring Pollution Control Measures Responsible,' 2023,
https://www.cseindia.org/coal-based-thermal-power-plants-ignoring-
pollution-control-measures-responsible-11969#:~:text=New%20
Delhi%2C%20November%2025%2C%202023,complying%-
20with%20emission%20control%20norms.

29 *Times of India*. 'Shut All 11 NCR Thermal Plants to Curb
Pollution: Delhi to Centre,' 2023, https://timesofindia.indiatimes.
com/city/delhi/shut-all-11-ncr-thermal-plants-to-curb-pollution-
delhi-to-centre/articleshow/78671719.cms.

30 *Hindu*. 'BSES Discoms Blamed for Power Cuts,' 2023, https://
www.thehindu.com/news/cities/Delhi/bses-discoms-blamed-for-
power-cuts/article6215725.ece.

31 Council on Energy, Environment and Water. 'Access to Electricity:
Availability and Electrification Percentage in India,' 2023, https://
www.ceew.in/publications/access-to-electricity-availability-and-
electrification-percentage-in-india.

32 *Times of India*. 'Just 4 Days to Grap 82 Condos in GGN; FBD
Still Rely on Gensets,' 2023, https://timesofindia.indiatimes.com/
city/gurgaon/just-4-days-to-grap-82-condos-in-ggn-fbd-still-rely-
on-gensets/articleshow/78609762.cms.

33 Commission for Air Quality Management. 'CAQM Press Release,'
2023, https://caqm.nic.in/WriteReadData/LINKS/CAQM%20

PR%2008%2006%202023%20014ba02f-c8d4-413f-b51b-
d02f75a8d3052889aac5-08b7-43f8-a7bb-b1c1c5c4b79b.pdf.

34 *Business Standard*. '85% of Delhi NCR Residents Reluctant to
Retrofit DG Sets with CNG: Survey,' 2023, https://www.business-
standard.com/india-news/85-of-delhi-ncr-residents-reluctant-to-
retrofit-dg-sets-with-cng-survey-123112200920_1.html.

35 Delhi Forest Department. 'Green Action Plan,' 2023, https://forest.
delhi.gov.in/forest/green-action-plan.

36 *Indian Express*. '2 Crore Trees, Shrubs Planted in Delhi Over 4
Yrs: Gopal Rai,' 2023, https://indianexpress.com/article/cities/
delhi/2-crore-trees-shrubs-planted-in-delhi-over-4-yrs-gopal-
rai-9210835/.

37 *Hindustan Times*. '7580 Saplings Planted in Delhi from 2016–
2019 Survived: Gopal Rai,' 2023, https://www.hindustantimes.
com/cities/delhi-news/7580-saplings-planted-in-delhi-from-2016-
2019-survived-gopal-rai-101646419644323.html.

38 'Green Action Plan for Delhi', Delhi Government eForest Portal,
2023, https://gap.eforest.delhi.gov.in/GAP.aspx

39 *Hindustan Times*, 'Land short: Alter compensatory plantation norms,
DDA to state', 29 October 2024, https://www.hindustantimes.com/
cities/delhi-news/land-short-alter-compensatory-plantation-norms-
dda-to-state-101652295281408.html

40 *Economic Times*, '9,000 hectare land available in Yamuna
floodplains for plantation: Delhi forest dept', 30 October 2024,
https://economictimes.indiatimes.com/news/india/9000-hactare-
land-available-in-yamuna-floodplains-for-plantation-delhi-forest-
dept/articleshow/93386671.cms?from=mdr

41 'City Forests', Delhi Forest Department, 2023, https://forest.delhi.
gov.in/forest/city-forestss

42 *Times of India*, '5 trees cut every hour in 3 years: Delhi HC says
act urgently', 30 October 2024, https://timesofindia.indiatimes.
com/city/delhi/5-trees-cut-every-hour-in-3-years-delhi-hc-says-act-
urgently/articleshow/97927426.cms

43 Delhi Forest Department, 'Tree Transplantation Policy
2020', 2020, https://forest.delhi.gov.in/sites/default/files/generic_
multiple_files/tpp-policy-2020.pdf

44 *Hindustan Times*, 'Understanding the rationale of Delhi's
tree transplantation policy', 30 October 2024, https://
www.hindustantimes.com/analysis/understanding-the-

rationale-of-delhi-s-tree-transplantation-policy/story-XHmgBLfq5MuGsx0HkCuwSM.html

45 Delhi Government, 'Outcome Budget 2023–24', 2023, https://delhiplanning.delhi.gov.in/planning/outcome-budget-2023-24

46 Department of Forests, Delhi Government, 'Delhi's Forests at a Glance Report, 2022', 2022, https://forest.delhi.gov.in/sites/default/files/generic_multiple_files/delhi_s_forest_at_a_glance.pdf

47 *Times of India*, 'At 9.6 square metres, Delhi has largest forest cover per resident: Rai', 10 August 2022, https://timesofindia.indiatimes.com/city/delhi/at-9-6-square-metres-delhi-has-largest-forest-cover-per-resident-rai/articleshow/90001747.cms

48 *Times of India*, 'Delhi joins UN-backed race, commits to 25% green cover in 5 years', 5 December 2023, https://timesofindia.indiatimes.com/city/delhi/delhi-joins-un-backed-race-commits-to-25-green-cover-in-5-years/articleshow/103874775.cms

49 *Times of India*, 'Marginal spike in Haryana forest area, but tree cover on the decline', 30 July 2022, https://timesofindia.indiatimes.com/city/chandigarh/marginal-spike-in-haryana-forest-area-but-tree-cover-on-the-decline/articleshow/88886835.cms

50 *Times of India*, 'Farm fire share in PM2.5 close to 50% in peak season', 2 November 2021, https://timesofindia.indiatimes.com/city/delhi/farm-fire-share-in-pm2-5-close-to-50-in-peak-season/articleshow/87724822.cms

51 'Year Wise Residue Data', Punjab Remote Sensing Centre, 2023, http://gis-prsc.punjab.gov.in/residue/Year_Wise.aspx

52 Council on Energy, Environment and Water, 'CEEW Study on Paddy Stubble Burning in Punjab: How to Solve Challenges with Solutions', 2021, https://www.ceew.in/sites/default/files/ceew-study-on-paddy-stubble-burning-in-punjab-and-how-to-solve-challenges-with-solutions.pdf

53 The Wire, 'Delhi Plays Role Model, Adopts IARIS Pusa Decomposer Solution to Combat Stubble Burning', 2024, The Wire, https://thewire.in/government/delhi-plays-role-model-adopts-iaris-pusa-decomposer-solution-to-combat-stubble-burning.

54 *Deccan Herald*, 'Stubble Burning Audit by Central Agency Shows Pusa Bio-Decomposer Highly Effective, Says Kejriwal', 2024, *Deccan Herald*, https://www.deccanherald.com/india/stubble-burning-audit-by-central-agency-shows-pusa-bio-decomposer-highly-effective-says-kejriwal-1029843.html.

55 *Indian Express*, 'Economics of Punjab's Paddy Varieties: Case of Banned Pusa 44 and the Promoted PR 126', 2024, *Indian Express*, https://indianexpress.com/article/cities/chandigarh/economics-of-punjabs-paddy-varieties-case-of-banned-pusa-44-and-the-promoted-pr-126-9310587/.

56 PRSC, 'Year Wise Residue', 2024, *PRSC*, http://gis-prsc.punjab.gov.in/residue/Year_Wise.aspx.

57 *The Economic Times*, 'Centre Rejects Punjab's ₹2,500/Acre Cash Sops to Stop Stubble Burning', 2024, *Economic Times*, https://economictimes.indiatimes.com/news/india/centre-rejects-punjabs-2500/acre-cash-sops-to-stop-stubble-burning/articleshow/94036296.cms?from=mdr.

58 Official notification of Odd-Even in January 2016: http://it.delhigovt.nic.in/writereaddata/egaz20157544.pdf

59 'Odd-Even Formula: Volunteers to Win Over Violators with Flowers', 2024, *Times of India*, https://timesofindia.indiatimes.com/city/delhi/odd-even-formula-volunteers-to-win-over-violators-with-flowers/articleshow/50386695.cms.

60 'Delhi Model: Good Environment Policies Also Make Good Politics', 2024, *Hindustan Times*, https://www.hindustantimes.com/analysis/delhi-model-good-environment-policies-also-make-good-politics/story-BmQ4SeDNGm3315xwO8vlcK.html.

61 'Odd-Even: A Step Towards Cleaner Air or a Political Gimmick?', EPW (Economic and Political Weekly), 2 July 2017, https://epic.uchicago.in/wp-content/uploads/2017/07/Odd-Even-EPW-draft-02072017.pdf

62 ResearchGate, 'Traffic Intervention Policy Fails to Mitigate Air Pollution in Megacity Delhi', 2024, *ResearchGate*,https://www.researchgate.net/publication/316676552_Traffic_intervention_policy_fails_to_mitigate_air_pollution_in_megacity_Delhi.

63 *Hindustan Times*, 'Delhi govt cites studies to back odd-even in affidavit to SC', 30 October 2023, https://www.hindustantimes.com/cities/delhi-news/delhi-govt-cites-studies-to-back-odd-evenin-affidavit-to-sc-101699552679996.html

64 *Ideas for India*, 'Driving Delhi: The impact of driving restrictions on driver behaviour', 5 September 2023, https://www.ideasforindia.in/topics/environment/driving-delhi-the-impact-of-driving-restrictions-on-driver-behaviour.html

65 https://cpcb.nic.in/uploads/final_graded_table.pdf

66 Commission for Air Quality Management, 'GRAP Schedule', 5 October 2023, https://caqm.nic.in/WriteReadData/LINKS/ GRAP%20Schedulebc030504-9c75-4773-8c69-9942a9175aab.pdf

67 ANI News, 'Delhi Minister Gopal Rai writes to Centre urging ban on entry of vehicles non-compliant with BS-VI norms', 4 November 2023, https://www.aninews.in/news/national/general-news/delhi-minister-gopal-rai-writes-to-centre-urging-ban-on-entry-of-vehicles-non-compliant-with-bs-vi-norms20231104135819/

68 Centre for Science and Environment, 'Only 12 per cent of India's census cities and towns have air quality monitoring stations', 23 October 2023, https://www.cseindia.org/only-12-per-cent-of-india-s-census-cities-and-towns-have-air-quality-monitoring-stations-11779

69 Commission for Air Quality Management, 'Policy to curb air pollution in NCR', 19 October 2023, https://caqm.nic.in/ WriteReadData/LINKS/Policy%20to%20curb%20air%20 poluution%20in%20NCR_8bc1ddf1-b34a-4506-b29f-34390650e053.pdf, pg.19

70 Department of Environment, Government of Delhi, 'Air pollution control & pollution hotspots', 2 November 2023, https:// environment.delhi.gov.in/environment/air-pollution-control-pollution-hotspots

71 *Hindustan Times*, 'Kejriwal unveils study devices to help combat air pollution in Delhi', 3 February 2023, https://www.hindustantimes. com/cities/delhi-news/kejriwal-unveils-study-devices-to-help-combat-air-pollution-in-delhi-101675104001475.html

72 'The highest total attributable mortality due to air pollution in India', *BMJ*, 25 October 2023, https://www.bmj.com/content/383/ bmj-2023-077784#:~:text=The%20highest%20total%20 attributable%20mortality,to%202.81)%20deaths%20per%20 year

73 '5–6 lakh people are dying due to sudden cardiac deaths in India, finds study', *The Week*, 1 October 2023, https://www.theweek. in/news/health/2023/10/01/5-6-lakh-people-are-dying-due-to-sudden-cardiac-deaths-in-india-finds-study.html

74 'Delhi air pollution is cutting lives shorter by almost 10 years: report', *Air Quality Life Index*, 25 October 2023, https://aqli.epic. uchicago.edu/news/delhi-air-pollution-is-cutting-lives-shorter-by-almost-10-years-report/

75 'Air pollution in India and the impact on business', Clean Air Fund, 25 October 2023, https://www.cleanairfund.org/resource/air-pollution-in-india-and-the-impact-on-business/

76 'The world's most polluted cities are in India', Statista, 25 October 2023, https://www.statista.com/chart/3670/the-worlds-most-polluted-cities-are-in-india/

77 'What Delhi pollution tells us about smog and air quality', *Indian Express*, 14 November 2023, https://indianexpress.com/article/opinion/columns/what-delhi-pollution-smog-air-quality-index-aqi-mexico-4930351/

78 'CSE says India needs to adapt a regional air quality management framework', Centre for Science and Environment, 25 October 2023, https://www.cseindia.org/cse-says-india-needs-to-adapt-a-regional-air-quality-management-framework-11408

79 'Beat air pollution', United Nations Environment Programme, 25 October 2023, https://www.unep.org/interactive/beat-air-pollution/

80 'Air pollution: Prakash Javadekar's remarks raise eyebrows', *The Wire*, 25 October 2023, https://thewire.in/politics/air-pollution-prakash-javadekar

81 'Action Plan for Control of Air Pollution in NCR', Commission for Air Quality Management, 25 October 2023, https://caqm.nic.in/WriteReadData/LINKS/0031dcb806e-8af7-4b38-a9bc-65b91f2704cd.pdf

82 'Government of India launches National Clean Air Programme (NCAP)', *Press Information Bureau*, 25 October 2023, https://pib.gov.in/PressReleasePage.aspx?PRID=1989207

83 'Five years of the National Clean Air Programme', *Climate Trends*, 25 October 2023, https://climatetrends.in/wp-content/uploads/2024/01/5-years-NCAP.pdf

84 'Prakash Javadekar postponed air pollution meetings in Delhi', NewsLaundry, 7 November 2019, https://www.newslaundry.com/2019/11/07/prakash-javadekar-postponed-air-pollution-meetings-delhi

Chapter 5: Transport

1 Budget Speech 2015–16. Delhi Government, 2015.

2 'RTO Most Corrupt Body, Loot More Than Chambal Dacoits: Nitin Gadkari', *Economic Times*, 26 Nov. 2015, https://economictimes.indiatimes.com/news/politics-and-nation/rto-most-

corrupt-body-loot-more-than-chambal-dacoits-nitin-gadkari/
articleshow/50126446.cms?

3 'Delhi Metro's Daily Ridership Soars to 60 Lakh, Receives ₹500
Crore in 2024-25 Budget', CNBCTV18, 30 Oct 2024, CNBCTV18,
www.cnbctv18.com/economy/delhi-metros-daily-ridership-soars-
to-60-lakh-receives-500-crore-in-2024-25-budget-19193791.htm.

4 'Government of India Announces New Initiatives for Skill
Development', Press Information Bureau, 6 Oct 2023, https://pib.
gov.in/PressReleaseIframePage.aspx?

5 Economic Survey of Delhi 2020-21. Delhi Government, https://
delhiplanning.delhi.gov.in/sites/default/files/Planning/12._
transport.pdf.

6 Ibid.

7 'Waiting for a Bus,' Centre for Science and Environment, 2024,
p. 17, https://www.cseindia.org/waiting-for-a-bus-8114.

8 'After China and Santiago, Delhi's E-Bus Fleet Third Biggest
in World, Says Govt.' *Indian Express*, 20 Feb. 2023, https://
indianexpress.com/article/cities/delhi/after-china-and-santiago-
delhis-e-bus-fleet-third-biggest-in-world-says-govt-9162264/.

9 'Delhi Boards E-Bus in Pursuit of Clean Air.' *Hindustan Times*,
27 August 2023. https://www.hindustantimes.com/opinion/delhi-
boards-e-bus-in-pursuit-of-clean-air-101695306116481.html.

10 Ibid.

11 'Delhi Will Procure Only E-Buses in Future', *Hindustan Times*,
6 June 2023, https://www.hindustantimes.com/cities/delhi-news/
delhi-will-procure-only-e-buses-in-future-transport-minister-
kailash-gahlot-101635357758983.html.

12 'Delhi Government Launches One Card for Commute on Metro,
Buses', *Business Standard*, 3 December 2018, https://www.business-
standard.com/article/news-ians/delhi-government-launches-one-
card-for-commute-on-metro-buses-118120300994_1.html.

13 Delhi Government, Department of Transport. 'Official Website',
https://otd.delhi.gov.in/

14 'Delhi Govt Launches 'Connect Delhi' to Increase Reach of
Transportation Facilities', *Financial Express*, 4 December
2019, https://www.financialexpress.com/india-news/delhi-govt-
launches-connect-delhi-to-increase-reach-of-transportation-
facilities/1231521/

15 'Govt Begins Trial Run of Mohalla Buses in Delhi', *Hindustan
Times*, 25 October 2023. https://www.hindustantimes.com/

cities/delhi-news/govt-begins-trial-run-of-mohalla-buses-in-delhi-101721067758333.html.

16 'Delhi Govt Introduces Nation's First Ever Premium Bus Aggregator Scheme', LiveMint, 18 November 2021. https://www.livemint.com/news/india/delhi-govt-introduces-nation-s-first-ever-premium-bus-aggregator-scheme-11700737799261.html.

17 'Premium Bus Service Likely to Launch This Month', *Hindustan Times*, 21 October 2023. https://www.hindustantimes.com/cities/delhi-news/premium-bus-service-likely-to-launch-this-month-101720545510631.html.

18 'Free Metro for Women: A Safety Bonanza?' *Indian Express*, 29 January 2020. https://indianexpress.com/article/opinion/columns/free-metro-for-women-safety-gender-violence-rapes-bonanza-5781490/.

19 'Labour Force Participation Rate, Female (% of Female Population Ages 15+) (Modeled ILO Estimate)' World Bank, 2020, https://data.worldbank.org/indicator/sl.tlf.cact.fe.zs?end=2020&locations=IN&start=2001.

20 'In Delhi, More Women Are Taking Free Bus Rides. Is AAP's Scheme Making Them Feel the City Is Safer?' Scroll.in, 15 January 2020, https://scroll.in/article/944568/in-delhi-more-women-are-taking-free-bus-rides-is-aaps-scheme-making-them-feel-the-city-is-safer.

21 'Arvind Kejriwal Made Travel Free for Women Instead of Buying a Plane.' NDTV, 9 March 2020, https://www.ndtv.com/delhi-news/delhi-chief-minister-arvind-kejriwal-made-travel-free-for-women-instead-of-buying-a-plane-2134105.

22 'Understanding the Gender Wage Gap in the Indian Labor Market.' Ashoka University, 2021, https://dp.ashoka.edu.in/ash/wpaper/paper105_0.pdf.

23 '7 Years of DDC: A Comprehensive Report.' Delhi Development Commission, 2022, https://ddc.delhi.gov.in/sites/default/files/reports/7_years_of_ddc_report.pdf, pg. 39

24 'Delhi Electric Vehicles Policy 2020.' Delhi Transport Department, 2020, https://transport.delhi.gov.in/transport/delhi-electric-vehicles-policy-2020.

25 'Union Cabinet Approves the Establishment of National Land Monetization Corporation.' Press Information Bureau,

9 February 2022, https://pib.gov.in/PressReleaseIframePage.
aspx?PRID=1987802

26 'Delhi Had Highest Share in Total EV Sales in Country in December:
Minister.' *Business Standard*, 2 January 2024, https://www.
business-standard.com/industry/auto/delhi-had-highest-share-in-
total-ev-sales-in-country-in-december-minister-124010200936_1.
html.

27 Data from Transport Department, Delhi Government

28 'EV Charging Points, Battery Swapping Facilities to Soon Cross
5,000 Mark in Delhi: Discoms.' Zee Business, 21 February 2024,
https://www.zeebiz.com/automobile/news-ev-charging-points-
battery-swapping-facilities-to-soon-cross-5000-mark-in-delhi-
discoms-269480#:~=According%20to%20the%20latest%20
report,charging%20points%20across%20the%20country..

29 '42 New Sites to Get EV Charging Points.' *Times of India*, 30 April
2023, https://timesofindia.indiatimes.com/city/delhi/42-new-sites-
to-get-ev-charging-points/articleshow/101248649.cms.

30 'Delhi Motor Vehicle Aggregator and Delivery Service Provider
Scheme 2023.' Delhi Transport Department, 2023, https://
transport.delhi.gov.in/transport/delhi-motor-vehicle-aggregator-
and-delivery-service-provider-scheme-2023.

31 'Delhi's Motor Vehicle Aggregator Scheme Enrolls Over 1
Lakh Vehicles, Including Ola, Uber, Zomato.' CNBC TV18, 24
April 2023, https://www.cnbctv18.com/auto/delhis-motor-vehicle-
aggregator-scheme-enrolls-over-1-lakh-vehicles-including-ola-
uber-zomato-19442932.htm.

32 Budget Speech 2016–17, Delhi Government.

33 https://www.youtube.com/watch?v=47NCjQo9pp4

34 Budget Speech 2023–24, Delhi Government.

35 Ibid

36 Budget Speech 2015–16, Delhi Government

37 'Public Transportation in India: Part 1.' AIF, 2024, https://aif.org/
public-transportation-in-india-part-1/.

38 'Urban Transport Project White Paper.' The Infra Vision
Foundation, December 2023, https://theinfravisionfoundation.
org/wp-content/uploads/2023/12/Urban-Transport-Project-White-
Paper.pdf

39 'Domestic Review Report on ESCBS', Ministry of Housing
and Urban Affairs, 9 June 2019, https://mohua.gov.in/upload/

uploadfiles/files/PC1_ESCBS_Domestic_Review_Report_(09_ Jun_19).pdf

40 'India Is Failing Its Public Bus Commuters', The Morning Context, 2023, https://themorningcontext.com/chaos/india-is-failing-its-public-bus-commuters

41 'Urban Development Report', Parisar, 2023, https://parisar.org/ images/Copy_of_Digital_-_Urban_Development_Report.pdf

42 'Free Public Transportation is a Reality in 100 Cities—Here's Why.' CNBC, 2 March 2020, https://www.cnbc.com/2020/03/02/ free-public-transportation-is-a-reality-in-100-citiesheres-why. html.

43 'Delhi Metro Fare Hike: A Step Backward.' *Indian Express*, 9 October 2018, https://indianexpress.com/article/opinion/ columns/delhi-metro-fare-hike-dmrc-metro-ticket-arvind-kejriwal-4916163/.

44 Ibid

45 'India Walks to Work: Census.' *The Hindu*, 16 March 2022, https://www.thehindu.com/data/India-walks-to-work-Census/ article60346511.ece.

Chapter 6: Electricity

1 'Electoral War Over Electricity Bills in Delhi.' *The New York Times*, 18 July 2013, https://archive.nytimes.com/india.blogs. nytimes.com/2013/07/18/electoral-war-over-electricity-bills-in-delhi/.

2 'Delhi Government Agrees to ₹500 Crore Bailout for BSES Discoms.' *Economic Times*, 25 January 2012, https://economictimes. indiatimes.com/industry/energy/power/delhi-government-agrees-to-500-crore-bailout-for-bses-discoms/articleshow/11261658. cms?from=mdr.

3 'Supreme Court Halts Potential Blackout in Delhi.' Moneycontrol, 17 February 2023, https://www.moneycontrol.com/news/business/ companies/supreme-court-halts-potential-blackoutdelhi-1202229. html.

4 'BSES Discoms Blamed for Power Cuts.' *The Hindu*, 19 June 2014, https://www.thehindu.com/news/cities/Delhi/bses-discoms-blamed-for-power-cuts/article6215725.ece.

5 'Electoral War Over Electricity Bills in Delhi.' *The New York Times*, 18 July 2013, https://archive.nytimes.com/india.blogs.

nytimes.com/2013/07/18/electoral-war-over-electricity-bills-in-delhi/.

6 'The Transformative Story of Delhi's Power Sector.' *Hindustan Times*, 22 April 2023, https://www.hindustantimes.com/analysis/the-transformative-story-of-delhi-s-power-sector/story-EpBaBzKrHBZRotHtNBD9gK.html.

7 'Analysis of Tariff Orders of DERC 2014–15 to 2020–21.' DERC Website, 2021, https://www.derc.gov.in/tarriff-orders.

8 'Press Release.' Press Information Bureau, 15 February 2023, https://pib.gov.in/PressReleaseIframePage.aspx?PRID=1997977.

9 'BSES Discoms Blamed for Power Cuts.' *The Hindu*, 19 June 2014, https://www.thehindu.com/news/cities/Delhi/bses-discoms-blamed-for-power-cuts/article6215725.ece.

10 'Delhi's Power Pangs.' *The Hindu*, 18 June 2014, https://www.thehindu.com/news/cities/Delhi/delhis-power-pangs/article6211523.ece.

11 'Delhi to Face 10-Hour Blackouts from February: BSES Yamuna Power Limited.' *India Today*, 31 January 2014, https://www.indiatoday.in/india/north/story/delhi-to-face-10-hour-blackouts-from-february-bses-yamuna-power-limited-179142-2014-01-31.

12 'Power Cuts Add to Delhi's Summer Misery.' *Hindustan Times*, 1 June 2019, https://www.hindustantimes.com/delhi/power-cuts-add-to-delhi-s-summer-misery/story-IjZi32wxG1rHwv93sPLw4H.html.

13 'Access to Electricity: Availability and Electrification Percentage in India.' Council on Energy, Environment and Water, 2022, https://www.ceew.in/publications/access-to-electricity-availability-and-electrification-percentage-in-india.

14 Economic Survey of Delhi 2023–24, p. 224: https://delhiplanning.delhi.gov.in/sites/default/files/Planning/economic_survey_of_delhi_2023-24_english.pdf

15 'Delhi Power Cut, Electricity Disruptions Down by 70% but Pinches Inverter Sellers', Millennium Post, 2019, https://www.millenniumpost.in/delhi/delhi-power-cut-electricity-disruptions-down-by-70-but-pinches-inverter-sellers-388710

16 'BSES Finds Innovative Grid Solutions for Space Crunch.' *Statesman*, 18 May 2017, https://www.thestatesman.com/business/bses-finds-innovative-grid-solutions-for-space-crunch-1495041620.html.

17 'Economic Survey of Delhi, 2014–15 and 2023–24.' Delhi Government, 2024, https://delhi.gov.in/.

18 Ibid.

19 'Economic Survey of Delhi 2023–24.' Delhi Government, 2024, https://delhi.gov.in/.

20 Outcome Budget 2023–24, Delhi Government, 2024, https://delhi.gov.in/.

21 'Fine: Discoms for Power Cuts, Delhi Tells Regulator.' *Indian Express*, 15 May 2019, https://indianexpress.com/article/cities/delhi/fine-discoms-for-power-cuts-delhi-tells-regulator/.

22 'Now, Discoms to Pay Up to ₹100 per Hour for Long Power Cuts in Delhi.' *Hindustan Times*, 17 May 2019, https://www.hindustantimes.com/delhi/now-discoms-to-pay-up-to-rs-100-per-hour-for-long-power-cuts-in-delhi/story-Of9AezfxVHgK53Y5VjtcrN.html.

23 'Delhi: Penalty for Unscheduled Power Cuts Unlikely to Be Implemented This Year.' *Hindustan Times*, 30 July 2019, https://www.hindustantimes.com/delhi-news/delhi-penalty-for-unscheduled-power-cuts-unlikely-to-be-implemented-this-year/story-BKARSzcY1zAaPADrv3yTIN.html.

24 'Proposal to Compensate Delhi Residents for Unscheduled Power Cuts Gets Final Nod from Anil Baijal.' *Economic Times*, 24 May 2018, https://economictimes.indiatimes.com/news/politics-and-nation/proposal-to-compensate-delhi-residents-for-unscheduled-power-cuts-gets-final-nod-from-anil-baijal/articleshow/63835211.cms?from=mdr.

25 'CM Wants Discoms to Pay Compensation for Power Cuts.' *The Tribune India*, 5 July 2019, https://www.tribuneindia.com/news/archive/delhi/cm-wants-discoms-to-pay-compensation-for-power-cuts-418681/.

26 'Power in Delhi to Cost More,' *Business Standard*, 27 August 2011, https://www.business-standard.com/amp/article/economy-policy/power-in-delhi-to-cost-more-111082700004_1.html.

27 'Use Less Power If You Cannot Afford Hiked Charges: Sheila Dikshit,' *DNA India*, 31 January 2014, https://www.dnaindia.com/india/report-use-less-power-if-you-cannot-afford-hiked-charges-sheila-dikshit-1803920.

28 'Delhi to Face 10-Hour Blackouts from February: BSES Yamuna Power Limited,' *India Today*, 31 January 2014, https://www.

indiatoday.in/india/north/story/delhi-to-face-10-hour-blackouts-from-february-bses-yamuna-power-limited-179142-2014-01-31.

29 'Power Tariffs Will Not Increase, Come What May: Satyendar Jain,' *Indian Express*, 31 January 2024, https://indianexpress.com/article/cities/delhi/power-tariffs-will-not-increase-come-what-may-satyendar-jain/.

30 'Tariff Orders for 2014–15 and 2020–21,' *Delhi Electricity Regulatory Commission*, https://www.derc.gov.in/tarriff-orders.

31 Ibid.

32 As per latest tariff orders in respective cities/states

33 'AAP Likely to Surrender Power,' *The Hindu*, 10 July 2015, https://www.thehindu.com/news/cities/Delhi/aap-likely-to-surrender-power/article7401286.ece.

34 'CEEW Research on Delhi Power Purchase Agreements and Procurement Costs,' Council on Energy, Environment and Water, 2021, https://www.ceew.in/sites/default/files/ceew-research-on-delhi-power-purchase-agreements-and-procurement-costs.pdf.

35 'Economic Survey of Delhi 2023–24,' Delhi Planning Department, 2023, https://delhiplanning.delhi.gov.in/sites/default/files/Planning/economic_survey_of_delhi_2023-24_english.pdf.

36 'Delhi discoms' regulatory assets down by ₹3,029 cr in 5 years,' *Economic Times*, 2020, https://energy.economictimes.indiatimes.com/news/power/delhi-discoms-regulatory-assets-down-by-rs-3029-cr-in-5-years/71037619.

37 'The transformative story of Delhi's power sector,' *Hindustan Times*, 2023, https://www.hindustantimes.com/analysis/the-transformative-story-of-delhi-s-power-sector/story-EpBaBzKrHBZRotHtNBD9gK.html.

38 'Systematic Review of the Socio-economic Impacts of Rural Electrification,' UNESCAP, 2023, https://www.unescap.org/sites/default/d8files/knowledge-products/Systematic-Review-of-the-Socio-economic-Impacts-of-Rural-Electrification%2026%20Feb.pdf.

39 'More Than a Third of Power Consumed in Delhi is Green,' *Times of India*, 2024, https://timesofindia.indiatimes.com/city/delhi/more-than-a-third-of-power-consumed-in-delhi-is-green/articleshow/105972288.cms.

40 'Domestic Consumers Installing Rooftop Solar Panels Will Get Zero Power Bills in Delhi: Arvind Kejriwal,' *Economic Times*, 2024, https://energy.economictimes.indiatimes.com/news/power/domestic-consumers-installing-rooftop-solar-panels-will-get-zero-power-bills-in-delhi-arvind-kejriwal/107247522.

41 Ibid.

42 2014 Tariff Data: Report of Central Electricity Authority', Central Electricity Authority, March 2015, https://cea.nic.in/wp-content/uploads/2021/03/tariff_2015.pdf; '2024 Tariff Data: Latest Tariff Orders of the Respective States'.

43 PTI, 'NPA: Banks Write Off ₹14.56 Lakh Crore NPAs in Last Nine Financial Years,' *Economic Times*, 7 August 2023, https://economictimes.indiatimes.com/industry/banking/finance/banking/banks-write-off-rs-14-56-lakh-crore-npas-in-last-nine-financial-years/articleshow/102503282.cms?from=mdr.

44 Lucknow: *Hindustan Times*, 'Amid Protests Over Frequent Power Outages, LESA to Reassess Load on Substations,' https://www.hindustantimes.com/cities/lucknow-news/amid-protests-over-frequent-power-outages-lesa-to-reassess-load-on-substations-101717346374539.html.
Gurugram: *Times of India*, 'Outrage Over Power Outages in Gurgaon Amid Heatwave,' https://timesofindia.indiatimes.com/city/gurgaon/outrage-over-power-outages-in-gurgaon-amid-heatwave/articleshow/110477042.cms.
Indore: *Free Press Journal*, 'Indore Power Outages Irk Residents, Reaching Zones for Resolution,' https://www.freepressjournal.in/indore/indore-power-outages-irk-residents-reaching-zones-for-resolution.

45 *Times of India*, 'Adityanath Government Orders 18-Hour Power Supply in UP Villages,' 3 April 2017, https://timesofindia.indiatimes.com/city/lucknow/adityanath-government-orders-18-hour-power-supply-in-up-villages/articleshow/58129427.cms.

46 Ministry of Power, Government of India, 'Power Sector at a Glance – All India,' https://powermin.gov.in/en/content/power-sector-glance-all-india.

47 Lok Sabha Secretariat, 'Report of the Standing Committee on Energy,' 29 January 2022, https://loksabhadocs.nic.in/lsscommittee/Energy/17_Energy_29.pdf

48 *The Tribune*, 'State opposes Centre's directive on blending of imported coal,' 4 March 2022, https://www.tribuneindia.com/news/patiala/state-opposes-centres-directive-on-blending-of-imported-coal-556819/.

49 *PRS India*, 'What is fuelling power sector losses,' 8 April 2022, https://prsindia.org/theprsblog/what-is-fuelling-power-sector-losses.

50 *Times of India*, 'Developers not to build power infra as Hry brings in major policy change,' 16 February 2023, https://timesofindia.indiatimes.com/city/gurgaon/developers-not-to-build-power-infra-as-hry-brings-in-major-policy-change/articleshow/104482216.cms.

51 Press Information Bureau, 'Press Release,' 25 October 2022, https://pib.gov.in/PressReleaseIframePage.aspx?PRID=1947709

Chapter 7: Water

1 'City's tanker mafia makes killing', *Deccan Herald*, 5 January 2014, https://www.deccanherald.com/archives/citys-tanker-mafia-makes-killing-2169707

2 Associated Press, 'Water Shortages Lead to Tanker Mafia in New Delhi', NDTV, 8 September 2014, https://www.ndtv.com/delhi-news/water-shortages-lead-to-tanker-mafia-in-new-delhi-660794

3 Sai Manish, 'Black Market for Water Expands in Delhi', *The New York Times*, 18 September 2013, https://archive.nytimes.com/india.blogs.nytimes.com/2013/09/18/black-market-for-water-expands-in-delhi/

4 Ibid

5 Ibid

6 'Why are Water Bills Skyrocketing in Delhi?', Uploaded by Aam Aadmi Party, 16 February 2013, https://www.youtube.com/watch?v=OIl6LSSOfK4

7 Anil Swarup, Kartikey Singh, 'Why Delhi struggles with water shortage–and how this problem can be fixed', *Indian Express*, 3 June 2024, https://indianexpress.com/article/opinion/columns/delhi-water-shortage-problem-how-can-it-be-fixed-9369435/

8 'Water meters in capital increase by 75,000, says Jal Board', *Indian Express*, 2 September 2015, https://indianexpress.com/article/cities/delhi/water-meters-in-capital-increase-by-75000-says-jal-board/

9   Paras Singh, '"Free water" impact: Meters up, usage dips',
     Times of India, 20 March 2018, https://timesofindia.indiatimes.
     com/city/delhi/free-water-impact-meters-up-usage-dips/
     articleshow/63373594.cms

10   Finance Department, Government of NCT of Delhi website,
     https://finance.delhi.gov.in/finance/budget-speech

11   Planning Department, Government of NCT of Delhi website,
     https://delhiplanning.delhi.gov.in/planning/economic-survey-
     delhi-2014-15

12   Finance Department, Government of NCT of Delhi website,
     https://finance.delhi.gov.in/finance/budget-speech

13   Planning Department, Government of NCT of Delhi website, https://
     delhiplanning.delhi.gov.in/planning/budget-delhi-2023-24-1

14   'CM waives individual water, sewer charges', *The Hindu*, 23
     November 2019, https://www.thehindu.com/news/cities/Delhi/cm-
     waives-individual-water-sewer-charges/article30055631.ece

15   *Hindustan Times*, 'Delhi govt plans to expand RO ATMs across
     different locations, how will this help?,' 3 January 2023, https://
     www.hindustantimes.com/cities/delhi-news/delhi-govt-plans-
     to-expand-ro-atms-across-different-locations-how-will-this-
     help-101696069316089.html.

16   Paras Singh, 'Tenure of watershed deal nears end: Yamuna
     sharing talks to start next year', *Hindustan Times*, 5 July 2024,
     https://www.hindustantimes.com/cities/delhi-news/tenure-of-
     watershed-deal-nears-end-yamuna-sharing-talks-to-start-next-
     year-101720116907160.html

17   'Jat stir damage to Munak canal highlights Delhi's water vulnerability',
     Hindustan Times, 23 February 2016, https://www.hindustantimes.
     com/delhi/jat-stir-damage-to-munak-canal-highlights-delhi-s-
     water-vulnerability/story-I2Zo5ORKFluPdjeJAAvctO.html

18   Prathna T.C., Ankit Srivastava, 'Wetland Rejuvenation: Early
     Experiences from the National Capital Territory of Delhi',
     Wetlands International South Asia, February 2021, https://south-
     asia.wetlands.org/publications/sarovar-newsletter-series/

19   Prathna T.C., Ankit Srivastava, 'Urban water resource
     management: experience from the revival of Rajokri lake in
     Delhi', *AIMS Environmental Science*, 2021, 8. 421-434. 10.3934/
     environsci.2021027.

20 'Rajokri Lake revived by Delhi governments wins Jal Shakti Ministry award', New Indian Express, 31 August 2020, https://www.newindianexpress.com/cities/delhi/2020/Aug/31/rajokri-lake-revived-by-delhi-government-wins-jal-shakti-ministry-award-2190558.html

21 'Delhi: 159 dying lakes to get fresh lease of life as Jal Board begins ambitious ₹376-crore project', *Indian Express*, 25 December 2018, https://indianexpress.com/article/cities/delhi/delhi-159-dying-lakes-to-get-fresh-lease-of-life-as-jal-board-begins-ambitious-rs-376-crore-project-5508352/

22 Priyangi Agarwal, 'Tables Turned! How lakes project is helping recharge groundwater in Delhi', *Times of India*, 27 June 2024, https://timesofindia.indiatimes.com/city/delhi/delhi-govts-successful-lakes-project-helps-recharge-groundwater/articleshow/111298154.cms

23 Department of Environment, Government of NCT of Delhi website, https://environment.delhi.gov.in/environment/data-djb

24 Sonal Matharu, 'Toxic Delhi is turning into a city of lakes. Jal Board has just created 14 new ones', ThePrint, 22 February 2023, https://theprint.in/feature/toxic-delhi-is-turning-into-a-city-of-lakes-jal-board-has-just-created-14-new-ones/1389546/

25 Ibid

26 Planning Department, Government of NCT of Delhi website, https://delhiplanning.delhi.gov.in/planning/budget-delhi-2023-24-1

27 'Delhi Jal Board to offer financial assistance for rainwater harvesting system', *Hindustan Times*, 14 September 2021, https://www.hindustantimes.com/cities/delhi-news/delhi-jal-board-to-offer-financial-assistance-for-rainwater-harvesting-rwh-system-101631555611378.html

28 Planning Department, Government of NCT of Delhi website, https://delhiplanning.delhi.gov.in/planning/2024-25

29 Planning Department, Government of NCT of Delhi website, https://delhiplanning.delhi.gov.in/planning/2023-24-0 Economic Survey of Delhi 2023-24

30 Anup Verma, 'Delhi water crisis: Atishi writes to PM to intervene & mitigate water woes, will go on indefinite fast if situation is not resolved', New Indian Express, 19 June 2024, https://www.newindianexpress.com/cities/delhi/2024/Jun/19/delhi-water-crisis-

atishi-writes-to-pm-modi-says-will-go-on-indefinite-fast-from-june-21-if-situation-not-resolved-2

31 'After waterlogging brings city to a halt, CM Kejriwal holds meeting to assess draining master plan', *Indian Express*, 25 August 2021, https://indianexpress.com/article/cities/delhi/delhi-after-waterlogging-brings-city-to-a-halt-cm-holds-meeting-to-assess-drainage-master-plan-7469170/

32 Ankit Srivastava, Prathna T.C., 'Yamuna Action Plan-III: Impact on Water Quality of River Yamuna, India'. *Fine Chemical Engineering, 10 November 2021,* https://ojs.wiserpub.com/index.php/FCE/article/view/1032

33 Delhi Jal Board website, https://delhijalboard.delhi.gov.in/

34 Planning Department, Government of NCT of Delhi website, https://delhiplanning.delhi.gov.in/planning/budget-delhi-2023-24-1

35 Delhi Jal Board website, https://delhijalboard.delhi.gov.in/

36 'Delhi govt looking to scale up treatment of water in major drains', *Times of India*, 8 April 2023, https://timesofindia.indiatimes.com/city/delhi/delhi-govt-looking-to-scale-up-treatment-of-water-in-major-drains/articleshow/99325495.cms.

Chapter 8: Democracy Under Attack

1 Saba Naqvi, *Capital Conquest*, Hachette Book Publishing, 21 April 2015 and Ashutosh, *The Crown Prince, the Gladiator and the Hope: Battle for Change*, HarperCollins, 5 March 2015

2 Ministry of Home Affairs website, https://www.mha.gov.in/sites/default/files/video_87.pdf

3 Krishandas Rajgopal, 'Supreme Court okays Centre's proposal to grant Delhi Chief Secretary six months' extension of service', *The Hindu*, 29 November 2023, https://www.thehindu.com/news/cities/Delhi/supreme-court-okays-centres-proposal-to-grant-delhi-chief-secretary-six-months-extension-of-service/article67587724.ece

4 Jasmine Shah, 'The SC verdict in the Delhi services case is a boost for democracy', *Hindustan Times*, 14 March 2023, https://www.hindustantimes.com/opinion/delhis-fight-for-democracy-supreme-court-verdict-gives-elected-government-control-over-bureaucracy-101684068130006.html

5   'Services dept a circus, L-G the ringmaster, says Sisodia'. *Hindustan Times*, 26 February 2019, https://www.hindustantimes.com/ delhi-news/services-dept-a-circus-l-g-the-ringmaster-says-manish-sisodia/story-JtSCrJiKHtiI2h8FS71cfP.html

6   '"Funds stopped for Farishtey scheme", AAP govt claims in plea; SC issues notice to L-G office', *Indian Express*, 9 December 2023, https://indianexpress.com/article/cities/delhi/funds-stopped-for-farishtey-scheme-aap-govt-claims-in-plea-sc-issues-notice-to-l-g-office-9060610/

7   Anup Verma, 'Delhi Deputy CM accuses govt officers of stopping funds for mohalla clinics', New Indian Express, 16 January 2023, https://www.newindianexpress.com/cities/delhi/2023/Jan/16/ delhi-deputy-cm-accuses-govt-officers-of-stopping-funds-for-mohalla-clinics-2538258.html

8   'Saxena Threatened Officers to Stall Bus Marshal Scheme: Delhi CM Kejriwal', Business Standard, 29 February 2024, https://www. business-standard.com/politics/saxena-threatened-officers-to-stall-bus-marshal-scheme-delhi-cm-kejriwal-124022900470_1.html

9   PTI, 'SC notice to Delhi finance secy on plea alleging non-release of DJB funds', *Business Standard*, 1 April 2024, https://www. business-standard.com/india-news/sc-notice-to-delhi-finance-secy-on-plea-alleging-non-release-of-djb-funds-124040100903_1.html

10   'Officials not taking our calls, skipping meetings: Delhi govt affidavit to SC', *Indian Express*, 15 November 2022, https:// indianexpress.com/article/cities/delhi/officials-not-taking-our-calls-skipping-meetings-delhi-govt-affidavit-to-sc-8259592/

11   'Delhi Health Minister highlights 30% shortage of doctors, criticises LG for inaction', *Economic Times*, 9 March 2023, https://health.economictimes.indiatimes.com/news/policy/delhi-health-minister-highlights-30-pc-shortage-of-doctors-criticises-lg-for-inaction/112861677

12   Directorate of Education, Delhi Government.

13   Outcome Budget 2023–24, Delhi Government, Link: https:// delhiplanning.delhi.gov.in/planning/outcome-budget-2023-24

14   'AAP targets Lt Governor Jung: "doing Centre's bidding"', *Indian Express*, 16 September 2016, https://indianexpress.com/article/ cities/delhi/aap-targets-lt-governor-jung-doing-centre-bidding/

15   'NCT of Delhi, Union of India: The Lieutenant Governor and the NCT Delhi case background', *SC Observer*, 2018, https://

www.scobserver.in/cases/nct-delhi-union-of-india-the-lieutenant-governor-and-the-nct-delhi-case-background/

16 'Delhi Govt-LG: Why GNCTD ordinance nullifies Supreme Court judgment, unconstitutional', *LiveLaw*, 26 May 2023, https://www.livelaw.in/articles/delhi-govt-lg-why-gnctd-ordinance-nullifies-supreme-court-judgment-unconstitutional-229569

17 'State vs Centre: Who Holds the Reins?', *The Indian Express*, 2024, https://indianexpress.com/article/opinion/columns/state-government-centre-rule-9492179/

18 'LG is administrative head of NCT Delhi, not required to act on advice of Cabinet: Delhi HC', *LiveLaw*, 8 August 2016, https://www.livelaw.in/breaking-lg-administrative-head-nct-delhi-not-required-act-advice-cabinet-delhi-hc/

19 'Special status of Delhi under Article 239AA of the Constitution', *Lok Sabha Secretariat*, 19 March 2021, https://loksabhadocs.nic.in/Refinput/New_Reference_Notes/English/19032021_172541_1021205239.pdf

20 'Who is LG to stop Kejriwal on tussle over teachers' training in Finland?', *Business Standard*, 17 January 2023, https://www.business-standard.com/article/current-affairs/who-is-lg-to-stop-kejriwal-on-tussle-over-teachers-training-in-finland-123011700775_1.html

21 'Delhi LG approves with riders city govt's proposal to send teachers to Finland for training', *The Hindu*, 27 June 2023, https://www.thehindu.com/news/cities/Delhi/delhi-l-g-approves-with-riders-city-govts-proposal-to-send-teachers-to-finland-for-training/article66580196.ece

22 'Delhi Development Commission (DDCD) dissolved: LG VK Saxena', *India Today*, 27 June 2024, https://www.indiatoday.in/cities/delhi/story/delhi-development-commission-ddcd-dissolved-lg-vk-saxena-aap-2559117-2024-06-27

23 https://www.youtube.com/watch?v=oaP5lCSmpOY

24 'From 60 per cent in UPA to 95 per cent in NDA: A surge in share of opposition leaders in CBI net', *Indian Express*, 16 October 2022, https://indianexpress.com/article/express-exclusive/from-60-per-cent-in-upa-to-95-per-cent-in-nda-a-surge-in-share-of-opposition-leaders-in-cbi-net-express-investigation-8160912/

25 'Since 2014, 25 opposition leaders facing corruption probe crossed over to BJP; 23 of them got reprieve', *Indian Express*, 15 February

2023, https://indianexpress.com/article/express-exclusive/since-2014-25-opposition-leaders-facing-corruption-probe-crossed-over-to-bjp-23-of-them-got-reprieve-9247737/

26 'False cases being filed against AAP leaders; campaign underway to end party: Delhi CM Kejriwal', *Times of India*, 30 October 2023, https://timesofindia.indiatimes.com/india/false-cases-being-filed-against-aap-leaders-campaign-underway-to-end-party-delhi-cm-kejriwal/articleshow/104335776.cms?from=mdr

27 'SC upholds amendments to PMLA, giving ED unbridled powers of summons, arrests, raids', *Hindu Business Line*, 25 July 2022, https://www.thehindubusinessline.com/news/sc-upholds-amendments-to-pmla-giving-ed-unbridled-powers-of-summons-arrests-raids/article65689464.ece

28 'Politics stalled Delhi's progressive excise policy', *Hindustan Times*, 30 September 2022, https://www.hindustantimes.com/opinion/politics-stalled-delhi-s-progressive-excise-policy-101661959437810.html

29 ibid.

30 'Delhi excise revenue set to double after licence auctions under new liquor policy', *Hindustan Times*, 8 August 2021, https://www.hindustantimes.com/india-news/delhi-excise-revenue-set-to-double-after-licence-auctions-under-new-liquor-policy-101628274483032.html

31 'Delhi excise policy: Aam Aadmi Party alleges corruption in change of decision by Centre's LG, seeks CBI probe', *The Hindu*, 5 August 2022, https://www.thehindu.com/news/cities/Delhi/delhi-excise-policy-aam-aadmi-party-alleges-corruption-in-change-of-decision-by-centres-lg-seeks-cbi-probe/article65735648.ece

32 'Who are Sharath Reddy, Raghav Magunta Reddy, Arvind Kejriwal mentioned in court?', *Hindustan Times*, 23 November 2022, https://www.hindustantimes.com/india-news/who-are-sharath-reddy-raghav-magunta-reddy-arvind-kejriwal-mentioned-in-court-101711639348717.html

33 'Punjab excise revenue increases: AAP', *Indian Express*, 8 April 2023, https://indianexpress.com/article/cities/chandigarh/punjab-excise-revenue-increases-aap-8543885/

34 'AAP govt slams "total confusion" in LG's office over subjects transferred to Delhi govt', *Economic Times*, 26 October 2023, https://economictimes.indiatimes.com/news/elections/lok-sabha/

Notes

delhi/aap-govt-slams-total-confusion-in-lgs-office-over-subjects-transferred-to-delhi-govt/articleshow/109142858.cms?from=mdr

35 'Delhi among most unsafe cities for women: NCRB data', *Hindustan Times*, 14 September 2022, https://www.hindustantimes.com/cities/delhi-news/delhi-among-most-unsafe-cities-for-womenncrbdata-101701714002746.html

36 NCRB data for crimes against women in Delhi: 2012–2022

37 'Delhi is in an utter mess: Supreme Court rebukes Centre on master plan delay', *Hindustan Times*, 23 November 2023, https://www.hindustantimes.com/india-news/delhi-is-in-an-utter-mess-supreme-court-rebukes-centre-on-master-plan-delay-101698070236272.html

38 'Arvind Kejriwal's challenges', *Mint*, 12 January 2015, https://www.livemint.com/Politics/hBrjGOgFsEmuk2tuqZ1qTO/Arvind-Kejriwals-challenges.html

39 'The Delhi debate: Local governance is vital to the national capital', *Hindustan Times*, 19 June 2023, https://www.hindustantimes.com/opinion/the-delhi-debate-local-governance-is-vital-to-the-national-capital-101687205726843.html

40 Ibid

41 'CM Kejriwal unveils draft bill seeking full statehood status for Delhi', *Hindustan Times*, 18 April 2016, https://www.hindustantimes.com/delhi/cm-kejriwal-unveils-draft-bill-seeking-full-statehood-status-for-delhi/story-hr6txd0aEoEnr1U89RV3tI.html

42 'Is it time to divide Delhi into two cities?', *Times of India*, 22 May 2023, https://timesofindia.indiatimes.com/india/is-it-time-to-divide-delhi-into-two-cities/articleshow/100400538.cms?pcode=462

Scan QR code to access the
Penguin Random House India website